Women's Work, Men's Property:

The Origins of Gender and Class

Edited by Stephanie Coontz
and Peta Henderson

VERSO
The Imprint of New Left Books

British Library
Cataloguing in Publication Data

Women's work, men's property : the origins of
gender and class.
1. Women——Social conditions
I. Coontz, Stephanie   II. Henderson, Peta
305.4'2   HQ1154

First published 1986
Second printing 1986
© Stephanie Coontz & Peta Henderson

Verso
15 Greek Street London W1V 5LF

Typeset in Palatino by
PRG Graphics Ltd. Redhill, Surrey

Printed by the Thetford Press Ltd.
Thetford, Norfolk

ISBN 0-86091-112-8
ISBN 0-86091-819-X Pbk

CONTENTS

Preface   xi

Introduction   1
Stephanie Coontz and Peta Henderson

**1.   In the Beginning . . .: The Origins of the Sexual   43
Division of Labour and the Development of the First
Human Societies**
Lila Leibowitz

**2.   The Dawn of Lineage Societies: The Origins of Women's   76
Oppression.**
Nicole Chevillard and Sébastien Leconte

**3.   Property Forms, Political Power and Female Labour   108
in the Origins of Class and State Societies**
Stephanie Coontz and Peta Henderson

4.   Slavery and Women   156
Nicole Chevillard and Sébastien Leconte

**5.   The Processes of Women's Subordination in Primitive   169
and Archaic Greece**
Monique Saliou

Bibliography   207
General Index   214
Index of Authors   219

IN MEMORY
OF
LILA LEIBOWITZ

Nicole Chevillard was born in Bois-Colombes, France, in July 1947. She lives in Paris, where she works as an economist specializing in African Affairs. She holds the 'Doctorat d'Etat' from the University of Paris X – Nanterre (1979). Her dissertation, 'Les Inégalités économiques entre sexes: Fondements – rôles et articulations', was written jointly with Sébastien Leconte.

Stephanie Coontz was born in Seattle, Washington in 1944. She received a B.A. in the history honours programme at the University of California and an M.A. from the University of Washington, where she was a Woodrow Wilson Fellow. She was an associate editor of the *International Socialist Review*, and has taught at The Evergreen State College in Olympia, Washington since 1975. She co-edited and contributed articles to *Life in Capitalist America* (Pathfinder 1974), and is currently completing a manuscript on the history of American families.

Peta Henderson was born in Belfast, Northern Ireland, in 1937. She holds a B.A. from Swarthmore College, an M.A. from McGill University, and a Ph.D. from the University of Connecticut (1976). She is a Member of the Faculty in Anthropology at The Evergreen State College, Olympia, Washington, where she has taught since 1974. She has done field research in Belize and Puerto Rico and has published articles on development and population policy.

Sébastien Leconte was born in Douala, Cameroun, in September 1949. He currently lives in Paris, where he works as an economist. He holds the 'Doctorat d'Etat' from the University of Paris X – Nanterre (1979). His dissertation, 'Les Inégalités économiques entre sexes: Fondements – rôles et articulations', was written jointly with Nicole Chevillard.

Lila Leibowitz was born in New York City in 1930. She was Associate Professor of Anthropology at Northeastern University from 1972 until her untimely death in June 1984. She was an honours graduate at Brooklyn College, and earned her M.A. and Ph.D. from Columbia University (1971). She authored *Females,*

Males, Families: A Biosocial Approach and numerous journal articles.

Monique Saliou was born in 1952. She graduated from the Ecole Normale Superieure, 'agrégée' in history. She specializes in the history of religions. She is the author of numerous articles in feminist journals and in theoretical journals of the Fourth International.

Preface

This book began as separate strands of research in America and France. We would like to thank the International Research Institute for Scientific and Democratic Socialism and the Robert H. Langston Foundation for bringing the authors together and providing travel funds so that we could meet and discuss our work. The Institute also funded the translation of the French articles into English, which was done by Aaron Barzman. The editors would also like to thank The Evergreen State College for providing us with research time, The Evergreen State College Interlibrary Loan Department for their remarkable ability to track down the many books and articles we requested, and our Evergreen State College students for their insightful comments and criticisms.

Introduction

'Explanations' of Male Dominance

Stephanie Coontz and Peta Henderson

Male dominance is one of the earliest known and most wide-spread forms of inequality in human history. To some, the very idea of a book on the origins of sexual inequality is absurd. Male dominance seems to them a universal, if not inevitable, relationship that has been with us since the dawn of our species. A growing body of evidence and theory, however, suggests that this is not the case, and a number of scholars have begun to address the issue of male dominance as a historical pheno-menon, grounded in a specific set of circumstances rather than flowing from some universal aspect of human nature or culture. The essays in this volume offer differing perspectives on the development of sex role differentiation and sexual inequality (the two are by no means identical), but share a belief that these phenomena *did* have origins, and that these must be sought in sociohistorical events and processes. Before turning to these theories, we would like critically to review some of the altern-ative explanations of sexual inequality.

A starting point for many theories of gender inequality is the assumption that biology is destiny: the roles men and women play in society, and the different privileges attached to these roles, are said to be fundamentally determined by our genes, which are in turn the product of natural selection. One common approach within this general framework of biological reduc-tionism is to explain human sex role patterns and inequalities by reference to our primate heritage. The most popular model for this approach is the baboon. The scenario is as follows: Male baboons are twice as large as females; this sexual dimorphism

(differentiation in secondary physical characteristics) is related
to differences in both function and status; male size, strength,
and aggression are adaptive traits for defending the troop and
maintaining order within it, and a tight male dominance hierarchy also reproduces this aggression, the most dominant/
aggressive animal being the one that gets the greatest access to
'receptive' females and to food. With minor differences in
emphasis and use of evidence, a whole series of authors imply
that male aggression and dominance (with their necessary
accompaniment, female passivity or dependence) are therefore
part of our genetic primate heritage. Male aggressive instincts
are also said to have served early humans well in their role as
'predators'.[1]

There are a number of problems with this approach. In the first
place, there is much more variability in primate behaviour than
these authors admit. Some species are highly dimorphic; some
are not. Mating patterns range from monogamy to promiscuity
(by both males and females), while parenting and socialization
behaviours are extraordinarily diverse among different species,
or even in the same species under different environmental conditions.[2] Forest baboons, for example, are very different from the
savannah baboons so beloved by the theorists cited above:
'Aggression in general is very infrequent, and male dominance
hierarchies are difficult to discern. Intertroop encounters are
rare, and friendly. When the troop is startled . . . it flees, and,
far from forming a rearguard, the males — being biggest and
strongest — are frequently up the trees long before the
females'.[3] Adult females, far from being passive followers of the
males, actually determine the direction and timing of troop
movement. Similarly, chimpanzees, with whom humans share
ninety-nine percent of our genes and from whom we may have

1. Robert Ardrey, *African Genesis*, New York 1961, p. 36. See also, Sherwood
Washburn and Irven DeVore, *Baboon Social Organization* (film), 1963; Washburn
and Chet Lancaster, 'The Evolution of Hunting', in Robert Lee and DeVore eds.,
Man the Hunter, Chicago 1968; Desmond Morris, *The Naked Ape*, London 1968;
Desmond Morris, *The Human Zoo*, London 1969; Lionel Tiger, *Men in Groups*,
New York 1969; Konrad Lorenz, *On Aggression*, New York 1966.

2. Lila Leibowitz, *Females, Males, Families: A Biosocial Approach*, North
Scituate, Mass. 1978; Ruby Rohrlich-Leavitt, Barbara Sykes and Elizabeth
Weatherford, 'Aboriginal Women: Male and Female Anthropological Perspec-
tives', in Rayna Reiter ed., *Toward an Anthropology of Women*, New York 1975.

3. David Pilbeam, 'An Idea We Could Live Without: The Naked Ape' in
Ashley Montagu ed., *Man and Aggression*, New York 1973, pp. 110–21.

diverged as little as five million years ago, are highly social animals who display a very low degree of male dominance, hierarchy, or aggression.[4]

Where aggression and male dominance are found in primate groups, there is some question as to how much of this is natural and how much a response to stress. The male dominant savannah baboons live in game parks where predators and humans are concentrated in numbers far beyond those likely in aboriginal conditions. There is considerable evidence that such stressful circumstances, especially captivity, markedly increase hierarchy and aggression. Indeed, the noted researchers who filmed 'Baboon Social Organization' (1963) only induced what they called 'latent' dominance behaviour by artificial feeding, while forest baboons placed in cages and fed with clumps of food that had to be competed for showed a great increase in fighting, aggression, and dominance behaviour.[5] Is such behaviour natural or pathological? Many scholars now suggest that the normal behaviour patterns of our primate ancestors involved sharing and cooperation rather than aggression, male dominance, and competition.[6]

Finally, there is little evidence that aggressive or dominant behaviour gives males privileged access to females, thus allowing them to pass on their supposedly more aggressive genes.[7] Gorillas and chimpanzees are not normally sexually aggressive and males tend to wait patiently for an oestrous female to make herself available. Among chimpanzees and orangutans, sex is usually initiated by the females, and their choices seem to have little to do with the males' rank.

Of course, the capacity for aggressive and dominant behaviour was undoubtedly an important part of primate survival, but this is not the same thing as having such behaviour deter-

4. Nancy Tanner and Adrienne Zihlman, 'Women in Evolution: Part 1', in *Signs*, no. 1, 1976, pp. 585–604.

5. Thelma E. Rowell, 'The Concept of Social Dominance', in *Behavioral Biology II*, 1974, pp. 131–54; Pilbeam, pp. 114–15.

6. Jane Lancaster, *Primate Behavior and the Emergence of Human Culture*, New York 1975; Leibowitz, *Females, Males, Families*; M. Kay Martin and Barbara Voorhies, *Female of the Species*, New York 1975; W. C. McGrew, 'The Female Chimpanzee as a Human Evolutionary Prototype', in Frances Dahlberg ed., *Woman the Gatherer*, New Haven 1981, pp. 35–74; Nancy Tanner, *On Becoming Human*, Cambridge 1981.

7. Ruth Bleier, 'Myths of the Biological Inferiority of Women', *University of Michigan Papers in Women's Studies* no. 2, Ann Arbor 1976, p. 50; Thelma E. Rowell, 'The Concept of Social Dominance', p. 131.

4

mined by our genes. In general, research is demonstrating that the primates are capable of highly adaptive learning. Not only have chimpanzees been taught to talk (sign) and rhesus males to parent in captivity,[8] but increasingly sophisticated techniques of wildlife observation have shown primates to be capable of inventing new cooperative behaviours.[9] If primate behaviour is this plastic, it is only reasonable to suppose that plasticity is more pronounced in humans, whose much longer period of neotony (physical immaturity at birth) makes them almost totally dependent on learning.

A no less reductionist approach to the origins of gender inequality is found in the theories of sociobiology.[10] Starting from species (such as ants, bees, and slime moulds) that operate only by instinct and whose members cannot make individual decisions or even survive alone, sociobiologists have come to believe that certain behaviours are determined by the genes and selected because of their survival value for the species. Individuals are believed to be driven by their genes to maximize their 'inclusive fitness'; they strive, that is, to maximize the number of their genes passed on to the next generation, even if this lessens their individual fitness. This explains why bees and ants engage in 'suicidal' behaviour that ensures the survival of their group (and therefore, since all are related, the survival of more of their genes than if they had saved themselves at the expense of this group). Thus there is a genetic base for altruism, and such behaviour will be directed toward those to whom the organism is most closely related, with proportionately less investment in more distant kin or strangers. Applying these theories to humans, E.O.Wilson suggests that occasional examples of helpful behaviour toward non-related persons are explained by an additional concept that takes care of the residual cases: 'reciprocal altruism'. This suggests that sometimes individuals will act favourably toward unrelated people from whom they can expect an equivalent or more generous response at a later date. Such behaviour is said to be genetically programmed, and Wilson also speculates that there may be a genetic basis for a number of other traits that he

8. Leibowitz, *Females, Males, Families*.

9. Emily Hahn, *On the Side of the Apes*, New York 1971.

10. Edward O. Wilson, *Sociobiology: The New Synthesis*, Cambridge, Mass. 1975; *On Human Nature*, Cambridge, Mass. 1978; Charles J. Lumsden and Edward O. Wilson, *Genes, Mind and Culture: The Evolutionary Process*, Cambridge, Mass. 1981; David Barash, *Sociobiology and Behavior*, New York 1982; Richard Dawkins, *The Selfish Gene*, New York 1976.

alleges to be universal, including 'spiteful intrigue', aggression, national chauvinism, female monogamy, male promiscuity, and the fact that humans 'are absurdly easy to indoctrinate' since they 'would rather believe than know'.[11] Through this combined theory of 'inclusive fitness', individual (Darwinian) fitness is translated into a theory of how cultures, rather than species, survive. Successful cultural behaviour is transmitted between generations and cultures through the genes.

Predictably, sociobiologists assume a biological/genetic basis for the division of labour by sex, male dominance, and the double standard. The origins of sexual inequality are seen as an outcome of genetically programmed male behaviour derived from the species' hunting heritage and continuously selected for since by war and imperialism. According to Wilson:

> In hunter-gatherer societies, men hunt and women stay at home. This strong bias persists in most agricultural and industrial societies and, on that ground alone, appears to have a genetic origin. . . . My own guess is that the genetic bias is intense enough to cause a substantial division of labor even in the most free and most egalitarian societies. . . . Even with identical education and equal access to all professions, men are likely to continue to play a disproportionate role in political life, business, and science.[12]

Thus sexual selection acting on the prehistoric division of labour by sex tends to create dominant, public-oriented males and passive, home-centred females. This is reinforced by the different genetic strategies required by males and females in order to maximize their inclusive fitness. Since males produce literally millions of sperm, any male has a better chance of fathering many individuals if he spreads his sperm widely rather than investing in a few children, who could be killed. There is thus a genetic base for male promiscuity. Females, on the other hand, can produce relatively few eggs over a lifetime. The sociobiologists thus argue that it is an adaptive genetic trait for females to desire a monogamous union. Women also, they assert, have a genetic bias toward concentrating their reproductive interest on men who are socially, economically, or educationally superior to them, as well as physically fit enough to provide for them and their children. Thus patterns of male

11. Wilson, *Sociobiology*, ch. 2.
12. Edward O. Wilson, 'Human Decency is Animal', *New York Times Magazine*, 12 October 1975.

6

domination and female subordination, as well as the sexual double standard, are seen as an outcome of genetically determined mate selection.

The fundamental assumption of sociobiology is that 'similar' behaviours are manifest in animals and humans (Wilson talks about ants having wars and slaves) and that they must therefore have similar origins (genetic programmes). This assumption suffers first of all from a confusion of analogy (similar traits due to similar functions) with homology (common genetic ancestry).[13] Even if we agree that there are behavioural similarities, this does not necessarily mean that there is a common genetic basis. As Richard Lewontin, specialist in population genetics at Harvard, notes: 'Certainly the fact that all human societies cook is a result of their genes, not because they have genes for cooking but because they have genes for solving problems in their world'.[14] Sociobiologists, moreover, draw very sloppy analogies between distinct animal and human behaviours, projecting anthropomorphic motivations onto animals, who are said to exhibit 'xenophobia', 'altruism' and 'spite'.[15] Since these 'traits' in animals have demonstrable genetic links, it is argued that they must have in humans as well. The logic is circular. Since 'the outcome of the model is determined by the assumptions underlying the model',[16] the possibility that there can be a cultural, as opposed to a genetic, explanation for similar behaviours is 'systematically excluded'.[17]

Furthermore, like the other biologically determinist theories, sociobiology tends to ignore the variability that exists among cultural systems and cultural behaviour. As one critic has shown,[18] nowhere do people actually behave in the manner predicted. For one thing, it is well known that in societies based on kinship as an organizing principle, expediency rather than actual blood relationship dictates the interactions between individuals. Through the fiction of adoption, complete strangers are assimilated into the group and treated *as if* they were

13. Stephen Jay Gould, *Ever Since Darwin*, New York 1977; *The Mismeasurement of Man*, New York 1981.

14. Richard Lewontin, interview, *Dollars and Sense*, December 1978, p. 9.

15. Gould, *Ever Since Darwin*.

16. B. J. Williams, 'Have We a Darwin of Biocultural Evolution?', *American Anthropologist* 84, 1982, p. 849.

17. Richard Burian, 'A Methodological Critique of Sociobiology,' in Arthur Caplin, ed. *The Sociobiology Debate*, New York 1978, pp. 376–95.

18. Marshall D. Sahlins, *The Use and Abuse of Biology*, Ann Arbor 1976.

brothers, sisters, aunts, uncles, etc. Although mutual aid is certainly a factor in most relationships between people, genetic relatedness is clearly not the primary factor in such kinship systems. Among the Trobriand Islanders, for example, a sister's son has more rights to a man's goods than his own son, though his own son carries more of his genetic material. Among the Lakher of Southeast Asia, a child is considered related to his mother only by virtue of her marriage to his father. If they are divorced, the cooperation and interaction of mother and child cease. In some African and Native American tribes a woman becomes a female husband, and is considered the parent of the children her wife bears by various lovers. The child's loyalty is to the social, not the biological, parent. And in many societies, of course, loyalty and sharing extend far beyond the family.

In answer to these criticisms, sociobiologists have recently attempted to explain cultural variability through the theory that genes and culture 'co-evolve'.[19] The implication of this theory is not simply that genes and culture interacted initially in the development of the human brain ('mind'), or even that cultural behaviour is limited and shaped by our biology (genes), both of which concepts are uncontroversial; what it purports to demonstrate is that even past and present *differences* among human cultures and behaviour have genetic origins.[20] This means that not only the aboriginal division of labour by sex, but also the variability found in male-female interactions throughout history today can be explained as outcomes of natural selection.

As various critics have shown, this theory is seriously flawed.[21] First, it rests on an inadequate knowledge of the precise relationship between our genetic structure (genotype) and our physical traits (phenotype), and of how these affect behaviour.[22] Genes are not the units of evolution and several genes, located on different chromosomes and acting in combination, influence the physical trait. Moreover, the mechanisms of inheritance are complex and poorly understood. Biologists are beginning to recognize that they are an outcome of the dialectical interaction of biology with environment.[23]

19. Charles J. Lumsden and Edward O. Wilson, *Genes, Mind and Culture; Promethean Fire: Reflections on the Origins of Mind*, Cambridge, Mass. 1983.

20. Stephen Jay Gould, 'Genes on the Brain', *New York Review of Books*, June 1983.

21. Williams; Burian; Gould, *Mismeasurement of Man*; Gould, 'Genes on the Brain'.

22. Burian.

8

The sociobiological theory of gene-culture 'co-evolution' also depends on an inadequate conception of culture that sees it as being composed of a series of unitary traits ('culturgens') each of which evolves independently of the others 'through populations by way of the adaptive force of natural selection'.[24] According to this view, culture traits such as a particular ritual, or a conception of women as polluting, are an outcome of natural selection working through the particular populations and facilitating the survival of the group. Such an atomistic view fails to take account of culture as a *system* of interrelated traits.[25] Moreover it is, once again, a basically circular argument: if institutions survive they are adaptive; if they are adaptive they were selected for; therefore institutions that survive derive in some measure from genetics. It is an explanation that discounts the inventiveness of human minds and ignores the fact that lack of genetic programming is probably the most important adaptation humans have made. There is evidence from recent ecological research, for example, that rates of change in the incidence of genetically determined traits in a population are very low, and that it takes even longer for a trait to become established at the level of the group than in the case of individual selection. If it took genetic changes in a population to adapt to new circumstances, humans would probably have died out long ago. Most acquired cultural behaviour is thus likely not genetic even if it is adaptive.[26]

In sum, although few would dispute that human behaviour is genetically constrained (humans can't fly without the aid of an aeroplane), sociobiological theory fails to provide a satisfactory demonstration that either similarities or differences in cultural behaviour can be explained by genetic determination. The evidence suggests only that the big brain provides the potential for problem-solving ability (such as the invention of the aeroplane), not the determination of specific behaviour (such as male promiscuity), however widespread its manifestations in time and place.[27]

It is true, of course, that there are some readily visible physical differences between men and women that seem to a large degree genetic in origin, and some would argue that these mandate

23. Richard Lewontin, 'The Corpse in the Elevator', *New York Review of Books*, January 1983.
24. Gould, 'Genes on the Brain'.
25. Williams.
26. Burian.

different roles and statuses for the sexes. In most (though not all) populations, the average male is taller than the average female, both at birth and after puberty, though the average difference between the sexes is a matter of inches, while the normal range of variation within each sex is more than two feet. Males are also heavier and seem to have greater physical strength, though again the variation among individuals of the same sex is far greater than the average variation between the sexes. But physical sexual dimorphism cannot explain the different roles of the sexes, and far less male dominance, as Leibowitz points out in this volume and elsewhere.[28] Although males tend to do the fighting in many primitive societies, women do as much 'heavy' work as men, if not more.[29] Western history testifies, moreover, that the strongest workers and best warriors often *serve* the dominant members of society, who may be physically very weak. Among a group like the seventeenth century Iroquois, a strong emphasis on male physical prowess was fully compatible with a high position for women, and indeed there is little evidence that men in most foraging societies use either their strength or their weapons as a means of controlling women.[30]

Some authors argue, however, that males are innately more aggressive than females. Although recent studies have repudiated the idea that there are significant sex differences in intellect, analytical powers, social skills, or personal motivation,[31] there does seem to be a strong difference in physical aggression that appears at least as early as the kindergarten years. Some

27. Gould, *Ever Since Darwin*; Science for the People: Sociobiology Study Group, 'Sociobiology – Another Biological Determinism', in *BioScience* 26, 3, pp. 182–90; Stuart Hampshire, 'The Illusion of Sociobiology', *New York Review of Books*, October 1978.

28. Lila Leibowitz, 'Perspectives on the Evolution of Sex Differences', in Reiter, *Toward an Anthropology of Women*; Leibowitz, *Females, Males, Families*.

29. Ann Oakley, *Sex, Gender and Society*, New York 1972, pp. 128–49.

30. Paula Webster, 'Matriarchy: A Vision of Power', in Reiter, pp. 141–156.

31. Irene Frieze, Jacquelinne Parson, Paula Johnson, Dian Ruble and Gail Zelman, *Women and Sex Roles: A Social Psychological Perspective*, New York 1978; Ruth Lowe and Miriam Hubbard, *Genes and Gender Two*, New York 1979; Eleanor Maccoby and Carol Jacklin, *The Psychology of Sex Differences*, Stanford 1974; Marie Richmond-Abbott, 'Early Socialization of the American Female', in Richmond-Abbott ed. *The American Woman: Her Past, Her Present and Her Future*, New York 1979. For a critical review of recent theories about differences in male and female brains, see Freda Salzman, 'Are Sex Roles Biologically Determined?' *Science for the People* 9, 1977, pp. 27–33; Joseph Alper, 'Sex Differences in Brain Asymmetry,' *Feminist Studies* 11, 1985, pp. 7–37.

10

observers suggest that this is partly biological in origin.[32]

Attempts to demonstrate a biological tendency toward aggression (as opposed to a biological capacity, which obviously exists) have centred on studies of hormones. High levels of the male hormone testosterone have been correlated with high levels of aggression, and injections of testosterone increase fighting behaviour in rats. But a hormonal explanation of sexual inequality is hardly admissible, since even in animals aggression does not guarantee dominance[33] and in many societies aggressive individuals are social outcasts or face severe sanctions.[34] In addition, cross-cultural studies show some important variations in rates of male aggression. Margaret Mead found that women among the Tchambuli were *more* aggressive than men, that women and men were equally fierce among the Mundugamor, and that neither men nor women were aggressive among the Arapesh.[35] The explanation for such variability can only be that socialization is more significant than hormones in determining appropriate behaviour among both men and women.

The explanation of social behaviour such as aggression by a single biological factor, moreover, reflects a central weakness of almost all biological determinism. The methodology of such reductionist theories generally involves introducing a disruption of the organism's normal functioning and then explaining the normal working of the organism by its response to the disturbance. The result 'confuses the nature of the perturbation itself with the "cause" of the system's normal functioning'.[36] If, for example, injection of a hormone increases aggressive behaviour, it does not follow that the ordinary levels of that hormone in the animal cause its other aggressive behaviour. Thus, injections of the female hormone oestrogen also increase fighting behaviour in rats while injections of testosterone into the pre-optic area of a male rat's brain stimulate maternal nest-building behaviour.[37]

10

32. Maccoby and Jacklin.

33. Robert Rose, Thomas Gordon and Irwin Bernstein, 'Plasma Testosterone Levels in the Male Rhesus: Influences of Sexual and Social Stimuli', in *Science* 178, pp. 643–45; Rowell, *The Concept of Social Dominance*; Maccoby and Jacklin, p. 274.

34. Ruby Rohrlich-Leavitt, 'Peaceable Primates and Gentle People', in Barbara Watson ed., *Women's Studies: The Social Realities*, New York 1976.

35. Margaret Mead, *Sex and Temperament in Three Primitive Societies*, New York 1963.

36. Lewontin, 'The Corpse in the Elevator', p. 34; Steven Rose ed., *Against Biological Determinism*, New York 1982; Rose ed., *Towards a Liberatory Biology*, New York 1982.

Studies of humans do not show consistent correlations between hormone levels and aggression.[38] Even where correlations are found, it is unclear whether the aggression or the hormone level came first. When low dominance monkeys are placed with monkeys toward whom they can safely act aggressively, their testosterone levels go up; when they are returned to an established group to whom they must defer, their testosterone levels fall dramatically.[39]

Even granting that hormone levels or other chemical changes in the body affect mood, the interpretation of that mood and the behaviour it 'induces' depends upon the social environment. Researchers at Yerkes Primate Centre, for example, were able to locate an 'aggression centre' in the brain of chimpanzees. When this was stimulated electrically in laboratory animals, increased fighting resulted. However, when this was done in monkeys who were released into the wild the result was increased grooming behaviour.[40] Similarly, people injected with adrenalin (the 'fight or flight' chemical), but placed in a peaceful setting, displayed sociable behaviour.[41] As one of the pioneers in hormone research has concluded: 'Hormones are often necessary but never sufficient cause for the occurrence of behaviour.'[42]

All human behaviour, of course, has a biological base, else it could not exist. But the dominance in humans of the cerebral cortex means that what we do with our biological capacities is almost entirely a matter of learning. The difference in aggression between boys and girls should be considered in light of the different socialization given them. Significantly, Sears, Maccoby, and Levin[43] found that the greatest parental distinctions between kindergarten boys and girls were made in the area of permitted aggression. Many studies have shown that people's sex role expectations determine their earliest assessment of infants' capacities and behaviours (even at one day old), creating differences where none can in fact be measured by any objective criteria,[44] and undoubtedly establishing a number of self-

37. Bleier; Frieze et al. p. 85.

38. Oakley, p. 26; Carol Tavris and Carole Otis, *The Longest War: Sex Differences in Perspective*, New York 1977; Frieze et al, p. 88.

39. Rose, Gordon and Bernstein.

40. *New York Times*, 11 September 1974.

41. Stanley Schacter and Jerome Singer, 'Cognitive, Social and Physiological Determinants of Emotional State', in *Psychological Review*, no. 69, pp. 379–99.

42. Beach, 1974, quoted in Bleier, 1976, p. 48.

43. R. R. Sears, E. E. Maccoby and H. Levin, *Patterns of Child Rearing*, Evanston 1957.

fulfilling prophecies. The vital impact of expectations can be seen in studies of persons born as hermaphrodites: in ninety-five percent of the cases the person's sexual identity and correspond-ing social behaviour depended not on actual genetic makeup but on the choice the parents had made in rearing the child as either male or female. This was true 'even for those individuals whose sex of rearing contradicted their biological sex as determined by chromasomes, hormones, gonads, and the formation of the in-ternal and external genitals.'[45]

We conclude that evidence is lacking for clearcut mental or temperamental differences between the sexes. Even where such differences may be established, it is by no means justified to assume, as most of these theories do, that a sex difference ex-plains a sex inequality. This is a conceptual leap made by a number of other authors, who start from the fact that most societies do recognize and define different social and symbolic functions for the sexes. These authors argue that the origins of inequality lie not in naturally different abilities or tempera-ments, but in cultural attempts to explain or control women's central role in reproduction. Woman's biology does not make her weaker, less intelligent, or more submissive than man, but it does make her society's source of new members. According to this school of thought, cultures tend to interpret or organize motherhood in ways that accentuate differences between the sexes and lead to sexual assymetry. There are quite a number of variations on this theme, offering a cultural or symbolic explan-ation for gender inequality.

One such variation is the psychoanalytical interpretation that postulates a universal male fear of female reproductive powers. Starting from the fact that large numbers of primitive societies believe menstruating women to be dangerous to men and animals, proponents of this view argue that men fear and hence attempt to control female sexuality and reproduction.[46] One problem with this theory is that such beliefs have often been interpreted in a male biased and ethnocentric fashion, leaving the impression that *women* are unclean or evil instead of recog-

44. Letty Pogrebin, *Growing Up Free*, New York 1980, pp. 123–8; C. A. Deavey, P. A. Katz and S. R. Zalk, 'Baby X: The Effect of Gender Labels on Adult Response to Infants', in *Sex Roles*, no. 2, 1975, pp. 103–11.

45. Oakley, p. 164.

46. H. R. Hays, *The Dangerous Sex: The Myth of Feminine Evil*, New York 1964; Wolfgang Lederer, *The Fear of Women*, New York 1968.

nizing that certain substances, such as blood, are considered dangerous, whether shed by women or men.[47] Another problem is that some of the simplest foraging societies lack such beliefs altogether, while in other societies males try to imitate rather than avoid female reproductive practices. Elizabeth Zelman[48] has argued that female pollution beliefs validate extreme sex segregation while male rituals imitating female reproduction, such as the couvade, support a high degree of role flexibility. This suggests that fears about female sexuality and reproduction are less cause than symptom of social tensions in male-female relations.[49] A suggestive finding is reported by Raymond Kelly, who notes that pollution beliefs abound in areas of New Guinea where male power and prestige depend on female labour.[50]

A richer psychoanalytical perspective is taken by Nancy Chodorow,[51] who suggests that the primary role of women in bearing, nursing, and socializing children leads to a different psychological dynamic for each sex. Girls learn their gender identity by imitation of a particular, individual female, which leads them, she argues, to relate to others in a particularized and personalized way. They become more present-oriented and subjective than boys, who must learn to identify with a sex that is frequently absent and less accessible and who can only do so by learning an abstract male role. In the attempt to gain this 'elusive' male identity, the boy tends to define himself as not-woman, repressing his own feminine qualities and denigrating femininity in general.

Although Chodorow perceptively analyzes the reproduction of sex roles in male dominant societies, her work does not really address the origins of male dominance, as she assumes much of what needs to be explained: for example, the confinement of

47. Elizabeth Faithorn, 'The Concept of Pollution Among the Kafe of the Papua New Guinea Highlands', in Reiter; Evelyn Reed, *Women's Evolution*, New York 1975, pp. 95–101.

48. Elizabeth Zelman, 'Pollution and Power', in Dorothy McGuigan, *New Research on Women and Sex Roles*, Ann Arbor 1976.

49. Edward Harper, 'Fear and the Status of Women', in *Southwestern Journal of Anthropology*, no. 25, 1959; pp. 81–95; Mary Douglas, *Purity and Danger*, London 1966.

50. Sherry Ortner and Harriet Whitehead eds., *Sexual Meanings: The Cultural Construction of Gender and Sexuality*, Cambridge 1981, p. 20.

. 51. Nancy Chodorow, 'Family Structure and Feminine Personality', in Michelle Zimbalist Rosaldo and Louise Lamphere eds., *Women, Culture and Society*, Stanford 1974, pp. 43–66; Chodorow, *The Reproduction of Mothering: Psychoanalysis and the Reproduction of Mothering*, Berkeley 1978.

women to a private domestic sphere cut off from the public sphere of male activity and authority. Even where women *are* primarily responsible for child care, however, and males do work away from the domestic arena, it does not follow, except in an already sexist society, that a boy should move from defining himself as not-woman to denigrating women in general; and it is even less logical that such childhood denigration (which females also frequently direct against males) could in and of itself produce the institutionalized subordination of adult women.

Another theory based on reproductive roles emphasizes symbolism rather than psychodynamics. Sherry Ortner[52] attempts to show how gender identification can lead to a denigration of adult women on the part of both sexes by arguing that women's biology and domestic role make her appear closer to nature. Nature, she argues, is in turn seen as lower than culture, so that women are perceived as lower in the social scale and subject to the restrictions that culture puts on both nature and the domestic unit. Other authors build on Ortner and Chodorow in suggesting that there is a 'universal, structural opposition between domestic and public spheres'[53] that juxtaposes the fragmented, private interests of women to the higher universalistic and integrative activities of men. Men are concerned with collective affairs — politics, governance, and external relations — while women individually tend hearth and children. Ortner and Whitehead assert that 'the sphere of social activity predominantly associated with males encompasses the sphere predominantly associated with females and is, for that reason, culturally accorded higher value.'[54]

Formulations such as those above, however, tend to impose a Western dualism and hierarchy that do not do justice to the complexity of other cultural behaviour and belief systems. In the first place, the association of women with nature and men with culture is far from universal. Many ancient societies had androgynous deities that reflected an integration of both male and female principles with natural and cultural forces.[55] Among the Mandan and the ancient Sumerians, the earth is a female symbol, but among the Iroquois and ancient Egyptians the

52. Sherry Ortner, 'Is Female to Male as Nature is to Culture?', in Rosaldo and Lamphere, pp. 67–88.
53. Rosaldo, 'Women, Culture and Society: An Overview', in Rosaldo and Lamphere, pp. 17–42.
54. Ortner and Whitehead, pp. 7–8.

sky — surely a transcendent symbol — is considered female. Among the Sherbro, children are considered close to nature, but both adult men and women are associated with culture.[56] Australian aborigines attribute such qualities as passivity, ferocity, and sweetness to membership in a kinship section rather than to gender. Sperm, incidentally, are thought to belong to a kin section designated as passive and associated with the moon, calm water, and temperate weather.[57]

Not all societies, moreover, devalue nature. For the Haganers, the wild and domestic 'are in an antithetical rather than a hierarchical, processual relationship. The . . . development of social consciousness in persons is not represented as culture transcending nature'.[58] The adversary approach to nature is linked to the rise of state society, as is the idea that both women and nature are forces to be tamed.[59] The latter is an effect, not a cause, of male domination.

It is true that men tend to be associated with the political sphere in most societies where this sphere exists. The political arena, however, is not the only public arena in non-state societies, for many vital collective decisions are made within the domestic grouping.[60] The idea that politics is a higher social sphere derives from state societies where the political realm can coerce the domestic one. But a remarkably consistent aspect of simple societies is the fact that political leadership confers

55. Joseph Campbell, *The Masks of God*, New York 1962, 1964; James Melaart, *Catal Huyuk: A Neolithic Town in Anatolia*, New York 1967; Eleanor Leacock and Jill Nash, 'Ideologies of Sex: Archetypes and Stereotypes', in *Annals of the New York Academy of Sciences*, no. 285, 1977, pp. 618–45; Peggy Sanday, *Female Power and Male Dominance*. Cambridge 1981.

56. Carol MacCormack, 'Proto-Social to Adult: A Sherbro Transformation', in Carol MacCormack and Marilyn Strathern, eds., *Nature, Culture and Gender*, Cambridge 1980, pp. 95–118.

57. Maurice Godelier, 'Modes of Production, Kinship and Demographic Structures', in Maurice Bloch ed., *Marxist Analysis and Social Anthropology*, New York 1975.

58. Marilyn Strathern, 'No Nature, No Culture: The Hagan Case', in MacCormack and Strathern, pp. 174–222.

59. Leacock and Nash; MacCormack and Strathern.

60. Eleanor Leacock, *Myths of Male Dominance*, New York 1981; Nicera Suderkasa, 'Female Employment and Family Organization in West Africa', in McGuigan, Judith Brown, 'Iroquois Women: An Ethnohistoric Note', in Reiter.

61. Robert Lowie, 'Political Organization Among the Australian Aborigines' in Ronald Cohen and John Middleton eds., *Comparative Political Systems*, New York 1967; Marshall Sahlins, *Stone Age Economics*, Chicago 1972.

neither power nor prestige, and is frequently ignored by domestic groups.[61] It might be more reasonable to describe political affairs as peripheral in such societies rather than as paramount.

Where male political activities do exert an important influence on wider social interactions, it is still not inevitable that males are exclusively associated with 'integrative, universalistic sorts of concerns'[62] that give them prestige and/or power. Denise Paulme points out that in many African societies

> . . . men never seem to conceive of ties other than those of kinship linked with common residence . . . [whereas] among women the mere fact of belonging to the same sex is enough to establish an active solidarity. An appeal addressed by a woman to other women will reach far beyond the boundaries of a single village, and a movement of revolt among women will always be a serious matter, even if its immediate cause should be of minor importance.[63]

In nineteenth century America it was men who were stereotyped as rebels against (or refugees from) the social order, whose continuity was often represented by women. Men may also be associated with the destructive acts of war and personal rivalry. Among the Iroquois, men were more likely to engage in individualistic behaviour that required social control, while 'feminine activities . . . coincided with the cooperative and pacific principles upon which the League was built.'[64] Indeed, it has been suggested that it is typically male-centred activities and organizational principles that are individuating, competitive, and fragmenting, while female ones are associated with integrative social concerns and cooperation.[65]

To be sure, there is much ethnographic evidence that women *are* perceived as particularistic and fragmenting in many societies. Once again, however, this is likely to be not cause but consequence of processes in which female labour and reproduction are privately appropriated for the aims of male household heads — aims often called 'social' but more appropriately labelled as clan or patriarchal family. Thus among the Haganers the view of women as particularistic, even anti-social, and men

62. Ortner, 'Is Female to Male', pp. 67–88.
63. Denise Paulme, *Women of Tropical Africa*, Berkeley 1960, p. 7.
64. B. H. Quain, 'The Iroquois', in Margaret Mead ed., *Cooperation and Competition Among Primitive Peoples*, Boston 1961, p. 277.
65. Karla Poewe, *Matrilineal Ideology*, London 1981.

as social, corresponds to the fact that women change residence at marriage and cannot always be counted on to place the interests of their husbands' clan ahead of their own.[66]

Attempts to explain women's low status by psychological or symbolic processes associated with female reproduction often provide insightful analyses into how male dominance is *perpetuated* and why male-female relations are so complex and fraught with tension. They help us understand the dynamics of sexual inequality in a way that the articles in this volume do not even attempt. Ultimately, however, they cannot explain the origins of gender inequality, as they assume universal psychological associations that do not withstand detailed examination. A seemingly more historical and materialist theory is presented by William Divale and Marvin Harris,[67] who believe that population pressure on resources, especially following the Neolithic Revolution (the transition from food collecting to food production; for example, horticulture and herding) led in an elaborate sequence of cause-effect to the subordination of women.

Divale and Harris assert 'the existence of a pervasive institutional and ideological complex of male supremacy in band and village sociocultural systems.'[68] This complex includes patrilineal inheritance and descent, patrilocal residence, marriage by capture, polygamy, brideprice, postmarital sex restrictions on women, property rights in women, male secret societies, male age grades, men's houses, and a preference for male babies. What, they ask, are the origins of such a phenomenon? They suggest that the origins of the male supremacist complex lie in warfare, which places high value on male qualities and allows women to be used as rewards for male valour. Warfare, in turn, stemmed from population pressure, especially after the Neolithic Revolution resulted in a more sedentary life style and starchy diets, causing an increase in fertility. The most efficient way to limit population, in the absence of birth control, was to reduce the numbers of potential mothers through female infanticide. To justify killing female babies, however, the male supremacist complex outlined above was necessary. Warfare, 'always' present in human societies, now became increasingly important to 'sustain' the male supremacist complex. Warfare elevated

66. Strathern.
67. William Divale and Marvin Harris, 'Population, Warfare and the Male Supremacist Complex', in *American Anthropologist* no. 78, 1976, pp. 521–38.
68. Ibid., p. 521.

maleness and allowed women, already in scarce supply due to infanticide, to be used as reward for male feats of war. This necessitated rearing females to be passive. In short, Divale and Harris argue that the subordination (devaluation) of women was necessary to justify female infanticide (required for population control), and that warfare functioned to sustain this system both by reinforcing 'macho' values and by keeping the adult sex ratio somewhat in balance, through male deaths in battle.

In important ways, the argument advanced here seems to us to be circular. In this analysis, warfare arises to enforce female subordination; yet warfare also presupposes female subordination, in order for women to be used as rewards for male warriors. Warfare is a consequence of female infanticide, helping to create balanced sex ratios through the death of adult males; but it is also a cause for such infanticide, providing its main justification. One reads Divale and Harris in vain for an actual explanation of the origins of male domination and warfare. We only learn their supposed functions. But to say that a phenomenon sustains male dominance is not to say that it caused it. And the consequences of a male supremacist complex or of warfare should not be used to explain their origins. Equating the two, as functionalist theories like this do, allows the specific historical developments to be interpreted as inevitable, when in fact the question is why alternatives were not chosen.

Indeed, a major flaw in the argument of Divale and Harris is the assumption that the route of warfare and patrilineal organization was the most common or most successful path for Palaeolithic and Neolithic societies. Their sample of band societies is drawn mostly from twentieth century ethnographies of collecting economies severely influenced by Western culture and imperatives; it undoubtedly distorts our concept of the nature of Palaeolithic band and Neolithic village society. Thus the prevalence of warfare asserted in their Table IX (p.532) is a likely consequence of the heightening of cultural stress due to capitalist penetration in many areas of the world in this century. For example, Napoleon Chagnon, the original ethnographer of that prototypical 'macho' and warlike society, the South American Yanomamo, suggests that warfare was a recent introduction, and this view has been corroborated by other researchers.[69] Similarly, in asserting the predominance of patrilineality, Divale and Harris fail to acknowledge recent research questioning the model of the 'patrilineal band' and suggesting, rather, that in

many instances collecting societies have a highly flexible bilateral organization which allows men and women to choose
their place of residence according to circumstances, and to move
freely between groups. The Bushman band, for example, has at
its core a group of related brothers and sisters, but its membership is highly variable and fluctuates according to seasonal conditions.[70] The patrilineal band that features in twentieth century
ethnographies may well have been introduced by trade and
colonialism.[71]

A more historically oriented study comes to quite different
conclusions, showing that warfare is frequent in only eight per
cent of hunting and gathering societies, becoming more
common in advanced horticultural systems but only 'endemic' in
the early agrarian states.[72] The archaeological record suggests
that high levels of warfare did not follow the adoption of horticulture or agriculture *per se*, but developed only after the evolution of complex sociopolitical systems.[73] Catal Huyuk, one of
the best-documented examples of an early Neolithic urban
settlement, was notably free of defensive structures.[74]

Furthermore, the precise relationship between warfare, food
production, and population growth is highly controversial.[75]
Divale and Harris cite only their own work as evidence for the
assertion that warfare in band and village societies 'represents a
systematic attempt to achieve stationary or near stationary populations'[76]. There is little evidence of endemic population pressures in Palaeolithic society and no reason to think that early
Neolithic cultures would have accelerated any problem that did
exist. Indeed, in the absence of evidence to the contrary, one
might assume that improved farming techniques might have
eased population pressures in some areas.

69. Napoleon Chagnon, 'Yanomamo: The True People', *National Geographic*
150, 1976, p. 213; Shelton Davis and Robert Mathews, *The Geological Imperative*,
Cambridge 1976.

70. Dorothy Lee, *Freedom and Culture*, Englewood Cliffs 1959.

71. Eleanor Leacock, 'Class, Commodity, and the Status of Women,' in R.
Leavitt, ed., *Women Cross-Culturally*, The Hague 1975, pp. 601–18.

72. Gerhard Lenski and Jean Lenski, *Human Societies*, New York 1974, p. 138.

73. Gordon V. Childe, *What Happened in History*, Harmondsworth 1942; Julian
Steward, *The Theory of Culture Change*, Urbana 1955; Robert M. C. Adams, *The
Evolution of Urban Society*, Chicago 1966.

74. Melaart.

75. Ester Boserup, *The Conditions of Agricultural Growth*, Chicago 1965.

76. Divale and Harris, p. 531.

In short, this 'theory' of the origins of male dominance is unsatisfactory at all levels of analysis. Even if we accept the assumption that population increase was the problem faced by Palaeolithic and Neolithic societies, we would question first whether female infanticide was the only solution. It is well known that pre-industrial cultures have many artificial means of controlling births, apart from infanticide.[77] Second, supposing a cultural need for female infanticide, why was it necessary to devalue adult women in the process of constructing such an elaborate complex of institutions and ideology? Many primitive societies abandon the aged and infirm without faltering in their extreme respect for old age.[78] We suggest that 'the male supremacist complex' arose under specific historical conditions interacting with particular types of social structures, not as a mechanical solution to justify killing female babies. (Indeed, one could as easily read the evidence presented by Divale and Harris to show that female infanticide arose to balance out deaths from warfare, though we decline to use the same mechanical approach even in reverse.) We must look elsewhere for an explanation of the historical evidence for increasing male dominance in advanced horticultural and early state societies.

A more complex theory purporting to explain that evidence is offered by Parker and Parker.[79] They propose that the early development of differential power and prestige for men was as reward for male risk-taking (in hunting, warfare, and so on), and that this was reinforced and intensified by technological developments in the first complex societies. The Parkers believe that human biology and sexual dimorphism predisposed men and women to play certain roles in the division of labour. They characterize the male role as involving men in work requiring greater physical strength, high levels of risk and danger, mobility, cooperation, and technological skill — in short, a combination of brains and brawn.[80] Women, on the other hand,

77. Carol Ember, 'The Relative Decline in Women's Contribution to Agriculture with Intensification', in *American Anthropologist*, no. 85, 1983, pp. 285–304.
78. Stephanie Coontz, 'Insult and Injury: Growing Old in America' in Coontz and Frank eds., *Life in Capitalist America*, New York 1975; Leo Simmons, *The Position of the Aged in Primitive Society*, New Haven 1946.
79. Seymour Parker and Hilda Parker, 'The Myth of Male Superiority: Rise and Demise', *American Anthropologist*, no. 81, pp. 289–309.
80. George P. Murdock and Caterina Provost, 'Factors In the Division of Labor by Sex: A Cross-Cultural Analysis', in *Ethnology*, no. 12, 1973.

tended to engage in activities that involved less danger and mobility, required less concentration or skills, and were more easily interruptable and substitutable.[81] While not saying that the tasks were intrinsically unequal in the sense that one sex made a more important contribution than the other, the Parkers believe that throughout most of history men have been asked to make consistently more difficult and risky contributions (p.299). The requirements of male tasks, combined with a bio-psychologically-based male vulnerability (greater susceptibility to disease, death, and so on) resulted in a situation where the male labour supply was relatively costly and inelastic (not easily substitutable). In order to induce males to come forward in adequate numbers and with the requisite skills to perform the social tasks needed by an increasingly complex socioeconomic system, it was necessary to devise some sort of reward. Thus the 'myth of male dominance' was created as compensation and reward (in a kind of social exchange).

In addition, the Parkers assert that male dominance had adaptive advantages which were reinforced through time as societies became more complex, requiring ever greater levels of technological skill. However, although they believe that this situation has prevailed since the establishment of a division of labour by sex, and, in fact, that it intensified with increased complexity, they think that 'efficient means of birth control and other technological aids' of modern industrial society can and will lead to its elimination, and thus to the demise of the 'myth of male superiority'.

Parker and Parker may be criticized for their uncritical acceptance of a universal patterning of sex roles as an outcome of sexual dimorphism. A growing body of research lends credence to the counter-assertion that women in collecting and in simple horticultural societies undertook tasks that demanded as much brawn, as well as brain, as did male tasks.[82] Other research suggests that women were just as mobile as men, at least when they were not pregnant or nursing, and that in band societies this was quite a bit of the time. In non-sedentary Bushmen bands, for example, a combination of birth-spacing (average of four years) and sharing of child care tasks enables many women to range far from home in search of food.[83] West African women are well-known for their success — and mobility — as traders

81. Parker and Parker, p. 293.
82. Frances Dahlberg, *Woman the Gatherer*, New Haven 1981.

and entrepreneurs in their own right, proving that women, even those with children, do not have to be sedentary. In any case, the cross-cultural record demonstrates more variability in the assignment of tasks, and much greater socio-political variation, than is suggested here.

We would not deny that there is a general pattern in the division of labour. Indeed, our own article suggests that there were some consistent patterns in early societies in which males took on more geographically far-ranging assignments that frequently involved more risk (though not more brain or brawn) than women's tasks. But the social exchange theory fails to explain why male tasks 'universally' receive recognition and valuation. If male supremacy was a reward, what precisely was being rewarded? The Parkers seem to think that in early societies it was the male capacity for heavy work, whereas they suggest that later it was male 'skill'. But females engage in heavy work along with men in many societies, and they certainly take risks in childbirth, which is surely a socially necessary kind of labour. Furthermore, skill is a matter of training, so we have to ask why males were given that training and assigned tasks requiring a high level of skill. It is commonly accepted that women were the first potters: How and why did pottery become a male-dominated craft, and why weren't the inventors of this important manufacture given social rewards? It was not skill, but the social relations accompanying the development of craft specialization that must have determined that men should be trained in these tasks.

Furthermore, in the more complex societies — where the Parkers say male dominance was intensified by rewards for male skill and risk — it was increasingly only some men, not all, who were given prestige and power. What kinds of work did slave owners or family patriarchs do that justified their power and prestige vis à vis slaves, wives, and junior men? Why did women have low status in slave societies, such as fifth-century Athens, where free men took few risks and did little work? Why, conversely, have women had high status in many societies, from ancient Crete to the seventeenth century Iroquois, where males undoubtedly did take great physical risks? The answers to these questions must lie not in the nature of the work itself, which the

83. Richard Lee, *The !Kung San: Men, Women and Work in a Foraging Society*, Cambridge 1979; Patricia Draper, '!Kung Women: Contrasts in Foraging and Sedentary Contexts,' in Reiter, 1975, pp. 77–109.

Parkers themselves admit is not intrinsically hierarchical, but in the origins of the hierarchy itself. These, we would suggest, lie in the relations of work, the issue of who controls whose labour. To explain the origins of female subordination we need a theory that accounts for the control of women's work by men. Such a theory cannot be derived from the nature of men's and women's tasks on their own, nor from any inevitable technological tendency, because human cultures have exhibited too much variation to postulate any necessary relation between a task or a tool, on the one hand, and a particular social relationship of superiority or subordination on the other.

This brings us to a central assumption of all the preceding theories that we have so far failed to challenge — the assertion that 'in every known society, men and women compose two differentially valued terms of a value set, men being as *men*, higher.'[84] Although this assertion seems supported by an extremely large body of anthropological and historical observation, there are good grounds for challenging the idea that male dominance has been a universal in human societies over time.

In the first place, many observers have simply been unable to divest themselves of their own cultural preconceptions. Male ethnographers have dealt with male informants, accepting any uncomplimentary remarks these may make about women as the social reality, and ignoring equally disparaging comments about men made by women.[85] A number of anthropologists have recently gone back to the original anthropological sources on various cultures and found that the 'masters' had reported almost exclusively on male activities and prerogatives, ignoring or downplaying equivalent female activities, rights, and prestige systems.[86] Among the pre-colonial Ashanti, for example, 'the head of state was a female position' but in accounts of Ashanti life this is often only 'mentioned in passing, designated by the misnomer "queen mother", although she was never the king's wife, and was not necessarily his mother. She did not hold her position by virtue of her relationship with him; indeed

84. Ortner and Whitehead, p. 16.

85. Naomi Quinn, 'Anthropological Studies on Women's Status' in *Annual Review of Anthropology*, no. 6, 1977, p. 183; Susan Rogers, 'Woman's Place: A Critical Review of Anthropological Theory,' in *Comparative Studies in Society and History*, 20, 1978, pp. 143–7.

86. Annette Weiner, *Women of Value, Men of Renown: New Perspectives on Trobriand Exchange*, Austin 1976; Quinn, p. 184; Rogers, p. 185; Rohrlich-Leavitt, Sykes and Weatherford.

24

it was she who appointed him, and was above him in the state hierarchy'.[87]

Proofs of male dominance, moreover, frequently rest on fuzzy or inconsistent criteria: if women are excluded from some activity, that is considered proof of male power; when males are excluded, it's considered evidence of women's 'restriction' to a subordinate sphere. Considerable selection is also used in choosing examples. While Rosaldo emphasizes Yoruba women 'bowing and scraping' before their husbands,[88] Suderkasa adds that the same behaviour is engaged in by males, who 'prostrate themselves before their mothers, older sisters, and other females whose age or position demand that they do so.'[89] Similarly, observers who stress that only males engage in trance dancing among the Bushmen neglect to mention that the dance cannot go on unless the women agree to make the music for it.[90]

Western authors also seem unable to understand a world that lacks a conception of hierarchical relations among different things. Pre-state societies often have a concept of 'separate but equal' that state societies lack[91] and male/female distinctions may best be described in terms of complementary functions rather than superordination/subordination.[92] Indeed, the very attempt to define 'equality' may obscure the dynamics of societies where 'equality exists in the very nature of things, not as a principle to be applied. . . . Often there is no linguistic mechanism whatever for comparison. What we find is an absolute respect for . . . all individuals irrespective of age and sex.'[93]

A second major problem with the collection of cross-cultural examples 'proving' the universality of male dominance is the ahistorical nature of such evidence. Two major geographical areas where extreme male domination of women is well-documented in non-state societies are Melanesia and South America. But Melanesia is an area where rapid socioeconomic and status differentiation had taken place prior to Western ob-

87. Rogers, p. 146.

88. Rosaldo, 'Women, Culture and Society'.

89. Suderkasa, p. 61.

90. Elizabeth Marshall Thomas, *The Harmless People*, New York 1959, pp. 131–5.

91. Karen Sacks, 'State Bias and Women's Status', in *American Anthropologist*, no. 78, 1976, pp. 131–54.

92. Suderkasa, p.52; Colin Turnbull, 'Mbuti Womanhood', in Francis Dahlberg, p. 219.

93. Lee, 1979, p. 40.

servations, and the status of women seems to have been declining from a previously higher position.[94] In South America, devolution from larger political entities had taken place[95] and there was extreme (and atypical) population pressure and warfare.[96] In both these cases, the low status of women should probably be related to the tensions and pressures consequent on economic, political, and demographic transformation, not to 'the state of nature'. On close examination, in fact, many cases of male domination in 'primitive' societies seem to have evolved only under the pressure of trade or warfare following contact with expanding groups, or under the direct impact of colonialism.[97]

Finally, there are examples of societies in which asymmetry between the sexes is difficult or impossible to discern. Among the Mbuti 'both men and women see themselves as equal in all respects except the supremely vital one that, whereas the woman can (and on occasion does) do almost everything the male does, she can do one thing no male can do: give birth to life.'[98] John Nance reports that among the Tasaday 'decision-making apparently was based on discussion in which men and women expressed views equally, with age and experience determining degree of influence.'[99] And Peggy Sanday describes five societies that offer or offered 'scripts for female power'.[100] Summing up a review of recent anthropological research on women, Naomi Quinn comments: 'Together, the bias of male informants in reporting, ethnographers in describing, and cross-cultural workers in interpreting various disparate customs . . . and the depressive effects of colonialism on many aspects of women's lives, may seem to leave very little cross-cultural female subordination to explain.'[101]

94. Irving Goldman, 'Status Rivalry and Cultural Evolution in Polynesia', in Cohen and Middleton eds.; Eleanor Leacock, 'Women, Power and Authority', in Leela Dube, Eleanor Leacock and Shirley Ardener eds., *Visibility and Power: Essays on Women in Society and Development*, Delhi forthcoming.

95. Kay Martin, 'South American Foragers: A Case Study in Devolution', in *American Anthropologist*, no. 71, 1969.

96. Leacock, 'Women, Power and Authority'.

97. Ester Boserup, *Woman's Role in Economic Development*, New York 1970; Leacock, *Myths of Male Dominance*; Rogers, p. 158; Rayna Rapp Reiter, 'The Search for Origins: Unravelling the Threads of Gender Hierarchy', in *Critique of Anthropology*, no. 3, 1977, pp. 13–14; Peggy Sanday, *Female Power and Male Dominance*, Cambridge 1981; Judith Van Allen,' "Sitting on a Man": Colonialism and the Lost Political Institutions of Igbo Women', in *Canadian Journal of African Studies*, no. 10, 1972.

This is, of course, an overstatement. Male dominance is a material fact, with concrete repercussions for women, in most of the world, and our egalitarian examples come from relatively isolated simple societies. Long before Western trade and colonialism had even arisen, ancient societies in the Middle East, Mediterranean, and British Isles had gone through earlier processes in which the position of women had deteriorated. What is required, then, is a theory that explains why male dominance, though not inevitable, was a likely outcome of processes connected with socioeconomic expansion and increasing social complexity.

One theory that has been advanced to explain the evidence suggesting a decline in a formerly high position for women is that of the matriarchy. According to this view, women were once pre-eminent in economics and politics, but matriarchal rule was overthrown by men at some early point in human history.[102] Engels asserted that 'mother right' was a general phase of human pre-history that was overthrown when men developed movable wealth and created patrilineal inheritance in order to pass it on to their own children.[103]

We do not have the space to consider the various theories of matriarchy here, but simply note that there is *no* evidence for a matriarchal stage in human history. The theories cited above all contain one or both of the following fallacies: 1) Matriarchy is confused with matrilineality, and traces of matrilineal descent in the historical record are, without other justification, asserted as proof of an ancient matriarchy; 2) The importance of women in ancient myths and religious artifacts is often said to reflect a 'survival' of prior matriarchal social organization. Pomeroy[104] points out, however, that the role of women in myths has been subject to much misinterpretation, and Monique Saliou (this volume) suggests that such myths may indicate greater equality

98. Turnbull, p. 206.

99. John Nance, *The Gentle Tasaday*, New York 1975, p. 24.

100. Sanday, pp. 15–34.

101. Quinn, p. 186.

102. Robert Briffault, *The Mothers*, London 1952; Johan Jacob Bachoven, *Myth, Religion and Mother-Right*, Princeton 1967; Helen Diner, *Mothers and Amazons*, New York 1965; Reed; George Thompson, *The Prehistoric Aegean*, London 1965.

103. Friedrich Engels, *The Origin of the Family, Private Property and the State*, New York 1972.

104. Sarah Pomeroy, *Goddesses, Whores, Wives and Slaves: Women in Classical Antiquity*, New York 1975.

for women in the past but are not evidence of actual female rule. Childe[105] asks: 'are female figurines any better evidence for matriarchy than are the Venus figures and Virgins of undeniably patriarchal societies?' (See Fleuhr-Lobban[106] for a further critique of theories of matriarchy).

The search for origins will never be definitively settled. But if we are to counter the assertions of inevitable and universal male dominance we must suggest some concrete reasons for the historical appearance and spread of male domination in ancient cultures. Probably no single historical account will suffice to explain every case: we will need to look at different time periods and processes, as Rapp points out in an excellent survey of the problem.[107] The two most important recent attempts at a historical explanation have been made by Peggy Sanday and Eleanor Leacock.[108] Both have combined a historical approach taking into account the variability of sociocultural experience with an explanatory framework that identifies underlying recurrent patterns of development.

Peggy Sanday focuses on the ways in which gender is used by many societies as an organizing principle on both the structural and symbolic levels. She has presented a complex account of the conditions under which balanced and symmetrical power relations between the sexes are replaced by asymmetry and male dominance. Basing her analysis on the evidence of both quantitative cross-cultural data and in-depth case studies, she finds that characteristic 'cultural configurations' result from the interaction of natural environments, child-rearing practices, and sex-role behaviour. For example, hunting societies and societies in which large animals play an important part tend to produce distant fathers, masculine creator symbols, and an 'outer', animal orientation toward the powers of the universe. Gathering societies, and societies in which animals are less important, tend to produce involved male parents, feminine or couple creator symbols, and an 'inner', plant orientation. A 'dual' orientation sometimes occurs in societies that combine 'a ritual concern with both plant gathering or incipient cultivation *and* the predatory activities of men.'[109]

105. Gordon V. Childe, *Social Evolution*, London 1951, pp. 64–5.
106. C. Fluehr-Lobban, 'A Marxist Reappraisal of the Matriarchate' in *Current Anthropology*, no. 20, 1979, pp. 341–8.
107. Reiter, 'The Search for Origins'.
108. Sanday; Leacock, 'Women, Power and Authority'.

Sanday believes that the natural environment and mode of subsistence fundamentally 'cause' the symbol system and sex role plan of any society. However, she is also concerned to emphasize the independent role that symbols play in determining subsequent sex role behaviour and authority relations. She suggests that there is an underlying bio-psychological basis for gender concepts that, in turn, provide 'scripts' for behaviour. For example, she suggests that in all societies women are associated with the power to give life, while men are associated with the power to take life. Depending upon natural and historical conditions, one or both powers may be culturally valued and receive ritual emphasis. Where food is abundant and fertility is desired, women tend to have *ascribed* power and female principles are stressed. On the other hand, where the taking of life is important, as in hunting or warlike societies, men tend to exercise power and male principles are elevated in ritual and social life. However, a high value on male aggression does not automatically or necessarily translate into male dominance, as women may *achieve* power under some circumstances.

According to Sanday, men and women tend to be more segregated and competitive in societies that have a masculine/outer configuration. Higher levels of integration and cooperative relations between the sexes are more likely to be found in societies with an inner/plant orientation.[110] Sexual segregation, like male aggression, does not necessarily create male dominance. Some societies may segregate the sexes but relations between them may still be balanced and cooperative. However, Sanday thinks that male dominance is a likely outcome of the outer/segregated configuration where historical conditions have favoured an expansion of the male sphere leading to increased dependence of women on men.

Such conditions have arisen in a variety of historical contexts. Increased technological complexity, warfare, famine, migration, and colonization — all conditions leading to heightened social stress — have resulted in an expansion of the male role. Here Sanday borrows from the 'social exchange' model in suggesting that 'real' male dominance arises from the political rights that are granted to males as compensation for their role and as 'a privilege for being the expendable sex'.[111] However she says 'adap-

109. Sanday, p. 248.
110. Ibid., p. 90.
111. Ibid., p. 9.

tation to stress does not always include the subjugation of women'.[112] In inner-oriented or dual societies, where women still exercise some power, stress may lead to 'mythical' male dominance where 'conflicting sexual power principles coexist'.[113] For example, external pressures may lead to the projection onto women of cultural fears associated with female fertility. Under such circumstances, women may voluntarily cede 'mythical' power to men because it is more reproductively efficient to do so and allows both sexes manoeuvering room. Thus for Sanday the determinants of male dominance are the conjunction of stressful historical circumstances with a prior cultural configuration.

The great value of Sanday's book lies in her attempt to show how gender is used as a 'powerful and available metaphor' to organize society, and how the system of sexual symbols interacts with environment and social institutions to influence the relations between the sexes. She offers interesting insights into the richness and complexity of sex role plans and the mechanics of sexual inequality. We do not, however, feel that she has been totally successful in her claim to explain the origins of inequality, even while she has done much to elucidate its dynamics. As we have seen, she seeks the origins of sexual inequality in the pressure of stressful historical conditions on prior cultural configuration/sex role plans. But since externally generated stress does not, she argues, automatically or necessarily lead to male dominance, in the final analysis it seems to be the prior cultural configuration that determines the outcome. We have some difficulty with her emphasis on the independent role of such configurations, which she tends to treat as separate from changing social relations within the culture. Rather than examining the dialectical interaction between a culture's internal evolution and its sex role configuration, Sanday treats the sex role configuration as though it arises independently from internal social processes, determines internal social relations, and changes those internal relations only when it interacts with externally generated sources of stress, such as famine, invasion, or colonialism. We remain unconvinced by her tendency to give primary emphasis to environmental factors in her analysis of the origins of those configurations. We also question her contention that societies react to stress in fundamentally different ways depend-

112. Ibid., pp. 185–6.
113. Ibid., p. 179.

ing upon their prior cultural configuration.

To explain the origins of the prior cultural configuration, Sanday relies on a somewhat awkward combination of environmental and bio-psychological factors, neither of which, taken separately or in combination, can account for the ambiguities of the data. Why, for example, do the Copper Eskimo, a hunting society *par excellence*, have an 'inner' orientation? Why do twenty-eight percent of societies with a feminine orientation hunt large animals? Why do seventy-three per cent of fishing societies have masculine orientation,[114] while fifty-four per cent of these same societies have equality between the sexes and only fifteen per cent have inequality?[115]

Furthermore, Sanday does not really demonstrate that societies with different cultural configurations have qualitatively different reactions to stress. She gives no examples of inner-oriented or dual societies that reacted to stress without undermining the status of women. Even the Cheyenne and the Iroquois failed ultimately to resist the social tensions of colonialism and the pressures toward male dominance. Her distinction between 'real' and 'mythical' male dominance does not really help to explain the ambiguities of the evidence. Does the fact that women cede power to men voluntarily make 'mythical' male dominance any less real than that which develops in outer-oriented societies? At times, Sanday herself seems to suggest that 'mythical' male dominance is but a transitional state: 'a waystation where opposing and conflicting sexual power principles may coexist'.[116] If so, then the critical issue in explaining the origins of male dominance lies less in the prior cultural configuration than in the nature and origin of the stress.

Although Sanday does show that certain kinds of stress, such as war, migration, or environmental conditions, elevate the male role and lead to new sexual fears and tensions, she tends to ignore internal sources of stress that may help to account for increased social competition and a fearful attitude towards the environment. These are most likely to be associated with the breakdown of community reciprocity, and with the development of differences in rank or property ownership. For example, in her discussion of the Bellacoola she suggests that they perceived the environment as hostile and threatening due to

114. Ibid., p. 69.
115. Ibid., p. 170
116. Ibid., p. 116.

seasonal food scarcity. This, in turn, accounted for the Bella-coola's cultural perception of women as dangerous. But it is unclear why this should have been a cultural response among the Bellacoola, while it was absent among the Bemba, a society which suffered more extreme seasonal food shortages, but where female principles were ritually elevated.[117] Surely the Bellacoola environment (the Pacific Northwest Coast of America) was lush by comparison with other societies where there was/is no in-stitutionalized 'need' to control or dominate women? In fact, it is by no means the case that environmentally-caused scarcity always results in increased conflict and competition within groups. In some, it may lead to heightened cooperation and sharing.[118]

In the case of the Bellacoola, Sanday might have considered both the control of women *and* the fear of the environment as consequences of other social tensions that were breaking down cooperative interaction and trust. Her own account mentions, in fact,[119] that they were a ranked society with slavery. This cer-tainly might indicate that they were suffering from heightened competition for resources and tensions over social status. Such internal socially-based sources of stress might help us explain the evolution of the group's sex role plan and the changes in women's position better than Sanday's environmental analysis, especially since the aggression was directed against only some women, while others participated as men's equals. In other instances too such an approach might better explain the anomalies in her data and would allow her to make better use of her valuable insights.

The primary achievement of Sanday's book is to show us that a mechanical explanation of sex roles and status is not possible. Because gender is such a powerfully charged way of organizing social interactions, and involves so many basic bio-psycholo-gical processes, disruption in social organization and male-female roles may have far-reaching and complex repercussions. Male dominance cannot be understood as simply a matter of economic interest or political power; it interacts with every

117. Audrey Richards, 'Some Types of Family Structure Amongst the Central Bantu' in A. R. Radcliffe-Brown and O. Forde, eds, 'African Systems of Kinship and Marriage,' London 1950; Richards, *Land, Labour, and Diet in North Rhodesia,* London 1940.

118. Sahlins, *Stone Age Economics.*

119. Sanday, pp. 102–3.

thread in the fabric of social life and may thus have a different dynamic in each society where it is set into motion.

No review of theories of the origins of sexual inequality would be complete without reference to Eleanor Leacock, who has done pathbreaking work in applying a historical materialist framework to the ethnohistorical record, and in formulating an alternative vision of the social relations of foraging societies. On the basis of her research among the Montagnais-Naskapi Indians (a society based on fur trapping), she challenged the widely-accepted model of the patrilineal band, with its accompanying assumption of sexual inequality, and proposed in its stead that relations between the sexes were both flexible and egalitarian.[120] She argued that there is no reason why there should be gender hierarchy just because there is a division of labour by sex; in fact, she has shown that the social relations of many foraging societies are necessarily egalitarian and communal.[121] Taking its cue from Leacock, a whole generation of feminist anthropologists has begun to explore the implications of her model of the 'primitive commune', which includes a rough equality in the social relations between the sexes.

Leacock has, in addition, taken a leading role in efforts to revise and build on Engels's original theories about the origins of the patriarchal state.[122] Again beginning with her own fieldwork among the Montagnais-Naskapi, she has explored the historical processes whereby formerly egalitarian cultures were transformed by contact with patriarchal state societies, and especially by capitalist colonization during the past two centuries.[123] Basing her early theory of the evolution of sexual inequality on Engels's central insight that it was connected with the breakdown of kinship (clan) social organization and successive transformations of the division of labour, she has worked for a decade to refine her model. Her most recent and evolved statement is presented in her article 'Women, Power and Authority'.[124]

Leacock believes that male dominance was a consequence of the development of commodity production, which accompanied

120. Leacock, 'The Montagnais Hunting Territory and the Fur Trade,' *American Anthropologist*, 78, 1954.

121. Leacock, 1957; 'Women's Status in Egalitarian Society,' *Current Anthropology*, 19, 1978, pp. 247–75.

122. Engels.

123. Mona Etienne and Eleanor Leacock, eds., *Women and Colonization*, New York 1980.

124. Leacock, 'Women, Power and Authority'.

the evolution of ranked, and then stratified, societies:

> The direct producers lost decision-making powers over their lives when the specialization of labor and production of commodities for exchange led to the formation of slave, aristocratic, and merchant classes. Women in particular lost out because the new economic relations based on exchange were in the hands of men (the first important commodity exchanged, in Engels' view, was men's responsibility, cattle); because these relations undercut the communal households women had controlled and transformed women's domestic work into private service; and because the privatization of property through individual inheritance in the budding upper class required control of women's sexuality.[125]

According to Leacock, as the importance of inter-group exchange increased, especially as groups became more sedentary, there was a growing need for products that could only be obtained through exchange. In the process, some people were better placed than others to take advantage of the new relations of production. Leacock, then, following Fried,[126] sees a close relationship between the development of social ranking and the institution of centralized redistribution of products. She believes that women lost public authority as exchange and economic inequality developed, in particular because they tended to provide the labour that produced the goods exchanged by men (for example cattle, or pigs in New Guinea). She also notes that warfare may have increased as ranked societies expanded, and this may have given males additional control. Furthermore, she suggests that women unwittingly participated in the process of their own 'commoditization' because it was in their interest to ensure that their own husband was a 'big man', successful in trade exchange, and because they, too, could benefit from the labour of low ranking men. In sum, women lost autonomy as labourers when processes of economic differentiation were already transforming labour into a commodity. Commodity production, in turn, aided in the process of subversion of kin-based organization and the development of private property, as described by Engels.

We are in basic agreement with Leacock on this overall outline of the historical evolution of male dominance, and of the effects of commodity production on the primitive commune. However,

125. Ibid.
126. Morton Fried, *The Evolution of Political Society*, New York 1967.

we see a need for a more detailed explanation of how and why, in the 'pristine' case, societies that were transitional between egalitarian and ranked began to produce for exchange, and of why women in particular seem to have lost political and economic autonomy in such societies. In other words, we need a theory of why, by the time that true ranking had emerged in the form of institutionalized inequalities of access to production, exchange, and distribution, it was already 'big' men, and only rarely 'big' women, who usually achieved the institutionalized leadership statuses. We agree with Leacock that women's status in ranked societies is quite variable, and that there is no reason to assume a 'conspiracy theory' of the emergence of sexual inequality. But the underlying question of what stimulated men to commandeer the productive activities of women in order to engage successfully in trade exchanges is still not clearly answered. Even if cattle were the first exchangeable commodity, they were certainly by no means the only trade item; nor was warfare inevitably the accompaniment of the transition to ranking. It is therefore necessary to examine more closely why men were able to privatize the services of women and why women in many societies did not successfully resist.

These questions and others are analysed by the authors in this volume from the standpoint of their respective disciplines (history and anthropology) and scholarly traditions (French and American). In the first contribution, Leibowitz, an American physical anthropologist, presents a model of the origins of the division of labour by sex, which she sees arising out of the early conditions of production and long antedating any formal or informal sexual inequality. Two papers, Chevillard and Leconte 'The Dawn of Lineage Societies: the Origin of Women's Oppression', and Coontz and Henderson 'Property Forms, Political Power, and Women's Labour in the Evolution of Class and State Societies', then offer contrasting analyses of the origins of sexual inequality in pre-state kinship-based societies. These are followed by a second contribution by Chevillard and Leconte, 'Slavery and Women', which discusses women's status in early slave-based state societies. Finally, Monique Saliou, a French historian of religion, looks at the evidence from pre-Classical and Classical iconography and literature concerning 'The Processes of Women's Subordination in Primitive and Archaic Greece'. We turn now to a consideration of the different views presented in these articles.*

It is striking that, though working independently within two different scholarly traditions, empirical data bases, and language systems, the authors find themselves in substantial agreement on many fundamental aspects of the development of female subordination. First, the point of departure for all is that the explanation of gender inequality must be sought in social rather than biological imperatives. Leibowitz argues that the division of labour by sex was not biologically determined but was a social construct arising from changes in the techniques and relations of production. The other authors emphasize various social determinants of different male and female activities, agreeing that biology does not mandate an invariable division of labour between the sexes. They also agree that even where a division of tasks and activities *does* occur, that is not grounds, in and of itself, for assuming gender inequality. Indeed, they point to various indications suggesting that the earliest societies were based on interdependence and egalitarianism.

Second, following their rejection of biological explanations for male-female social relations, the authors agree that the origins of sexual stratification should be sought in women's role in production, and not in her powers of reproduction. Women indisputably played a central productive role in early foraging and horticultural communities, and the authors suggest that the origins of male dominance were bound up with the struggle to control women's labour and products. Control of women's reproductive powers followed from this. There was no demographic reason, dissociated from this social one, for men to oppress women simply because women bear children.

A third point of agreement accompanies the authors' rejection of biological determinism in favour of explanations emphasizing social production. They agree that while male dominance was not present in the earliest communal societies, it was already present in the earliest class societies as defined in the traditional sense of the term (for example, slave societies). They thus reject analyses which move directly from communal societies to advanced class systems based on individual private property without identifying an intervening social formation or mode of production. Though differing in their conception of such intervening societies, the authors agree that societies based on true

*The following section of the Introduction was written jointly by us and two of the French contributors, Nicole Chevillard and Sébastien Leconte.

private property were preceded by other forms of social organization based on the development of collective or group property. In these lineage or kin corporate societies, ties of kinship determined the organization of work and the appropriation of goods, and it was in these societies that male domination was first elaborated.

It follows from this that the dialectic of kin relations must be relevant to the origins of gender inequality. Although diverging in their reconstruction of the processes involved, the authors agree in seeking the origins of male dominance in some aspect of the rise of these kin corporate or lineage societies. Specifically, they agree on the critical importance of post-marital residence rules in determining gender relations within unilineal kin corporate societies. They argue that patrilocality — the system in which women move to their husband's kin group at marriage — enabled men to utilize and appropriate women's labour and products in ways that ultimately enhanced the authority of the senior males within the husband's kin group.

The authors agree, in short, that without patrilocality, there were limits on the ability of any kin corporation to utilize or appropriate the labour and products of women. Because they stress the importance of residence rules over unilineal descent, they agree in characterizing matrilineal, virilocal systems, in which the woman after marriage goes to live with her husband's mother's brother, as equally conducive to male dominance as patrilineal, patrilocal societies, in spite of the rule of descent through females. The effect on adult women of such a residence rule is similarly to sever her ties with her natal kin group and to encourage her dependence on her husband's kin group. The authors interpret matrilineal, virilocal systems as a contradictory social formation, rather than as proof that 'natural' male dominance will assert itself even in matrilineal societies, as is often claimed. Instances of such societies, therefore, make interesting case studies of transitional processes at work.

Having located the source of female oppression in the mechanism of patrilocality, the authors were still faced with the need to explain why this became the dominant mode of organizing social relations in kin corporate society (and hence why male dominance, though not 'natural', became so widespread). Although differing as to how this happened, the French and American authors again find themselves in substantial agreement as to the overall evolutionary dynamic which led to the reinforcement and institutionalization of male dominance. They agree that patrilocal societies, where women moved at marriage, had greater potential for expansion because they offered more opportunities and incentives to intensify production beyond the level necessary for everyday subsistence. This was due to the greater value of women's labour and reproductive potential in pre-plow agricultural systems. The more productive the society, the more expansionary it could become, absorbing or conquering more stable, 'steady state' societies. It is important to stress, though, that this analysis implies no value judgment that patrilocal societies were somehow 'better'. Rather, they were simply more capable of exercising coercive power over their own members (women, junior men, children) to intensify production than were more egalitarian social systems.

The above points of agreement lead to one final area of commonality. The authors agree that female subordination actually preceded and established the basis for the emergence of true private property and the state. The historical processes involved varied in time and place, but once set in motion, the evolution of sexual and social stratification was closely intertwined. The oppression of women provided a means of differential accumulation among men, which in turn gave some men special access to the labour and reproductive powers of women, as well as to the services of other men. As class stratification became institutionalized, we find that lower class men were often assimilated to the status of women, while women as a category were assigned to the juridical status of the propertyless in a system increasingly based on private property. The authors of this book offer different historical and sociological perspectives on these processes, but they agree that the oppression of women was a foundation for the emergence of traditional class society, and that sex and class oppression have developed in ways that render them analytically virtually inseparable.

Despite these broad areas of agreement, the authors in this volume differ in important respects. One area of disagreement is over how to explain and analyse the development of a division of labour by sex. Leibowitz argues that the earliest hominid cultures rested on non-gender-specific production, while later an informal sexual division of activities developed with projectile hunting and other technological inventions that led to hearth-centred activities. A full-fledged sexual division of labour, with codified rules for males and females in marriage and work, she argues, arose when Exchange between groups began to take place, and served to facilitate and regularize this Exchange. (She uses the capital E to distinguish this from the informal exchange between individuals that would have taken place on an irregular basis.) Neither the sexual division of tasks nor the sexual division of labour, however, constitutes a cause or a symptom of male dominance, whose origins must be sought elsewhere.

Coontz and Henderson largely accept this account, in which a sexual division of work is related to diversification of productive techniques allowing some members to hunt, trap, or trade as others engage in hearth-based activities, while a more formal sexual division of labour develops as groups need to regularize the production and circulation of goods and services. They agree that the circulation of spouses, of whatever sex, among groups is a means to establish increased social interaction, not male dominance.

Chevillard and Leconte, however, believe that the presence of a well-defined social division of labour between men and women, if accompanied by the circulation of female spouses, is already a symptom of male dominance. They thus reject an analysis which places the origins of the sexual division of labour so far back in history. They argue that Leibowitz's analysis covers a very long period in the history of humankind. There was little chance of absolute continuity, especially in the realm of social behaviour, between peoples of such widely differing periods, and locations. One must therefore be cautious when analysing the role of technological inventions such as the use of fire or projectile weapons in social organization. The implementation of certain techniques was probably greatly influenced, or conditioned, by the social organization of the human groups in which they were 'invented'. In other words, the link that Leibowitz establishes between these inventions and the sexual division of tasks, then of labour and social roles, appears too rigid and minimizes the influence of other evolutionary factors. Chevillard and Leconte view the sexual division of labour as a concept that is neither very precise nor illuminating with regard to the dynamics of the structure and evolution of the first human groups.

Another area of difference among some of the authors concerns the degree to which male dominance was a conscious creation of men who wished to exploit female labour, or a less consciously planned outcome of social processes whose original dynamic did not rest on sex oppression. For Chevillard and Leconte, for instance, the central contradiction leading to the dissolution of the earliest communal societies lies in the relations between (some) men and (all) women. As primitive communities developed a higher material standard of living, a surplus and an accentuation of the division of tasks by sex and age, they began to codify kinship rules that permitted the formation of larger and more stable human groups. These societies came to be based on both matrilocality and matrilineality, and in them, therefore, there was a tendency for the surplus to accumulate under the control of women. This accumulation engendered contradictions that in the end led to confrontations between women and men (probably from different kinship groups), who desired to gain control of this surplus. Since the natural evolution of matrilocal and matrilineal societies would be toward a certain amount of female control, a reversal of this, they argue, can only be explained by some sort of masculine victory over women, which turned over to a group of dominant men the control of the surplus and also of the female labour force. Thus patrilocality was instituted. There need not have been a generalized confrontation between men and women, for even if this overturn occurred in only a few instances, patrilocality and male domination would then spread by virtue of example and force of arms. Monique Saliou suggests that Greek mythology and tragedy provide evidence of outright conflict between males and females over power.

For Coontz and Henderson, on the other hand, male domination is the outcome of more gradual and peaceful social and economic processes. As surplus accumulated or techniques of production changed, communal societies developed a variety of residence and descent rules, which in and of themselves implied no immediate subordination of one sex by the other. But the emergence of kin corporate property and a kin corporate mode of production created a potential contradiction between kinship and residence. The new kin corporate mode of production was based on the appropriation of the labour of non-owning producers — the in-marrying spouses — by the corporate descent group, or its head. Coontz and Henderson do not believe that patrilocality, where it occurred, developed out of any confrontation between men and women or was necessarily instituted in order to oppress women and appropriate their labour.

However, they list a number of features of patrilocality which, they argue, allowed the potential inequalities of the kin corporate mode of production to develop more rapidly than alternative methods of circulating labour (for example, matrilocality). And they argue that the resultant worsening of women's position was forcibly maintained, first by lineage heads and later by the state.

For Chevillard and Leconte, then, the emergence of male dominance, achieved by an overthrow of the older matrilocal system, inaugurates a new mode of production. They hold that there was a decisive rupture with the first egalitarian societies (which tended to be matrilocal and matrilineal). This rupture created a new mode of production based on the exploitation of the female labour force (with the understanding that a certain number of attempts were probably made before the new mode of production emerged in all its characteristics). Coontz and Henderson, by contrast, stress the development from within the communal society of a new mode of production based on kin corporate property and the circulation of labour through marriage. In their view, male dominance develops more gradually, after the rise of a new mode of production, out of the dynamics of labour, ownership, and exchange in kin corporate societies, matrilocal or patrilocal.

No final resolution of these differences appears likely. Proponents of the first approach can point to the prevalence of myths about a violent overthrow of women by men, suggesting that these myths represent historical memories of such events; proponents of the second would stress the actual variability in women's status among kin corporate societies, suggesting that an evolutionary continuum is involved. Even the same phenomenon can be interpreted in diametrically opposed ways. Chevillard and Leconte point to the contradictions of matrilineal virilocal societies (where descent is reckoned through the female line but residence is with the husband's maternal relatives) as evidence for the forcible imposition of patrilocality. Such societies are too illogical and contradictory to have arisen naturally, they argue: 'These complexities are, as we will see, the sign that patrilocality doesn't just evolve of its own accord, but that it intervenes as a radical rupture in societies that must formerly have been constituted on the basis of matrilineality and of matrilocality.'

Coontz and Henderson, conversely, hold that the contradictions of matrilineal virilocal societies testify to their transitional nature. The shift to virilocality, they argue, may take place gradually within a formerly matrilineal, matrilocal society, creating conflicts between the individuating tendencies of virilocal residence and the collective practices of matrilineal structures and ideology.

Despite their differences over the origins of male dominance and the character of early social formations, both sets of authors identify a category of pre-state society in which the primary forms of oppression are those of sex and age. They differ, however, over how to characterize the subordination of women in such societies. Though they are describing the same objective phenomenon — the appropriation of women's products — Chevillard and Leconte describe this as class oppression, while Coontz and Henderson call it sex oppression. Chevillard and Leconte prefer to treat women as an oppressed class because this stresses the permanence of women's exclusion from control over the means of production; Coontz and Henderson prefer the term oppressed sex because this leaves more room for analysis of what they consider to be significant variations in the status and interests of women according to their age and marital status.

This difference is purely semantic in discussions of kin corporate societies; it becomes significant, however, in relating the oppression of women to that of other social groups once kin corporate society gives way to a society stratified along other socioeconomic lines. Chevillard and Leconte think that socioeconomic class is modelled upon and derives from the subordination of women. Coontz and Henderson think that in post-kin corporate societies women are divided by class as well as united in a common experience of subordination to males.

According to Coontz and Henderson, the original contradiction in virilocal kin corporate societies is between, on the one hand, men and women of the corporate property-owning group, and, on the other hand, the women who marry in. The subordination of women as a sex is the outcome of social processes whereby patrilocal lineages begin to exercise control over the labour and reproductive power of in-marrying wives. Older women as well as men benefit from this labour, even though for most women the benefits come at the cost of having had to experience an earlier stage of oppression as a wife. Coontz and Henderson see women as having contradictory interests as owners in one kin corporation and producers in another. In this analysis, the growth of socioeconomic stratification may exacerbate these contradictory interests, even though women as a sex may remain inferior to men. For in early class societies, they argue, aristocratic women may exercise significant power over both men and women of the lower class, even if they remain permanent juniors in relation to male members of the aristocracy. Upper and lower class women may therefore be divided in their interests and their consciousness, at the same time that sexual oppression may disguise some of the common interests of men and women within the lower class.

For Chevillard and Leconte, on the other hand, the contradiction is between some men and *all* women as a social group. There are no contradictory interests among women in either kin corporate or aristocratic class society. Aristocratic women do not share the socio-economic status of aristocratic men, as they do not have independent access to the means of production and may even be reduced to slave or lower class status if they offend against male prerogatives. The interests of upper class women are not at all antagonistic to those of lower class men or women, but do conflict directly with those of upper class men. Like high ranking servants, aristocratic women are artificially attached to the class of their husband or father, while in fact they belong to the dominated classes of society, even if they are not conscious of this.

Again, this is probably not a difference that can be settled. It is a question of analytical emphasis. Clearly, the difference has implications for the analysis of the role of upper class women in any feminist or class struggle, but since upper class women constitute only a minority of the female population, both analyses still affirm the interconnections between the 'woman question' and the class struggle.

In the Beginning . . . : The Origins of the Sexual Division of Labour and the Development of the First Human Societies

Lila Leibowitz

Introduction

In current anthropological discussions the sexual division of labour is viewed in two ways: simply as a division of productive activities by sex, or, more comprehensively, as the totality of social relations between men and women joined together by production. This paper approaches the origins of the sexual division of labour from the latter perspective. It touches on factors as varied as production and productivity, population profiles, subsistence technologies, intergroup exchange, incest rules, alliances and sex role socialization. Consequently, though the paper focusses on the origins of the sexual division of labour it is in effect a holistic analysis of the development of the first human societies and their social formations.

The common sense explanation of the origin of the division of labour by sex is that it is related to size and strength differences between early hominid males and females and to the lengthened biological dependency of the young. This implies that the sexual division is protocultural, and therefore 'natural'. This notion does not, however, bear up under close inspection. In this paper I will try to show that early hominids of both sexes, despite their differences in size after reaching sexual maturity, engaged in the same kinds of productive activities. Adult females simply combined these productive activities with bearing and nursing the young. The sexual division of labour developed in conjunction with certain specific *cultural* innovations.

The explanation of the sexual division of labour offered here is built around three main points: 1) The quintessential human adaptation is the invention of and reliance on production. The preconditions for the 'organization' of reproduction are the elaboration of productive processes followed by an organization of differentiated productive activities. While production was unspecialized and undifferentiated a regular sexual division of labour was simply unlikely and unnecessary.

2) The regular division of labour became practicable with the emergence of technological innovations which led to the development of a number of different productive processes. The division of labour can either be the result of pragmatic (informal and situational considerations) or of proscriptive (formal and institutionalized) regulations. The complexity of the new processes initially only called for a pragmatic division of tasks. The reorganization of economic and social relationships associated with the new technologies, however, led to the proscriptive sexual division of labour. While the pragmatic division of tasks along sex lines was influenced by the different reproductive functions of men and women, a proscriptive division of labour was a social construct that arose out of the new techniques of production which created the conditions for a change in the relations of production.

3) The regularizing of the expansion of Exchange between groups* led to firm rules about the organization of production and the institutionalization of a socially mandated sexual division of labour. The expansion of Exchange was made possible by the new technology and was regularized by incest prohibitions, contractual marriage, kinship designations, and family arrangements, all of which are linked to the institutionalization of the sexual division of labour. All are the products of cultural processes. None is part of our 'natural' legacy.

The evidence I use to support this explanation is, necessarily, indirect. Two major pieces of that evidence come from biology. The first has to do with the fact that while early hominid males and females who were sexually mature were markedly physically differentiated (sexually dimorphic), life expectancies were short. Relatively few individuals survived for any length of time as

---

*I will use 'Exchange' with a capital 'E' to refer to moving goods between groups, and 'exchange' with a lower case 'e' to refer to what took place within groups.

sexually reproducing physically differentiated adults. Consequently many of the foragers were young and physically undifferentiated.

The second biological datum has to do with the fact that the differences in size between males and females diminished recently and rapidly. For eons size differences between females and males were marked, but when fire and projectile hunting techniques became widespread this aspect of sexual difference was reduced. Since dimorphic and non-dimorphic species have different mating patterns, this physical change seems to indicate that as production became complex, mating patterns were transformed. Exchange seems to have assumed great importance at this time and marriage contracts and kinship systems became the vehicles of political and economic transactions. The 'family' became part of the social landscape and the sexual division of labour was institutionalized.[1]

The Basic Data

All human societies today have some sort of division of labour along sex lines; that is to say, all of them have arranged matters so that there are some tasks men are supposed to perform regularly, and others that fall into the category of women's work. Societies differ a good deal, however, with respect to how labour is divided between the sexes. Nearly any anthropology text will offer up a list of societies which directly challenge Western notions of

1. This discussion deals only generally with the archaeological evidence which testifies to the simplicity of early foraging techniques, and makes little mention of sites used by early humans which have been interpreted by archaeologists as home bases. A paper read by Richard Potts of Yale University at the December 1982 meetings of the American Anthropological Association appears to justify the fact that I regard these sites as irrelevant to this discussion. Home base sites have been characterized as places where females and dependent youngsters spent much of their time while adult males foraged. Potts analyzed the detritus at these sites and the length of time they were used (five years or so), and compared that detritus with what is found at the temporary campsites of contemporary foragers. He concludes that the sites were not home bases but may have been safe places to which game was brought again and again by groups of foragers. The foragers ate the meat raw and scavengers consumed what they left, a very different pattern than that found at recent sites. Potts argues that a human home base was not likely to have evolved prior to the controlled use of fire, and suggests that the notion of a home base has become entrenched in human evolutionary theory only because the idea of home or community is central to modern human life.

46

what men and women are supposed to do. There are societies where anyone, regardless of sex, is expected to do almost, but not quite, everything that needs to be done, at times alongside members of the opposite sex, at times segregated from them. There are also cultures where nearly every conceivable task has been designated as either men's work or women's work. How strict such designations are also differs by time and place. Under different circumstances, a man who performs what a society designates as women's work may attract no attention at all, may be subtly ostracized or openly punished for his actions, or may be honoured in one way or another. Much the same difference in responses to women who pursue men's activities is documented in the anthropological literature. That cultures differ greatly in how much they separate what men and women do, and how strictly they observe and maintain these distinctions is not as generally recognized as the fact that what is women's work in one society is often men's work in another.

Despite all this variability the fact remains that all known human societies (with the temporary exception of the Tasaday)[2] have some sort of division of labour along sex lines. The sexual division of labour is indeed a social universal. Furthermore, the biological differences between men and women are universally recognized and recognizable. Though physical differences between human males and females are not as marked as they are in some other primate species, and although one can find women who are taller, or hairier or more muscular than some men in their own population and than all men in some other population, humans are nevertheless members of a sexually dimorphic species. This universality of biological sex differences plays a part in how the origin of the universal division of labour by sex is viewed. Some theorists regard the physical differences between men and women as providing the basic *reasons* for dividing productive work. Others regard these physical differences as merely a set of conditions which were taken into account when the techno-cultural innovations which encouraged a division of work roles emerged, when the advantages of dividing labour were recognized and the habit of dividing labour by sex was institutionalized.

2. Bernard Campbell, *Humankind Emerging*, Boston 1976.

The Two Basic Models

Theorists who have built models of early human situations agree on at least one point. They hold that underlying any division of labour is the concept — or practice — of exchanging goods,[3] and underlying any exchange of goods is production. Production implies that individuals actively get or make a good in greater amounts than they plan or are able to consume in order to provide others with that good[4]. The authorities agree that exchange is usual in situations in which people who do or make certain things provide others with a good and the others reciprocate either by returning the same good at another time, or returning some other good immediately or later. However, the models they build disagree as to how production arose.

There are two basic models:

1) Biodeterminists argue that exchange arose because the biological differences between males and females result in different natural propensities or different activity profiles. As a consequence the sexes produce different things. Typically, the model says that *women* (as well as primate and hominid females), because of their physical characteristics or because of their natural or normal involvement with pregnancy, nursing and/or care of the young, were inclined and ultimately required to refrain from certain subsistence activities, usually collecting game[5]. Men's biological traits, on the other hand, permitted them to pursue these activities, and the game. Men brought in meat, and women brought in vegetable foods. Producers who produced different products were the outcome of these 'natural' sex-differentiated subsistence activities. The need to exchange products was generated by this situation. In biodeterminist models the habit of exchange emerged *because* of product differences, which derived from gender differences, and the sexual division of labour existed prior to the emergence of Exchange.

2) Many Marxists, as well as other sociologically oriented theorists, explicitly, or (more often) implicitly, suggest a some-

3. Euclid D. Smith, 'Comment on "Variations in Subsistence Activities of Female and Male Pongids", by B. Galdikas and G. Teleki', *Current Anthropology* 22, 1981, pp. 252-53.

4. Jules De Raedt, 'Comment on "A Marxist Reappraisal of the Matriarchate", by C. Fluehr-Lobban', *Current Anthropology* 20, 1979, pp. 349-50.

5. M. F. Birute Galdikas and Geza Teleki, 'Variations in Subsistence Activities of Female and Male Pongids: New Perspectives on the Origins of Hominid Labor Division', *Current Anthropology* 22, 1981, pp. 241-47.

48

what different sequence of events. In their models they indicate that both production and Exchange must have been in place well before the institutionalization of a division of tasks or products along sex lines. The variability of incest rules which regulate mate Exchanges and the variability of rules governing the way labour is divided in recent human societies lead them to conclude that the bases of such rules are social and cultural. Their analyses lead to a model in which the sexual division of labour, incest taboos, marriage, kinship and kin groups all emerged to cement alliances and to sustain intergroup Exchanges of products and people. Sociological models, therefore, suggest that sex-undifferentiated production and distribution of products preceded within-group exchange, and that Exchanges of some sort between groups preceded the invention of the sexual division of labour and of sex-differentiated production or products.[6]

The sequence of events such analyses implicitly postulate is roughly as follows. First came 'production'; that is, individuals, both male and female, pursuing similar or identical subsistence activities began distributing to those around them what they did not themselves consume, and began consuming what others had produced. Relying on each other led them deliberately to produce goods for distribution and engage in what anthropologists call generalized reciprocity. Subsequently, when groups on the move met and their production exceeded local needs, intergroup Exchange occurred simply because the opportunity offered itself. Finally, as it became evident that it was advantageous to Exchange products, skills, or personnel on a regular basis, rules enforcing a sexual division of labour were institutionalized alongside incest rules and marriage rules. These rules maximized the advantages of Exchange and formalized patterns of within-group exchange.

From such a perspective, a satisfactory biosocial model of the evolution of the sexual division of labour should begin by explaining the way in which evolving hominids of both sexes became producers rather than self-feeders; then it should show the ways in which exchange (or Exchanges) of products and/or people arose; only in its last phase need the model deal with the

6. Janet Siskind, 'Kinship and Mode of Production', *American Anthropologist* 80, 1978, pp. 860-72. Lila Leibowitz, *Females, Males, Families: A Bio-Social Approach*, Massachusetts 1978. Toshisada Nishida, 'Comment on "Variations in Subsistence Activities of Female and Male Pongids", by B. Galdikas and G. Teleki', *Current Anthropology* 22, 1981, p. 251.

origins of the sexual division of labour. Such a model will be presented here.

Sharing and Production

The two most familiar explanations of why and how production came about do not deal directly with the concept of production but focus instead on sharing, and do so in a manner which I consider biodeterminist. The discovery that sharing is practiced by some chimpanzees and baboons who take game and either give out pieces of meat or eat side by side on a carcass is the basis of one such explanation. Primate hunting, though occurring in only a few settings, is cited as the kind of proto-hominid behaviour that must have given rise to production for distribution and exchange. The way these primates forage for game is tied to the sexual division of labour on the grounds that male baboons and chimpanzees take game more frequently than females do and expend more time and energy on taking game.[7] Yet, the data in fact show that — whether male or female — chimps or baboons who take game do not spend much time on this activity and don't get to eat much meat. In other words, game collecting and meat eating are rare and meat sharing is even rarer.[8]

Viewing meat sharing as the basis for production seems questionable on several grounds. For one thing, among social predators far from the primate line, meat often is consumed in a social setting by sharing. Lionesses and wolves even bring game back to their young, which is more like production than anything chimps or baboons have been seen to do. Furthermore, the basic staples of primate foragers, human and nonhuman, are plant foods. Among nonhuman primates, those that forage side by side *rarely* share fruits or roots they collect. Nevertheless individuals of *both* sexes have been seen to share such vegetable foods in response to gestures of request,[9] and nursing mothers

7. Geza Teleki, 'The Omnivorous Chimpanzee', *Scientific American* 228, 1973, pp. 32-42.

8. S. M. Hladik, 'Comment on "Variations in Subsistence Activities of Female and Male Pongids", by B. Galdikas and G. Teleki', *Current Anthropology* 22, 1981, pp. 249-50; Yukimaru Sugiyama, 'Comment on "Variations in Subsistence Activities of Female and Male Pongids", by B. Galdikas and G. Teleki', *Current Anthropology* 22, 1981, p. 253.

have been seen to give bits of vegetable foods to their infants.[10] The notion that production for exchange derives from the habit of sharing meat is based on confusing a sustenance behaviour found among many predators with a human activity that is qualitatively different, and exaggerates the role of males as providers of meat.

Some versions of this male-centred sharing model argue that the most successful male hunters are the most successful impregnators, and spread their genes for hunting around as they give out game. This notion is not borne out by the data on sexual activities among hunting chimps or baboons,[11] which show that hunting success and reproductive success are unrelated in the open mating systems of both species, where females have access to many males.

A less popular, feminist rather than masculinist, biodeterminist version of the origins of production for exchange and of the sexual division of labour credits plant-collecting females with inventing sharing. This explanation of the origins of the human habit of production states that mothers (females) began to share by giving their infants food, then began to gather enough food to give to their older children (inventing carrying devices in order to bring back enough plants for them), and eventually began giving some of what they had gleaned to males in exchange for the meat the males had collected. Aside from the fact that primate males have been observed sharing vegetables as well as meat,[12] this model, which calls for the transformation of maternal generosity and sharing into production for distribution should raise some practical questions: 'Why didn't males gather whatever vegetable foods they needed while they were out hunting, as they do routinely in foraging societies?'; or, 'Why didn't mothers systematically collect small game animals, as they do among the Tiwi, and skip the exchange with men entirely, as they do among the Hadza?' In essence, these two models of sharing as the basis for production revolve on the notion that there was somehow an

9. See photograph in Geza Teleki, 'The Omnivorous Chimpanzee', *Scientific American* 228, 1973, p. 40.

10. J. B. Silk, 'Patterns of Food Sharing Among Mother and Infant Chimpanzees at Gombe National Park, Tanzania', *Folia Primatologica* 29, 1978, pp. 129-41.

11. Thelma Rowell, *Social Behaviour of Monkeys*, Harmondsworth 1972; Jane van Lawick Goodall, 'The Behaviour of Free-Living Chimpanzees in the Gombe Stream Reserve', *Animal Behaviour Monographs*, 1968, pp. 165-311.

12. Nishida, 1981.

intrinsic, primordial sex division of products because of sex differences in activities as soon as our primate or proto-human ancestors began going after game. Sharing thus becomes the province of one or the other sex, and this sharing is mistakenly equated with production.

Both models are based on the initial assumption that physical differences dictate sex differences in behavioural and productive capacities. The data, however, do not support this generalization. Among primates sexual dimorphism does not mandate different tasks for males and females, though it permits males and females to engage in the *same* activities in slightly different settings, thus minimizing competition for scarce resources. Furthermore, production, as we shall see, seems to have risen under circumstances in which sex differences were of secondary importance.

Dimorphism and What It Tells Us

Although there is considerable debate about what should or should not be called an Australopithecine and/or a Homo habilis, there is an emerging consensus among palaeoanthropologists that the early hominids who walked on two legs were not only small — adults were only 3-1/2 to 5 foot in height — but also exhibited marked sexual dimorphism in size.[13] By the time Homo erectus types appeared, the height of members of the line leading to Homo sapiens had increased. A strong size dimorphism is still found in early Homo erectus populations. Male-female size differentials diminish only in late Homo erectus populations. For two million years, sexual dimophism in height remained marked as the species as a whole became taller.[14] However, despite many claims to the contrary, the presence of physical sex differences tells us little about social patterns. Size differences between the sexes among living terrestrial and semi-terrestrial primates do not correlate with any particular form of social organization, and correlate least of all, or rather not at all, with pairing arrangements.[15]

Dimorphic primate species live largely terrestrial or semiter-

13. D. C. Johanson and T. D. White, 'A Systematic Assessment of Early African Hominids', *Science* 203, 1979, pp. 321-30. Richard Leakey, 'New Evidence for the Evolution of Man', *Social Biology* 19, 1972, pp. 99-114.
14. Milford H. Wolpoff, *Paleoanthropology*, New York 1980.

restrial lives. Species in which males are big and have bigger teeth than the smaller females exhibit a variety of social organizations. Chimpanzees live in large, amorphous and variously organized populations.[16] Baboons live in a variety of settings, such as forests and savannahs,[17] and exhibit different patterns of social organization in the different places.[18] Groups of Patas monkeys include females who tolerate one or two males, while in the hamadryas baboon groups a male may be found 'herding' females.[19] Among orangutans, where dimorphism is extreme, each female with her young occupies a range. Males are 'isolated' and usually travel widely over several such ranges. Yet orangutans raised in captivity and returned to the wild become social, aggregating, tool-using apes.[20] In Sumatra, where small siamangs chase them from food, male orangutans ally themselves peacefully with a female for a while. In Borneo, where logging operations are displacing orangutan populations, lone males attack and 'rape' females.[21] Even parenting is variable. In some troops of Barbary Apes (who are actually monkeys) males have been observed carrying and caring for infants, while in other troops this has not been seen to occur.[22] Male Rhesus monkeys are rarely involved with infants in the wild, but turn out to be capable of concerned parenting in the laboratory setting.[23] Behaviours vary but among all of these primates provisioning others is not tied to their dimorphism. All the animals rely on feeding themselves. A sexual division of labour simply does not occur. Since different populations or groups of the same

15. Owen Lovejoy's hypothesis overlooks this information, and argues that pair bonding was characteristic of the sexually dimorphic early hominid. Males were selected for large size, he says, because each one foraged widely to get the foods (largely vegetable) he brought back to his mate and children.

16. Jane Goodall, *My Friends, the Wild Chimpanzees*, London 1967.

17. Yukimaru Sugiyama, 'Social Organisation of Chimpanzees in the Budongo Forest, Uganoa', *Primates* 9, 1968, pp. 225-58.

18. Rowell.

19. Rowell, p. 163.

20. Gary L. Shapiro, 'Reports from the Field: Orangutan Research and Conservation Project', *L. S. B. Leakey Foundation News*, no. 18, 1980, pp. 7-8.

21. John MacKinnon, *In Search of the Red Ape*, New York 1974.

22. M. H. MacRoberts, 'The Social Organisation of Barbary Apes (Macaca Sylvana) on Gibraltar', *American Journal of Physical Anthropology* 33, 1970, pp. 83-100. Frances D. Burton, 'The Integration of Biology and Behavior in the Socialization of Macaca Sylvana of Gibraltar', in F. E. Poirier, ed., *Primate Socialization*, New York 1972, pp. 29-62.

23. Gary Mitchell, William K. Redican and Judy Comber, 'Lesson from a Primate: Males Can Raise Babies', *Psychology Today* 7, May 1974, pp. 63–8.

dimorphic species do different things, it is eminently clear that the species' behaviour is malleable, adaptable and learned, and social behaviour is shaped by circumstances and experience. The 'fact' of sexual dimorphism among early hominids by itself cannot, therefore, be translated into conclusions about specific forms of social organization. Clearly many types of organization were possible, as they are among other dimorphic primates, and many have occurred. How, then, can we account for this dimorphism?

Sexual dimorphism is correlated with mating systems in which all females have equal opportunities to mate while the males differ from each other with respect to their mating opportunities. Despite the variability of the social arrangements of the sexually dimorphic terrestrial primates there are several conditions, biological and behavioural, characteristic of all of them that help explain how their dimorphism evolved. First, in all these species dimorphism becomes marked only at puberty, when males continue to grow and females usually become pregnant and slow down or stop growing. Secondly, this dimorphism occurs in conjunction with a reproductive cycle which makes adult females rarely available for insemination; females who are pregnant for many months and nurse for several years are out of the mating pool for long periods. Thirdly, the adult males usually range more actively and widely than encumbered adult females. This sex-difference in the size of ranging areas is *not* characteristic of non-dimorphic arboreal primate species.[24] These three conditions create a pattern of circumstances which leads to the differential distribution of mating opportunities among males.

The outlines of the pattern are as follows. Females become pregnant soon after puberty, stop growing and experience a decline in activity levels. The activity levels of males are usually very high during their adolescent growth spurt, and for a while thereafter. During this period, as the males become larger and otherwise differentiated from females, the males' food intake needs are quite high. Growing males find themselves competing for food with other animals, particularly in terrestrial settings, especially with females who are pregnant or nursing and also eating for growth, though not their own growth. Healthy, growing, active males who are experiencing a growth spurt usually

---

24. E. D. Starin, 'Monkey Moves', *Natural History* 90, no. 9 1981, pp. 36-44.

wander widely, presumably at least in part to satisfy their hunger. (In some places, at adolescence males begin to forage for foods females rarely eat.) If a male who wanders widely grows big enough to avoid or intimidate predators and survives, he is obviously in a position to bump into a female (or two or three) who is in one of her infrequent fertile periods. A male who is not as active as he, and/or fails to survive the trip, obviously has fewer mating opportunities. The hungry, growing, active male is more likely to father an infant (who, if male, may inherit a tendency toward his growth pattern) than his less fortunate peers. As he ages, his activity levels decline and his mobility may be reduced. Nevertheless the longer he lives the more infants he will have a chance to father. Over their life spans more mating opportunities are open to large males who are spurred to wander and manage to survive their wanderings than to smaller, less mobile males. (The fact that a male's growth and maturation rate affect his reproductive success has been documented in a dimorphic species of deer.[25])

By contrast, all females have similar mating opportunities, even though those who tend to be smaller apparently have a long-term reproductive advantage over larger females. (Data which will be reviewed below indicates that where the quality or quantity of food is a problem, females with lighter nutritional needs come to sexual maturity earlier, in better health, and have more and healthier babies than their sisters.) Whatever the adult size of a female, she inevitably can find a mate or mates, often transient ones, during her rare fertile periods.

Evidently, a major size difference between the sexes of a terrestrial primate species tells us only one thing about its social interactions: the sex difference reflects a pattern in which all females who survive to maturity have similar mating opportunities, while the mating opportunities among males are unevenly distributed. Those active males who tend also to be bigger have a reproductive advantage over other males. Having

25. In a report about the first field study to attempt to measure lifetime reproductive success in both sexes for any wild animal, Tim Clutton-Brock shows that in a population of deer observed for more than ten years a stag's breeding success is correlated with its growth rate as a juvenile. Those that grew rapidly were most successful. Interestingly, a stag's growth rate appears to depend on its mother's milk yield and body condition. While red deer are socially and biologically very different from primates, Clutton-Brock's findings, which are based on long-term data, are clearly relevant to the model of primate dimorphism presented here. 'The Red Deer of Rhum', *Natural History* 91, no. 11, 1982, pp. 42-7.

modern human populations indicate that there are three factors which influence human fertility: the amount of food an individual gets, the kind of food he or she eats, and the amount of physical activity the individual engages in. Modern human populations differ from other primate populations not only in their furlessness, but in the fact that though men and women are not very different in size, women, unlike other primate females, develop permanent deposits of breast and buttock fat on becoming adult. Let us deal with Frisch's data on females first.

Frisch found that the age at which puberty occurs and the maintenance of a regular menstrual cycle are correlated with the proportion of a woman's body weight that is invested in fat. Undernutrition slows body growth, delays the time at which puberty occurs and reduces fertility in females. Starving women stop menstruating. Underweight, malnourished and (surprisingly) obese women become amenorrheic — they do not menstruate. How much and what is eaten, together with the amount of her physical activity, determine how much fat a woman carries. Very active women on a poor or marginal diet stop menstruating, and on a healthy but marginally weight-sustaining diet do not menstruate while nursing infants. The birth weight of an infant is correlated with the pre-pregnancy weight of its mother, and an infant's survival is correlated with its birth weight. Consequently, an ill-fed, very active woman has few healthy children.

In males ' . . . severe undernutrition results in loss of libido, a decrease in prostate fluid, a decrease in sperm motility and longevity, and, eventually, the cessation of sperm production, in that order. Undernutrition . . . delays the onset of sexual maturation in boys.'[32] Furthermore, high rates of sexual activity reduce sperm counts (something men who are 'sexual athletes' may or may not appreciate). In addition, aging has a deleterious effect on quality as well as quantity of sperm. Finally, and far

31. Rose E. Frisch, 'Nutrition, Fatness and Fertility: The Effect of Food Intake on Reproductive Ability', in W. Henry Mosely, ed., *Nutrition and Human Reproduction*, New York 1978, pp. 91-122; 'Fatness, Puberty and Fertility', *Natural History* 89, no. 10, 1980, pp. 16-27; Rose E. Frisch, Grace Wyshak and Larry Vincent, 'Delayed Menarche and Amenorrhea in Ballet Dancers', *New England Journal of Medicine* 303, 1980, pp. 17-19; Rose E. Frisch and Janet W. McArthur, 'Menstrual Cycles: Fatness as a Determinant of Minimum Weight for Height Necessary for their Maintenance or Onset', *Science* 185, 1974, pp. 949-51.
32. R. E. Frisch, p. 20.

big males serves the species well. It allows the males, who are engaging in the same kind of food-getting activities as the females, to get more food by going abroad for it. This removes some of the pressures on females. Note here that their sexual dimorphism, far from reflecting even a casual or pragmatic division of labour by sex, allows both males and females to engage in the *same* foraging activities, only in different geographical ranges.

A Reconsideration of Growing Up Hominid

The above review of field observations of sexually dimorphic non-human primates reveals that male and female foraging activities are essentially alike, and forces us to conclude that early hominids, though dimorphic, were not 'naturally' prone to dividing tasks by sex. Other data from biology provide additional reasons for coming to this conclusion. Short life spans, a relatively late age of sexual maturation, and rates of population growth which suggest that fertility levels were low combine to indicate that early hominid populations were composed primarily of young, non-dimorphic members. Species survival could not, then, have hinged on the subsistence activities of the few adults in a group, but must have depended on the development of cooperative production by all and for all.

Leakey's casual observations on Zinjanthropus, as well as Mann's systematic analysis of the extensive Swartkrans fossils, indicate that Australopithecines matured at a rate closer to that of present-day human populations than to that of present-day large primates.[26] Early hominids took about as long to reach sexual maturity as we do. Among our sexually dimorphic ancestors, the small females, Mann estimates, became sexually mature around the age of twelve (and pregnant presumably shortly thereafter) if conditions were right.

Startlingly, Mann's analysis of over three hundred fossil specimens leads him to the conclusion that the average age of

26. L. S. B. Leakey and J. S. Prost, *Adam or Ape*, Massachusetts 1971. A. Mann, 'Paleodemographic Aspects of the South African Australopithecines', *University of Pennsylvania Publications in Anthropology*, no. 1, 1975.
27. Kelton R. McKinley, 'Survivorship in Gracile and Robust Australopithecines: Demographic Comparison and a Prepared Birth Model', *American Journal of Physical Anthropology* 34, 1971, pp. 417-26.

death among Australopithecines was also around twelve, though McKinley's analysis of the data suggests an average life span of about twenty years.[27] Despite the different life expectancy figures, which evidently reflect different estimates of infant mortality rates, a similar population structure is suggested by both analyses. Assuming, as both Mann and McKinley do, a somewhat shorter birth interval than that found in chimpanzees (a four to five year interval), a female who had a first infant around twelve had another one at about age fifteen, another one about three years later, and so on. Like the males of her generation who perhaps fathered one or another of her offspring, she probably died before all of her young were sexually mature. A few individuals of both sexes presumably survived into their thirties. What can we conclude from this?

It is all too easy to interpret the population profile which emerges from this pattern of late sexual maturation, early death, and high mortality rates as one overflowing with orphaned youngsters, missing the mothers on whom they would have been dependent. However we need to forget our biases about the dependency of human children and our preconceptions about the skills and information they must acquire before they become fully functional adults and look at the data.

Given what we know about dimorphic primates, the savannah groups of these early hominids would have been composed of a small number of fully adult large males (who presumably circulated widely between groups), a similarly small number of infrequently fertile adult females, most or all of them with infants and small youngsters, and a significant number of 'orphaned' individuals, males and females at different stages of pre-reproductive physical development. Individuals orphaned while young and pre-reproductive had to forage for themselves (or cooperatively) to survive. (The situation resembles one that has been observed in a population of vervet monkeys.[28]) Presumably, the physically similar males and females were able to forage in much the same ways. Since hominid populations were maintained, many of the orphaned individuals in this setting suc-

28. In a study of 'immature' animals in three groups of vervet monkeys it was found that throughout the period of study mortality was high and the birthrate low in all three groups. 'Family size (sic) was small and there was a large number of orphans', and 'All of the animals spent the greatest proportion of their days feeding and foraging.' Phyllis C. Lee, 'Socialization of Immature Vervet Monkeys', in L. S. B. Leakey Foundation News, no. 23, 1982, p. 7.

ceeded in surviving to a reproductive age — that is older. Only after puberty did females become less wid as a result of pregnancy and the encumbrances of in some of the males become much larger and more likel about outside the confines of a group. As we shall s from Frisch's studies, first pregnancies probably did immediately after puberty, births were probably mo spaced than Mann and McKinley propose, and adul probably had only a few successful pregnancies dur rather short lives. The survival of those few clearly dep cooperative foraging and feeding practices.

Both males and females had by age twelve experienc learning period in a group large enough to insure the For some, neither parent had been around for long. Befc ing maturity many must have been called upon to f themselves. If, in fact, an individual's mother lived lon to provide her or him with a half or full sibling, mothe tion probably was diverted to the new infant. Under cumstances she was as likely to benefit from what th forager found as the other way around, a situatio Tanner[29] envisions in her model of early gathering socie

Producing food for someone temporarily or pern unable to forage is a rudimentary way of dividing labo do it today and I'll do it tomorrow' is, after all, a div labour, though somewhat different from permanently tasks and saying 'You do one thing and I'll do somethi from now on'. Dividing labour by age, or physical state, considerations, temporarily or for prolonged periods may well anticipate dividing labour in other ways: for e along lines that generated different products. Tanner no 'The common assumption that it [a division of labour] v marily or exclusively by sex is an oversimplification' character of the apparent age distribution in early homin ulations suggests that dimorphism played an insignifica in differentiating foraging activities by sex. It also sugge maximum cooperation among all the foragers, includir ducing food for nonproducers (generalized reciprocity important for their survival.

Frisch's recent researches on fatness, puberty and fertil

29. Nancy Makepeace Tanner, On Becoming Human, New York 1981.
30. Tanner, p. 220.

from unimportant with respect to our early hominids, Frisch notes that experimental evidence drawn from laboratory animals indicates that substituting fat calories for carbohydrate calories hastens fat deposition and sexual maturation in males as well as females. Frisch's data are relevant here and will also be significant in the analysis of later events.

Let us return, now, to our populations of early hominids. What helped these predominantly youthful populations to survive, reproduce and achieve the slow but steady increase and dispersal of population that characterizes the early hominid evolutionary grade? What allowed individuals of either sex in a population with a high mortality rate (among the young), a late age of sexual maturation, infrequent mating opportunities, rare successful pregnancies and a low birth rate to leave a genetic legacy? How were populations so at risk of extinction able to survive, replace members, and eventually expand their numbers? Apparently by 'inventing' production. The archaeological evidence indicates that some of them were already taking small game — (that is substituting fat calories for carbohydrate calories) and making simple stone tools by somewhere between 2.9 and 2.7 million years ago.[33]

Production for Survival

Many of the important actors in the scenario I see emerging from this configuration of circumstances are the males and females between four and twelve years old, who are already weaned and capable of feeding themselves, but not yet sexually mature. While their range of sizes reflected the age differences among them, males and females of the *same* age were similar in size and body form, though adults were dimorphic. The remains in the ancient sites and evidence from contemporary human foragers and other primate groups suggest that these males and females engaged in several kinds of foraging activities. These rarely involve distinctions between what males and females (or young or old) are called upon to do. They include: 1) individual foraging for small game and vegetables; 2) group hunting (of either the surround or drive type, or of the 'chase and exhaust'

33. 'Science News of the Week, Oldest Tool Kit Yet', *Science News* 119, 1981, pp. 83-4; Donald Johanson and A. Edey Maitland, *Lucy: The Beginnings of Mankind*, New York 1981.

variety) focussing on small animals; and 3) killing or scavenging large animals that are, somehow, incapacitated. These foraging activities could have been accomplished with simple tools by the physically similar young foragers and the few sex differentiated adults who, if female, were not necessarily encumbered by either pregnancy or an infant. These activities — undifferentiated along sex lines — whether individual or cooperative, when rewarded by more than could be consumed on the spot become production if the surplus is distributed for later consumption. Production proves to be advantageous for all the actors involved.

There are two possible explanations for the spread of production. One simply refers to social advantages. Another suggests it became biologically programmed into human populations. The survival values of production and of giving away goods without expecting an equal or immediate return for them (a form of Exchange called 'generalized reciprocity') can be looked at as genetically selfish and a result of kin selection. Recent bio-determinist evolutionary models of behaviour might explain an 'instinct' for production and exchange in these terms: individuals are geared toward maximizing their genetic legacy; achieving sexual maturation as early as possible and in good health is, therefore, an 'advantage' sought by individuals; diversifying food supplies and getting to eat as much meat as possible would help achieve this advantage. Both of these are easier to accomplish if the individual belongs to a wide ranging, co-operating group. Presumably individuals should strive to assure themselves that an opposite-sexed individual also survives to sexual maturity. Provisioning peers of the opposite sex is therefore worthwhile. Provisioning same-sexed peers is also worthwhile not only because of the rewards of reciprocity but because the chances are high that among those same-sexed peers are half siblings or 'cousins' who carry some of the individual's genes. Helping feed one's own mother, or caring for any of her other offspring, would serve to enhance the chances of some of one's genes surviving, though one may never reach sexual maturity. Provisioning older adults, whatever their sex or relationship, pays off in another way, too. The older, more experienced members of the community are the repositories of non-genetically transmitted information useful for one's own survival. While helping each other stay alive and eat well is particularly important for orphans 'trying' to reach a reproductive age, anybody who helps anybody is bound to be maximizing the chances of his/her genes surviving, since the populations are so small nearly everybody is more or less related to everybody else.

While the above sociobiological explanation makes it clear that production increased the survival chances of early hominids, it does not validate the view that 'genes for production' became prevalent because of kin selection. For one thing, kin selection is effectively irrelevant in small populations in which all or most are kin. Furthermore, discriminating between degrees of relatedness in distributing largesse seriously jeopardizes the survival of a species barely able to replace its members. Lastly, non-kin-based reciprocity, or cooperation among unrelated individuals, is evident elsewhere among animal species.

More than one hundred species of birds exhibit patterns of cooperative breeding. For instance a flock of green wood-hoopoes may consist (though rarely and temporarily) of only a breeding pair, or may have as many as sixteen members but only one breeding pair. Sexually mature non-breeding flock members serve as nest helpers, bringing food to the incubating female, to nestlings and to fledglings. Ligon and Ligon[34] observed a number of flocks in which there were helpers that were not related to the nestlings they were tending or the incubating females they fed. The merger of unrelated individuals either to increase the size of the flock or to form new flocks suggests that genetic relationships are not all important to the woodhoopoes' form of cooperation. The Ligons argue that the immediate rewards of reciprocity and not kin selection account for the occurrence of these cooperative behaviours. Surely, early hominids must have been able to perceive those rewards.

To sum up, then, it appears that undifferentiated production, provisioning others, or generalized reciprocity — or whatever one wants to call it — must have played a part in maintaining the small, overwhelmingly young populations of early hominids whose marginal replacement rates kept the species hovering precariously on the edge of extinction. Inventing production evidently improved the ability of the species to survive and even permitted a very gradual increase in its numbers.

34. J. David Ligon and Sandra H. Ligon. 'The Cooperative Breeding Behavior of the Green Woodhoopoe', *Scientific American*, 247, no. 1, 1982, pp. 126-35.

The Emergence of Interlocal Exchange

The functions and effects of dividing labour and Exchanging as well as exchanging products have received enormous attention ever since the Enlightenment and will not be examined here. The model explored here departs from commonly held views about the origins of exchange primarily in seeing formalized and systematic Exchange between groups as an economic arrangement which emerged *before* the proscriptive sexual division of labour was institutionalized and exchange standardized within groups. Sociological analyses of the arbitrary ways in which tasks are divided along sex lines usually point out that this arbitrariness occurs because the primary function of the sexual division of labour is that of helping cement the bonds of Exchange networks.[35] While Durkheim[36] clearly says that proscriptions governing the sexual division of labour emerged as an instrument for cementing inter-group bonds, few other sociologists are so explicit. The notion that the practice of the sexes exchanging goods within groups was a precursor of, and one of the conditions that led to, regularizing a sexual division of labour is either implicit or, as is evident in Parsons' works,[37] absent. Two lines of evidence suggest that Durkheim was correct and that a proscriptive sexual division of labour arose *after* Exchange became important.

The available cultural evidence strongly indicates that in the populations we have been discussing, male and female food-getting activities were undifferentiated during the period in which sub-groups of the population began Exchanging goods. The simple artefacts and food detritus associated with early human groups show little change for nearly two and a half million years. These remains reflect the use of foraging techniques which are simple, involve both sexes, and call for similar activities on the part of both. The evidence, therefore, indicates that the foraging activities of male and female producers remained undifferentiated for a long time.

Though the cultural evidence indicates that foraging patterns

35. Claude Lévi-Strauss, *Elementary Structures of Kinship*, Boston 1969.
36. Emile Durkheim, *The Division of Labor in Society*, New York 1964.
37. Talcott Parsons, 'The Incest Taboo in Relation to Social Structure', in R. L. Coser, ed., *The Family, Its Structure and Functions*, New York 1964, pp. 48-69. Talcott Parsons, *Societies: Evolutionary and Comparative Perspectives*, New York 1966.

did not change much for two and half million years, a gradual increase in the population, evident in slow dispersal over an ever-widening area, took place. Ranging ever more widely and producing and distributing diverse foods probably helped increase survival rates, but the extreme slowness of the rate of population growth in the face of a somewhat improved diet indicates that reproductive rates remained low. According to Frisch's analysis,[38] maintaining high activity levels acts as a brake on female fecundity. Data supporting her analysis[39] show that women who lead sedentary lives become pregnant more quickly, give birth more often and have more children than women who are highly mobile and engage in strenuous activities. The low reproductive rate, consequently, supports the idea that while foraging tools and techniques remained essentially simple, women's activities remained strenuous, and that women, like men, spent little time at the so-called home base sites of this period. The maintenance of marked sexual dimorphism in the populations indicates further that no change took place in the way mating opportunities among males were distributed. There are thus good reasons for concluding that foraging activities were not differentiated along sex lines and that mating arrangements remained essentially amorphous. During this period intergroup Exchanges were probably based on chance meetings (by groups or individuals) and were haphazard with respect to what goods were Exchanged.

How and why did incorporated groups and a pattern of systematic inter-group Exchange emerge? Dispersal and local specializations in technology and in the food products which became more diverse must have set the stage for frequent and regular inter-group Exchange. The dispersal of the slowly enlarging populations within larger range areas results in localized groups, loosely articulated to each other, with different resources and perhaps differentiating skills. The exchange of different products between localities or for products that are temporarily scarce in one area merely involves an extension of productive patterns. It is possible, then, that the pattern of Exchanging products arose before male and female products and production activities had become differentiated. The next part of this dis-

38. R. E. Frisch, 1980.
39. Nancy Howell, *Demography of the Dobe Area !Kung,* New York 1979. Gina Kolata, '!Kung Hunter-Gatherers: Feminism, Diet and Birth Control', *Science* 185, 1974, pp. 932-34.

cussion shows why this seems likely.

The Institutionalization of the Sexual Division of Labour and the Exchange of Sex-Differentiated Products

There are three lines of evidence which lead me to believe that a sexual division of labour, along with incest taboos and marriage Exchanges, appeared late — well into Homo erectus times. The first involves the appearance of fire hearths and fire-hardened spears, followed by stone-tipped spears, atl atls, and bows and arrows.

Projectile hunting by itself created new conditions. It permitted a major increase in the amount of meat in the diet of what soon became a rapidly proliferating and quickly spreading human population. Innovations made it possible for hunters to shift from an early concentration on taking a few middle-sized and larger herd animals, to taking more middle-sized and smaller animals with solitary habits.[40] How game was pursued changed. Injuring or killing game from a distance calls for sustained quiet as the pursuer stalks an animal. One or a few individuals can bring in good-sized animals to feed a number of others. Furthermore, projectile hunting tools can be used as defensive weapons against cornered game and predators, making it safer to hunt in small groups. The hunters themselves had to change. The techniques of projectile weapon hunting demand both training and self-control. Where earlier technologies had called upon large groups of the unskilled for surrounds, drives or chases, and these participants saw much action and made a lot of noise, projectile hunting calls for silence and stealth and demands skill, experience, patience and strength. These are attributes of older individuals. Projectile weaponry seems to have changed the character of the hunt in a way which transformed children or youngsters into dependents. In populations which were living longer the youngsters' roles as primary producers declined.

Another consequence of the introduction of projectile weapon hunting was the elaboration of processing technologies that are fire- and hearth-centred. Thick-skinned medium-sized game

40. David Frayer, 'Body Size, Weapon Use, and Natural Selection in the European Upper Palaeolithic and Mesolithic', *American Anthropologist* 83, 1981, pp. 57-73.

posed problems. Preparing and cooking these products of the chase are time-consuming activities. Far more demanding of skill and experience are the other new activities: processing skins and hides; converting them into clothing and carrying devices, and making hunting equipment and the tools to process foods and hides. Setting up and maintaining the shelters *cum* workshops where all of these activities take place were even more demanding. The new skills and techniques required for the hearth-bound activities required training and experience. Consequently, the time it took to become a fully productive participant in the progressively more elaborate social setting expanded. The young became dependent on fully productive adults for the first time. The invention of projectile hunting weapons and the control of fire established the underlying conditions for dividing labour by sex and by age.

The complexity of these tasks was a significant factor in dividing labour and broadening the scope of the generalized reciprocity operating within camps or groups. Not only does this complexity call for teaching skills to youngsters, it puts a premium on making sure that the skills and knowledge of the disabled or elderly are not lost. The aged and incapacitated, whether or not able to undertake hearth tasks, become indirect producers by virtue of being repositories of information. The new techniques created distinctions between the activities of the young and unskilled, the adults who could venture forth and bring back necessary supplies, and the knowledgeable elderly or incapacitated members of the community who could perform hearth-bound processing tasks and/or perform the socially important job of transmitting information. While a proscriptive division of labour along sex lines was ultimately an outcome of the complexity of the new technology, its initial effects must have been only to encourage a pragmatic division of tasks, for example by ability, age, or current circumstance. Though a pragmatic division of tasks might have become prolonged and stabilized it was not enforced by clear cut social sanctions and therefore remained essentially flexible. A proscriptive division of labour — one which divided the sexes — implemented by social sanctions and ideological mechanisms such as early socialization was to appear only later.

The diversity of environments which human populations came to occupy by the Upper Palaeolithic indicates that foraging and processing tasks must have differed both in technical content and social form from place to place. Hearth-oriented tasks and fire itself must have differed as to their importance for the groups and communities scattered across the Eurasian and African landmasses. Siberian foragers who hunted mammoth must have relied in different ways on fire and developed a different repertoire of hearth tasks than African foragers in warmer climates who had richer and more varied flora and fauna to exploit. With the emergence of Mesolithic technologies in communities which exploited the resources of shores, lakes, rivers and seas, even greater variability of foraging and processing tasks, and the way they were organized, must have developed. The allocation of tasks undoubtedly depended in part on local circumstances and in part on local traditions. However the division of labour was institutionalized, though, the *need* for dividing tasks ultimately derived from the emergence of new foraging techniques and strategies, and the new processing problems that arose from them.

The second line of evidence that suggests that the emergence of a sexual division of labour is related to the appearance of this complex of social and technological innovations concerns the population expansion which occurred. The increase in meat and animal fats apparently contributed to a marked increase in female fertility as well as to increased longevity. But the increase in the birth and survival rates seems to reflect an additional factor, a behavioural change. It is obvious that those adults who did not go out on a stalking-type hunt must have assumed the responsibility for performing hearth-centred tasks and overseeing the activities of the dependent youngsters excluded from the hunt. Women in late pregnancy and those encumbered by nursing infants probably were non-hunters for prolonged periods. Engaging in time-consuming hearth-centred activities involves a degree of sedentism. This is associated with increased female fertility, and higher birth and survival rates. The population increase may, therefore, reflect a change in the activities women pursued. The increase suggests that women in earlier settings, which were not complex enough to generate a sexual division of labour, were not as hearth-bound or sedentary as the women in those later cultures where sophisticated forms of projectile hunting were practised. An informal or circumstantial division of labour along sex lines seems likely.

The third line of evidence suggesting that the sexual division of labour was institutionalized as projectile hunting developed and hearth activities became complex concerns sexual dimorphism. The size differences between the sexes are large in the Early Upper Palaeolithic, but approximate modern differences by the Mesolithic. The change indicates that for some reason small males were in the latter period getting a chance to mate they had not enjoyed in earlier periods. Though other analysts have seen this change as related to an increase in the survival of smaller males because of safer or more specialized hunting techniques,[41] together these three lines of evidence indicate something quite different: they suggest that rules equalizing male mating opportunities and rules *institutionalizing* the sexual division of labour emerged in conjunction with the expansion of Exchange.

How and why are reduced dimorphism and the institutionalization of the sexual division of labour linked to Exchange? A casual arrangement whereby hunters hunt and non-hunters undertake hearth tasks does not constitute an institutionalized sexual division of labour even if the majority of non-hunters happens to be women, and most or all of those going on hunts are male. Allocating the responsibility of supervising the activities of older children to women who are engaged in tasks that permit them to assume that responsibility more nearly approximates the institutionalized division. Still, there is something missing. While mothers occupied with new hearth skills probably found themselves involved with their youngsters for much longer than had previously been the case, hunters too assumed responsibilities toward the young. In addition to providing others with foods mothers and children normally did not produce, the need to undertake the responsibility for transmitting their hunting skills must have been self-evident. The sexual division of labour not only designates which productive tasks men and women pursue, it allocates the responsibilities for socializing youngsters into those tasks to both men and women. The division, when fully articulated, calls for recognizing early on who will be a 'mother' and who will not, deciding which set of skills a youngster is most likely to use as an adult, and training the youngsters accordingly. Girls and boys as well as women and men are distinguished from each other. Girls learn their skills from women, boys from men. By the time hunting and hearth

41. Alice M. Brues, 'The Spearman and the Archer', *American Anthropologist* 61, 1959, pp. 457-69.

tasks had become both time-consuming and skill-based the activities of all males and females, young and old, were differentiated and gender distinctions were created. But the institutionalization of such distinctions (rules insisting on their maintenance) and the emergence of a proscriptive sexual division of labour seem to have occurred as the result of the following dynamics.

One aspect of the interdependence between the sexes that emerged was the *need* for the exchange of the different goods produced by the sexes. This sort of exchange resembled the ongoing Exchange of different products between local groups or bands, with one notable difference. Within-group exchange based on a sexual division of labour involved men and women in inescapable interdependency. Intergroup Exchanges, while mutually beneficial, occurred irregularly, and depended on occasions when groups or individuals from different bands met, what products they had on hand, whether they needed each others' products, and whether those needs had been satisfied by Exchanges with other groups. The extension of the inescapable interdependence of the pragmatic sexual division of labour to intergroup relations was accomplished by instituting incest rules. Because the incest rules required men and/or women to move from one group to another at marriage, a certain amount of rigidity in the tasks undertaken by both was useful. Incest rules provided the conditions for codifying what had been casual. A pragmatic division of labour which only flexibly followed sex lines became the proscriptive sexual division of labour as sanctions and socialization were brought to bear on who was permitted to perform particular tasks. Incest and exogamy rules made proscriptive rules governing the sexual division of labour inevitable.

The incest rules, which forbade taking mates from among kin, or those who were members of the local group, called for groups to send skilled individuals of either sex away in contractual marriages and to attract mates to the band or group. Marriages established obligations and bonds, and, if contracted for a long term, stabilized Exchange relationships. Marriages also made it possible to establish and maintain loose and far flung networks of Exchange ties. Where projectile weapon hunting permitted the pursuit of solitary animals as game, a skilled man hunting as an individual with a skilled woman performing complementary tasks could survive. Monogamous marriages occurred frequently. The invention of incest taboos and marriage thus created a situation in which every or nearly every male, regardless of whether he was robust or tall or especially active at adolescence, was of potential value as a spouse if he had acquired adult men's skills. Similarly, a marriageable female was one who had acquired women's skills. (The uniquely human practice of postponing a first pregnancy for a while after a female reaches sexual maturity seems to have roots in this situation, since mating and marriage were delayed until a woman was adequately trained, or until non-kin mates were readily accessible, or until a worthwhile Exchange link presented itself.) Incest taboos and contractual marriage evidently led to the institutionalization of the sexual division of labour, along with an equalization of male mating opportunities and a reduction in dimorphism as monogamous unions served to stabilize exchange.[42]

The Model in Brief: The Early Foragers

Physical sex differences between adults appear to have been quite marked in early hominid foraging populations.[43] The hominids resembled other primate species where adult males and females are physically differentiated in that their mating relationships were temporary, variable in form and content, and rarely exclusive. Foraging activities were pursued in much the same ways by members of both sexes, and a sexual division of labour was absent. Adulthood appeared only after late sexual maturation (later than is characteristic of other large primates). Consequently, a large proportion of the foraging hominid population was made up of physically undifferentiated pre-adult females and males.

42. Devra Kleiman's examination of 'Monogamy in Mammals' is a succinct summary of the data demonstrating that a lack of dimorphism among mammals is associated with monogamous mating systems in which all males have an equal opportunity to find mates. Devra Kleiman, 'Monogamy in Mammals', *Quarterly Review in Biology* 52, March 1977, pp. 36-69.

43. C. Loring Brace, 'Sexual Dimorphism in Human Evolution', in C. L. Brace and J. Metress, eds., *Man in Evolutionary Perspective*, New York 1973, pp. 238-54. M. H. Wolpoff,

Sharing

The reliance on vegetable foods was nearly total at first, and, as happens among other primates with food habits similar to those of these early hominids, an individual of either sex would occasionally share an item it was eating.[44] As shown earlier such behaviour is analogous to the sharing found among social predators, and suggests that sharing was probably more frequent when and where unencumbered individuals killed small animals frequently, or joined with others to chase or hunt small game.[45] It is likely, then, that it was in places where taking game became a regular activity that early hominids learned to share food. Unlike social predators who regularly share game, however, the overwhelmingly youthful hominid populations had a very low reproductive rate. Their populations remained small and at risk. (Populations of social predators are adequately maintained by sharing.) The development of production, a peculiarly human social adaptation which rests on a kind of foresight unnecessary for sharing, appears to have been a critical factor in hominid survival and allowed orphaned and incapacitated individuals to survive. Thus production contributed to sustaining a species with a low replacement rate.

Production

Production appeared when individuals or groups deliberately set out to collect goods to give (or distribute) to others. The practice may have arisen when groups setting out to chase game found themselves surrounding or driving their prey and harvesting more than could be eaten on the spot. Carrying food back to share with others is production. Engaging in such actions provides obvious and immediate nutritional and social rewards. The perception that production is worthwhile (though I doubt that its *long*-term survival advantages were perceived) encouraged the development of productive surround-and-drive hunting techniques.

These techniques normally call for the active participation of all able-bodied individuals irrespective of their age or sex. Many of these individuals are likely to have been too young to have

44. Hladik, pp. 249-50.
45. Nishida, p. 251.

developed the sex differences of adulthood. Dividing labour (for example, undertaking different individualized activities which produce different goods) presumably only occurred whenever immediate situations or individual circumstances called for it. Whatever their sex or physique, individuals usually engaged in the same sorts of group or individualized foraging and hunting activities.

Exchange

The regular production and distribution of small quantities of game made animal proteins and fats dietary staples. The changed diet somewhat reduced the foetal, infant and adult mortality rates, and extended life spans. The population gradually increased. Members of the sexually dimorphic species spread themselves over an ever widening area. Fluidly organized groups with loose social and sexual ties to each other became more numerous and occupied ecologically differentiated settings. Localized populations found themselves producing different products. The goods produced for local distribution were sometimes Exchanged for different goods collected elsewhere or for similar goods in short supply locally. Exchanging goods increased and diversified what was available to the local groups. Production (undifferentiated by sex) continued, and in conjunction with Exchange (involving goods differentiated by locality) changed diets. The post-pubertal life span increased. The increased longevity wrought a change in the demographic profiles of successive populations and was also accompanied by an increase in adult heights and weights. The taller and heavier populations continued to be markedly sexually dimorphic. Over the many millenia during which foraging tools and techniques show but slow and slight changes, physical sex differences remained large.

The Sexual Division of Labour and Mate Exchange

The invention and elaboration of projectile hunting tools along with the growing use of fire[46] created a new and

46. Catherine Perles, 'Hearth and Home in the Old Stone Age', *Natural History* 90, no. 10, 1981 pp. 38-41.

72

revolutionary set of conditions. Following their introduction large numbers of medium-sized game animals began being taken regularly. Carcasses were prepared and processed in elaborate ways, and animal fats and proteins became a significant part of the human diet. The population expansion which occurred is apparent in the rapidity with which groups carrying the new tool kit spread over vast areas.[47] (Significantly, during this relatively recent spread of 'big' game hunting the size and skeletal difference between adult males and females first increased[48] then diminished[49] to current levels. This diminution of sexual dimorphism, occurring as it does in conjunction with the development of big game hunting (in populations which already included many sexually able adults) indicates that a radical change took place in the way the opportunities for reproductive success were distributed. The conditions which made small females more reproductively successful than larger females, and large males more reproductively successful than smaller ones, no longer existed. The chain of circumstances leading from the invention of projectile hunting tools to the reduction of physical sex differences includes a number of links: among them the emergence of the sexual division of labour, the establishment of rules governing mating, and the creation of more stable and extended exchange networks. The links are articulated as follows.

Projectile hunting changed how production within a local population was pursued. Projectiles made it possible for one or a few individuals skilled in their use to supply many individuals with meat from good sized animals. Inexperienced youngsters were excluded from the new kind of hunting but continued to engage in other kinds of foraging activities. The new game began being processed in time-consuming and complex ways so that fire and hearth-centred skills now required considerable training and experience, just as the new hunting did. Consequently, it took longer for youngsters to become fully productive adults. The ongoing responsibility for supervising dependent youngsters along with hearth tasks fell to non-hunters. As foetal and infant mortality declined, more and more often non-hunters were the encumbered women. The risky tasks of stalking and pursuing big game fell more and more often to

47. Chester S. Chard, *Man in Prehistory*, New York 1975.
48. Frayer, op. cit.
49. Wolpoff, op. cit.

unencumbered, able-bodied and expendable men. The pragmatic division of some tasks along sex lines was more frequent. The exchange of sex differentiated products produced *within* a local population became common practice. This internal exchange firmly established the interdependence of the activities pursued by men and women, and created the dependence of youngsters on adults of both sexes.

The exchange of products within groups mirrored many aspects of the Exchange of products between localities. Interlocal Exchange, however, lacked the element of ongoing interdependence generated by dividing tasks along sex lines. Interdependence *between* groups was assured by creating incest rules and establishing exogamy (the custom of marrying outside of one's own social group). Insisting that men and women were not permitted to have sex partners and/or long-term spouses except from groups other than their own, forced groups to Exchange producers as well as products. Though an individual who moved from one group to another for marriage was not necessarily Exchanged for someone with similar or equivalent skills, the person did have to possess skills which allowed the Exchange to be worthwhile. By codifying the tasks women and men were more or less consistently pursuing, and socializing girls and boys to perform them as adults, the complementarity and interdependence of spouses from different groups, and hence of the groups themselves, was guaranteed. The proscriptive sexual division of labour which replaced the pragmatic division of tasks by sex thus served to stabilize and extend Exchange networks. It cemented and helped make permanent the interdependence between groups created by exogamy and incest rules, transformed the mode of production, and, as we shall see in review below, helped reshape patterns of reproduction.

Projectiles provide safety from predators as well as being efficient hunting tools. Consequently, as projectile techniques and tools were refined, small hunting parties and ephemeral small foraging groups became more common. Scattering the males and females (of whatever physiques) who had acquired the appropriate sex-differentiated skills through such groups, and assigning each of them as 'spouses', expanded Exchange networks and simultaneously stabilized mating relationships. It also equalized the distribution of mating opportunities among males, irrespective of whether they were large, small, or of medium height and weight. Nearly every man who could use the tools was of use in the mate Exchange networks. The ongoing distribution of diversified resources through these networks added significantly to everyone's food supply, and thus effectively equalized the chances of reproductive success for women with different physiques and nutritional needs. A delay in a female's first pregnancy may have had a similar effect. The reduction of sexual dimorphism in human populations followed. The emergence of different tasks for men and women (and presumably of gender roles with differentiated behaviours) ironically set the stage for a *decrease* in physical sex differences.

Epilogue

Physical sex differences are often regarded as the foundation on which the sexual division of labour rests. The biosocial model outlined above, however, argues that the institutionalization of the sexual division of labour created the conditions which *reduced* physical sex differences. The model also proposes that production for distribution is fundamental to the human condition. It says that production not only precedes the sexual division of labour, but also precedes incest taboos, marriage and kinship systems. The model, therefore, departs from the structuralist view that these institutions are the benchmarks of human society and define it. This model differs from the Lévi-Straussian model espoused by most structuralists in another way as well. While Lévi-Strauss sees the Exchange of women by men as a first step in the process of culturalization, I argue here as elsewhere[50] that individuals of *either* sex were moved from one group to another to regularize Exchange. Thus, I do not go along

50. Lila Leibowitz, 'Founding Families', *Journal of Theoretical Biology* 21, 1968, pp. 153-69. 'Dilemma for Social Evolution: The Impact of Darwin', *Journal of Theoretical Biology* 25, 1969, pp., 255-75; 'Breasts, Buttocks and Body Hair', *Psychology Today* 3(9) 1970, pp. 16-22; 'Perspectives on the Evolution of Sex Differences', in Rayna Reiter, ed., *Toward an Anthropology of Women*, New York 1975, pp. 20-35. See also: Judith Brown, 'A Note on the Division of Labor by Sex', *American Anthropologist* 72, 1970, pp. 1073-78; Chester S. Chard, *Man in Prehistory*, New York 1975; Catherine Perles, 'Hearth and Home in the Old Stone Age', *Natural History* 90(10), 1981, pp. 38-41; Richard Potts, 'Behavioral Reinterpretation of Lower Pleistocene Sites from Olduvai', read for the American Anthropological Association; 'Universals and Male Dominance Among Primates: A Critical Examination', in Ruth Hubbard and Marion Lowe, eds., *Genes and Gender II: Research Pitfalls on Sex and Gender*, New York 1979, pp. 35-48.

with the structuralist argument that women were subordinated to men as soon as basic cultural institutions emerged. The idea that women are and always have been subordinated to men is not expressed in the model just presented. I do not subscribe to the view that the subordination of women is a 'basic' part of our heritage, but share the belief with the authors of this book that eradicating the oppression and exploitation of women is as worthwhile a goal as eradicating other forms of systemic exploitation and will not undermine the foundations of human society.

Acknowledgements

I would like to express my gratitude to Nathanial Raymond, Ruth Hubbard, Marian Lowe, Alan Klein, Ellice Gonzalez, Carolyn Fluehr-Lobban, Stephanie Coontz, and Peta Henderson for reading and commenting on earlier drafts of this paper.

The Dawn of Lineage Societies
The Origins of Women's Oppression

Nicole Chevillard and Sébastien Leconte

Certain societies have actually existed without wage-slavery, serfdom or slavery, without kings or bosses, societies in which all relations were expressed in terms of kinship, and really *experienced* as relations of kinship. Since these social systems did not have private property and did not give rise to any of the alienations we are most familiar with, we are tempted to assume that they were egalitarian and free of any form of women's oppression.[1]

Unfortunately, reality cannot be so easily explained. In the first place, all these stateless and classless societies (in the usual sense of the word 'class'), do not belong to the same category and therefore cannot be interpreted in terms of the same analytical models.

Some of these societies, the best-known, the ones that are still the favourite targets for anthropological studies — namely, classical or lineage societies — are already highly structured. Although both lineages and clans (which combine several lineages) are based on descent from a single ancestor, their organizational form includes surprisingly far-reaching genealogies and strict rules (for marriage, succession and alliance) that distinguish them from other less complex and probably more primitive social structures. We shall return to this point

1. See Friedrich Engels, *The Origins of the Family, Private Property and the State*, London 1972, for whom women's oppression is linked to the origins of private property. (In this and following sections, the authors see 'lineage' societies as identical with viri-, patri-, or avunculocal systems, where women move at marriage. – Editors.)

later.

There is, moreover, nothing egalitarian about these lineage societies, at least in terms of the relations between men and women. On the contrary, they offer proof that women's oppression is indeed the oldest of all forms of oppression.

By drawing on the wealth of anthropological investigation of this type of society, both in Africa and in America, we shall attempt first to identify the mechanisms through which women are subordinated, and ask certain key questions: Are women simply oppressed, for instance, kept out of certain positions? Or is their labour exploited? If so, how does this alienation actually operate in concrete terms?

These questions will subsequently prove useful when we try to analyse the genesis of this subordination, and to raise other questions: Was there a slow evolution toward increasingly pronounced forms of exploitation, with lineage societies appearing as the last phase in a transitional period preceding class societies proper? Or did the inegalitarian society that lineage society represents come into being as a result of a break, an upheaval? In this context, what was the role played by the sexual division of labour and the development of the idea of property?

We will move backwards, starting with the most recent and trustworthy data (that concerning clan societies) to the most ancient, concluding with some discussion of the social structures that may have preceded the oppression of women.

The Exploitation of the Female Work Force in Lineage Societies

'In Black Africa, most of the agricultural work is carried out by women . . . Food-producing farming remains entirely in the hands of married women.' This observation of French anthropologist Denise Paulme[2] is reinforced by her male colleagues, such as Georges Balandier,[3] who emphasizes the 'vital functions performed by women . . . who ensure *the main part of productive tasks.*'

'Agriculture is women's work,' declare the lagoon dwellers of the Ivory Coast, thereby summing up 'an obvious truth' so widely accepted in all of traditional Africa that Uganda's Thema

2. Denise Paulme, ed., *Classes d' Age et Associations d' Age en Afrique de l'Quest,* Paris 1972, and *Une Société de Côte d'Ivoire Hier et Aujourd'hui,* Paris 1971.
3. Georges Balandier, *Anthropo-Logiques,* Paris 1974.

Awori[4] could explain to a European public that 'in Western society, a man works to feed his family. This is not the case in traditional Africa where that responsibility is incumbent upon the women. . . . Whereas goods, land, children, and the woman herself can be regarded as the property of the father or his agnatic group, the responsibility to preserve and fructify these "possessions" of her husband rests with the woman.'

In predominantly agricultural societies, women's work is all the more essential in that these societies' food supply, their very survival, depends on food-directed farming. Women are also responsible for the major part of the daily work in cattle-breeding countries. Among the Nuer, for instance, they perform the main tasks: milk the cows and the goats, churn the butter, pound the millet, prepare meals. And since the livestock is looked after by young herdsmen, adult men have practically no 'routine' work to carry out. Evans-Pritchard merely remarks that 'in order to overcome their boredom . . . men make tools, ornaments, or do their hair'.[5] This is in the dry season. In the rainy season, men busy themselves with preparations for ceremonies (initiations particularly) and warfare. Compared to women and children, men behave as members of a predominantly idle group.

Agricultural advisors sent by bilateral or multilateral aid organizations to the countries of sub-Saharan Africa are quite familiar with this situation. They are the first to recognize that programmes introducing light agricultural motorization in bush country chiefly aim to promote men's interest in agriculture. Women are now threatening to leave for the cities and in countries such as Gabon, or the Congo, the female rural exodus is massive. With their departure, agriculture is waning. The same phenomenon prevails throughout almost all sub-Saharan Africa; even countries which used to export agricultural foodstuffs, with quite low populations which have never been threatened by drought or desertification, now have to import food.

The predominant role of women in traditional Black African societies is replicated in all Third World societies with lineage

4. Thema Awori, General Secretary of the Federation of Women's Organizations of Uganda. The quotation is taken from an article published in *Croissance des Jeunes Nations*, no.165, November 1975.
5. Edward E.Evans-Pritchard, 'Daily Life of the Nuer in Dry Season Camps', (1936), in Edward E. Evans-Pritchard, *The Position of Women in Primitive Societies*, London 1965, pp.188-96.

economies. Westerners have taken years to come to terms with this obvious fact (we will return later to the reasons for, and the consequences of, such blindness). It was not until the Wellesley international conference in the United States, that Third World aid institutions finally accepted that funds intended for agriculture and handed out to men in the form of proficiency classes or subsidies, had had no concrete impact on agriculture. Aid programmes worked out by men had not taken into account the real producers, women.

In Latin America, Indian tribes practice agriculture wherever the soil permits, in other words in most cases. 'The mode of subsistence of forest societies,' writes Pierre Clastres, 'is essentially agricultural; this agriculture is actually limited to gardening but, almost everywhere, its contribution is at least as important as that of hunting, fishing, and gathering.'[6] Taking the Tupi-Guarani tribe as an example, Pierre Clastres delights in 'the little time men devoted to what we know as work.'[7] Indeed men would be content with clearing gardens that were subsequently used for four to six consecutive years. Practically all other agricultural tasks — planting, weeding, harvesting — were the women's responsibility in accordance with the sexual division of labour. 'The resulting cheerful conclusion is this: men, i.e. half the population, worked about two months every four years! They devoted the remaining time to occupations experienced not as effort but as pleasure: hunting, fishing, feasting and drinking; and lastly to the satisfaction of their passionate taste for warfare.'[8]

1) A Rational Explanation of the Female Labour Force

Women thus play an essential role in traditional agriculture, which is the kind still practised by most lineage societies. Their day-to-day repetitive tasks ensure the survival of the entire human group. We sometimes tend to believe that this vital function should give them a correspondingly significant social role. But, in fact, the opposite is true. The importance of their responsibility is hidden and their productive labour (women's work) is downgraded. The only way they could perhaps make

6. Pierre Clastres, *Society against the State*, translated by Robert Hurley, Oxford 1977, p.45.
7. Clastres, p.165.
8. Ibid, p. 165.

their voices heard would be by using the product of their work, 'capitalizing' on it, as it were. But they have absolutely no control over this product, and no say in its distribution, nor even in the organization of their own tasks. Here we come to the crux of the mechanism that regulates the productive function of women in such societies.

A useful illustration is provided by the Jivaro, the famed head shrinkers, who recognize no chiefs except in time of war. In their predominantly agricultural society (sixty-five percent of food production, with the rest divided between the product of hunting, fishing, gathering, and a little herding), the organization of day-to-day life offers few surprises. 'Women do most of the laborious garden work, being exclusively responsible for planting and harvesting manioc, Araceae species, sweet potato, *papa china*, red pepper, sugar cane, onion and pineapple.'[9] (Note in passing the wide range of agricultural knowledge and practice.) Women alone weed the gardens, which is the most tedious task. They also raise chickens, hogs, cook, make pottery, prepare the beer and look after the children. Not surprisingly, in Jivaro society men have much more free time than women do. This would teach us nothing new if the author of this study on the Jivaro did not go on to present an exhaustive analysis of the organization of labour. The total surface of a garden (in other words, field or cultivated strip of land) depends essentially, for the man (he is the one who clears the land), upon the number of women he has to farm it. A man trying to enhance his prestige may clear even larger areas (that is to say, larger than normal) for each of his wives. In fact, men clearly prefer having two or more wives. Productivity, in terms of subsistence goods, is in direct relation to the number of women a man possesses, since women are responsible for most agricultural production. Hence, these women are no doubt thought of as 'labour power' capable of being rationally exploited.

This way of thinking about women extends far beyond the agricultural domain: when hunting, a man will bring along one of his wives to carry his supplies, in particular, the inevitable beer. Female labour also makes possible the formation of a surplus intended for social use. 'The importance of wives in producing food and beer goes far beyond the subsistence requirements of the household itself . . . The Jivaro place a high

9. Michael J.Harner, *The Jivaro*, New York 1972, p.52.

value on drinking and eating . . . so that one's status in a neigh-
bourhood is greatly affected by one's generosity with beer or
food.'[10]

Men clear the land . . . women do the rest. Men make a
rational calculation of the surface that can be cultivated by their
wives. But a question remains: how are women made to work on
that land? Marriage is certainly one answer; but are things that
simple? Why shouldn't women stay and work on their parents'
land, as they did during their childhood and adolescence? What
is it that makes women move out to live with their spouse? Have
they not worked enough at their father's and mother's to receive
in return a share of their land? In most Amazonian tribes it is
quite the opposite. 'The distance between long houses', writes
Pierre Clastres, 'is such that it gives a woman's departure a
practically definitive character . . . For a woman, marriage is
akin to a disappearance.'[11]

This rule bears a name: that of exogamy (marriages are only
allowed between persons of different lineages), which is practised by the vast majority of lineage societies. In this instance,
the rule is combined with a second principle, equally widespread, that of patri- or virilocality whereby a woman must
follow her husband and the place of residence is dictated by the
man and/or by his family.

2) The Components of Female Status under Customary Law

In Black Africa, as among the Indian tribes of Latin America,
residence, allowing for exceptions, is patrilocal whether one is
dealing with a matrilineal or patrilineal society (we will return to
this point later). The girls are thus destined to leave. Hence, they
cannot participate in the collective ownership of the land of the
lineage into which they were born. Boys, on the other hand,
receive some land from the elders of the lineage (father, uncle or
older brother in ch ge of managing the lineage community),
which, although it is not owned 'exclusively' by them, at least
enables them to live. They are generally awarded this land when
they get married, in other words at the same time as the woman
who will work it.

The principle is the same, whether the land needs to be cleared
or not. To obtain the means to work and her own subsistence, a

10. Harner, p.81.
11. Clastres, p.60.

woman has to resort to a man — father or husband — whom it will be her responsibility to feed. Her almost total lack of economic and social rights is akin to what we would call under modern law permanent 'legal incapacity'. Generally, a woman cannot inherit anything — except a few household goods and in certain matrilineal societies some female religious symbols (we will return to this point later). Nothing belongs to her exclusively. The IDEF congress on women's condition in Africa[12] was unambiguous on the status of women under customary law in countries south of the Sahara: in essence, women are supposed to have nothing. And they cannot own anything because they have no inheritance.

In a comparison with modern law, congress participants even noted that women's status under customary law was very paradoxical: most of the time a woman is the only one to have contributed to the accumulation of the household's goods through her labour, while the man has only had to lend her the means of production (a field, agricultural and cooking implements). Yet, when a marriage is dissolved (repudiation, divorce, widowhood), she is entitled to nothing. Michel Monuel Dah, magistrate, and Brigitte Kabore, a Ministry of Justice official — both from Upper Volta — have even pointed out that among the various ethnic groups of Upper Volta a father is not expected to provide food or clothing to his wife and children. Yet the opposite is true: a woman must feed her husband and children, and provide clothing for herself and her children.

There are many such examples: there are, for instance, all those mentioned during the Tunis congress. They recur and fit the description no matter the country or ethnic group considered. Black African jurists recognize that customary law regards women as 'instruments' or 'goods' rather than 'persons' or legal subjects.

It is less surprising then that African contributions to the Tunis congress accepted the term *'capital'* (which may seem inappropriate to us) or 'women-capital' when speaking of women in the traditional family system. The word, which appears in all the discussions, refers to the same haunting fear of being short of women that emerges from African customary law and palaver rituals (always male). The instrumental character

12. Congress of the Institut International de Droit d'Expression Française, held in Tunis from May 27 to June 3 1974, on the theme: 'The legal, political and social status of women'.

associated with femininity spreads to all domains: a woman's beauty or intelligence or courage is always regarded as secondary. Quantity prevails over quality.

For Jivaro, Béti, or Fang men, as for all other men in traditional lineage economies, the road to success is through women. A first wife enables the accumulation of a surplus which, if it is a good year, will permit the acquisition of a second wife. Polygamy is not only a sign of wealth, it creates wealth.

This observation needs further clarification: it is not the man and the man alone who grows rich from a woman's labour, but all the men of the same lineage. In the same way as there is no individual property in the lineage system, women, who are regarded as property or goods, do not belong to a single individual. In fact, the custom known as the levirate stipulates that at the death of her spouse a woman should be given as inheritance. She will then marry the heir, brother, son, nephew, or cousin of the deceased husband, and remain — *de facto* — within his lineage.

When a lineage, that is, the men of the lineage, wants to acquire a woman whose 'use' will be entrusted to one of its members, it must come to an agreement with another lineage, in accordance with the exogamy principle. This is the very essence of the principle of women's exchange. In general, the circulation of women is regulated by the elders of the lineage who, in theory (but it isn't always that simple), have to ensure that the system works to no one's (namely no male's) detriment.

When the exchange of women amounts to a barter (a lineage exchanges one woman for another, a system also known as the 'exchange of sisters'), the elders are in charge of accounting the 'incoming' and 'outgoing'. When the exchange is performed by means of symbolic goods, these goods are in the hands of the elders who can thus make their accounting more precise.

But a lineage will never agree to let go of a woman, to cut into its 'women-capital', without compensation. This is the meaning of the bride price, which makes women's instrumental character even more obvious. It is the reverse of the dowry practised by European bourgeois families; the lineage bride price is owed by the family that intends to acquire a woman for one of its members. This bride price is still practised in Black Africa today, and as a result of successive distortions can reach colossal amounts far beyond the available funds of an average young man.

Although a woman is acquired collectively by a lineage, the young man for whom she is intended is frequently made to contribute. The donor lineage sometimes demands to be paid 'in labour', a contribution which can take more or less time to complete (several years, several months over several years) and which is meant to compensate for the loss of labour caused by the departure of the girl. The Jivaro, in particular, practice this form of exchange 'in kind'. In other tribes or ethnic groups (especially in Africa), the elders sometimes take responsibility for all reciprocal relations with the lineage of the bride-to-be (or brides-to-be) but demand in compensation a certain amount of labour from future grooms. In fact, this will often prove to be the only moment in their lives when adult men are forced into productive work: by using women as blackmail![13]

Finally, the bride price system considerably curtails the freedom of women. They may not divorce without reimbursing the bride price, but they own nothing.

3) Homogeneous Groups of Exploited Working Women

All the elements that make up female status in lineage society — the rule of patrilocal residence; the exchange of women; the obligation for women to perform most agricultural tasks although they have no rights over the land which they farm; women's legal incapacity — form a coherent whole. The pattern of these devices, the way in which they fit together, demonstrate that they have one main objective, namely, the rational exploitation of the female labour force.

Lineage societies do not limit themselves to oppressing women. In fact they also oppress boys and young men (more or less severe sexual repression, respect and duties owed to elders, religious or political oppression and so on.)

On the other hand, it is only *women who perform alienated work* throughout their lives. This alienation makes possible the creation of a surplus which women do not control. In general they receive only the equivalent of what is necessary to renew

13. These systems also have the advantage of postponing the age of the first marriage for men. This type of arrangement goes hand in hand with the practice of polygamy — since boys and girls reach puberty in practically equal numbers among all the peoples of the world, polygamy presupposes that girls are married much earlier than boys (except in case of war, raiding, or considerable social inequality between men themselves).

their labour power; sometimes they receive less. A study by FAO shows that women are more affected than men in cases of malnutrition. A series of mechanisms (women fasting during menstruation, various food taboos, segregation during meals and so on) enables men to claim nearly all the rare proteins.[14] Many observers have noted this customary rule. Thus, French anthropologist Robert Jaulin writes in *La Mort Sara:* 'Meat — in particular that of chicken — is the privilege of men. Only on rare occasions are women entitled to it.'[15] And yet women are the ones who breed the chickens! It is worth adding that those thereby excluded from meat consumption are those who need it most: growing children and pregnant or breast-feeding mothers.[16]

In each basic economic unit, whether lineage or lineage segment, the female group represents the group of permanent producers. Other groups, also female, correspond to this group within other lineages. In all the basic units, the goods produced are frequently quite similar, but their quality or quantity varies over time. In the exchange of goods between lineages, the only unit of measure is 'labour value', a labour value easier to evaluate in these societies than in ours because it is known to all. Hence the universal measuring instrument is merely the labour power of a woman, the bride price.

Therefore, women in lineage societies form a homogeneous group of exploited working people. This labour force is the only one used rationally, thanks to mechanisms that affect the organization of production as well as the distribution of goods and social status. These mechanisms are self-reproducing from one generation to the next: they regulate the life of women from birth to death. Indeed they amount to a 'relation of production' specific to lineage society. Women are the only category of people subjected to this type of alienation prior to the invention of slavery. Are we not dealing, then, with a distinct *'mode of production'* (which we shall call the 'lineage mode of production')? A mode of production which is all the more 'dominant' in

14. We do not believe, as Evelyn Reed does, that women themselves refused meat consumption because they rejected cannibalism. Women of lineage societies are not systematically vegetarian. There is only a difference of degree between their meat consumption and that of men; in fact it all depends on the quantity of meat available. (Reed, *Woman's Evolution*, New York 1975.)

15. Robert Jaulin, *La Mort Sara*, Paris 1976.

16. See Claude Meillassoux, *Maidens, Meal and Money*, Cambridge 1981.

that it is the only known mode of production which was actually put into practice as a coherent system which acted both through the economic, the social and the ideological realm? Do women in lineage societies constitute a social class, the first alienated social class? Or are we faced with a transitional period that paves the way for other forms of alienation — such as slavery — and precedes class society proper?

Before answering these questions, we need to:

a) identify the key or keys to women's alienation in lineage systems;

b) trace the history of these determining factors: was there a slow evolution, in which women may perhaps have taken part (a thesis expounded by Stephanie Coontz and Peta Henderson)? If such is the case, it is indeed likely that lineage structures are transitional social formations. If the opposite is true, if there was a sudden break somewhere, be it even in a small number of human groups, then the transition thesis is more difficult to accept;

c) identify the actors of this history: do men form a homogeneous group which confronts women? In the event that women make up an alienated class in lineage societies, would men, all men, belong to the ruling class?

The Foundations of Women's Alienation in Lineage Systems

Any analysis of a relation of alienation leads to a certain discouragement. Whether it be the wage relationship in wage-slavery, or slavery in slave systems, or women in lineage systems, the coherence of the mode of production appears so strong, so 'ineluctable' that the system seems to be a product of 'the way of the world' or of the laws of nature. Yet, slavery did wither away and wage-slavery only arose at the time of the Industrial Revolution. Only the oppression of women still seems to be eternal. But that is in part a result of our ignorance.

Other contributions in this book state how necessary it is to reject all explanations based on biological determinism. But this rejection leaves room for two contradictory hypotheses: either men and women have gradually, since the beginning, evolved a division of labour that increased their differences and made women's alienation, step by step, more effective; or the division of labour along sex lines is essentially the result (and not the cause) of a social mutation.

The role played by the division of labour by sex

Let us consider the first hypothesis. It presupposes, albeit with qualifications, that biological factors had some impact: due to motherhood women were less mobile than men. They were increasingly confined to gathering activities, activities which as a matter of fact would have led them to the invention of agriculture. Then it seems that gradually, the more men exerted pressure upon women, the more the latter group managed to produce surpluses. These encouraged the idea of a first form of property, the collective property of a kin group. Lineage society was thus created.

This hypothesis faces five serious objections:

a) It is by no means proven that women are naturally more sedentary than men. If this were a 'natural propensity', logically it should exist in some form or another in all so-called primitive societies. This, however, is not the case; the opposite can often be established: women move great distances whether to get water, to cultivate fields or to sell their products in the marketplace. They are *par excellence* the bearers of heavy burdens over long distances (among some groups men explain that women's heads are stronger than those of men). Today they are often the first to leave the bush for the city. They are the ones who go away, who leave their parents for distant marriages. If these bonds are broken in some cases, they will return to their families but without the right to bring their children with them (which shows that the mother-child ties are not as binding as they are sometimes said to be). Women in lineage societies in all respects are characterised by their extreme mobility.

b) It has not been proved that women have a greater propensity for gathering than for hunting; even if this were the case, it would not make them less 'mobile', since gathering implies moving over long distances, nor less 'vigorous' in countering the attacks of large predators. Gathering obviously requires physical training as well as precise knowledge of plants, locations and wild animals.

c) In numerous lineage societies women fish and hunt. They capture small animals or participate in large collective hunts; the sole major difference to men is that they are not armed, or even trained in the use of weapons. This restriction (to which we will return) seems to arise more as the result of a prohibition than out of natural inclination. Collective memory, in histories transmitted mainly through men, tends systematically to hide all historical evidence of women bearing arms. Thus, taking a particularly vivid example, Semiramis, princess of Assyria (around 800 BC), to whom ancient historians attributed warlike deeds and the construction of numerous cities, was long regarded as a purely mythical figure, until in 1910 Assyrologist Lehman Haupt discovered a column where she is mentioned. Distinguished archaeologists have even been known to try and demonstrate that a Hittite statue of an armed woman was that of an armed man with the breasts, though very visible, a symbolic way of indicating a grown man as opposed to an ephebe! In the face of such distortions it is hardly surprising that the version of our prehistory (men hunt mammoth while women gather at the cave) given to us from primary school onwards is so questionable, let alone utterly impossible to substantiate!

d) Furthermore, the notion of a natural division of labour between men and women explains nothing. To give it explanatory value, one would have to assume (as French authors Edgar Morin and Serge Moscovici do) that hunting activities have an inherent social value which enabled men to *structure* themselves away from women — to 'civilize themselves' even, by forming the first stable and coherent human groups — while women, poor backward 'gatherers', allegedly remained at a 'protohuman' stage.[17] Thus men gradually imposed their laws upon women, while integrating them into their own social structures. This model does not stand up to analysis. The fact is, hunting societies, whether or not they are mixed, are unstable. Gathering, on the other hand, is carried out in a group and presupposes small, rather stable societies, which ensure collecting, sharing and the passing on of experience (such groups may or may not be mixed).

e) In agricultural lineage societies, women are involved in farming the land. But does that imply sexual division of labour, a division that derives from the natural division of labour between

17. Serge Moscovici, *La Société Contre Nature*, Paris 1972.

men and women? Obviously not, since what characterizes the status of women is not so much 'what they do' as the relation of production in which they do it. The woman who milks cows and churns the butter in herding societies, and the woman who fishes in lakeside societies, do not necessarily work with the hoe used by the agriculturalist. Yet both carry out their activities within the same alienated relation as the latter. Here what we have is not an equal division with each member, man or woman, contributing his or her share of work, but the exploitation of women's labour by the others. The male/female dichotomy appears above all as the result of changing social obligations. It does not derive from a division of labour dating back to the dawn of humankind.

Moreover, it is difficult to see why women would have quietly accepted a changeover from a (quite hypothetical) sexual division of labour based on reciprocity to such blatant imbalance. Indeed, even in the most firmly established lineage societies, women do not always behave as passive, submissive and resigned females. On the contrary, the domination exerted upon them is recurrent and repressive, and violence is frequently used, as we shall see.

Violence against Women: The Sudden Break Hypothesis

In lineage societies, male initiation always has the same objective: to distinguish men from women, to separate boys from their mothers and their sisters. Even the practice of sexual mutilation aims at that dichotomy. It is said among the Bambara that 'circumcision defeminizes men while excision devirilizes women.' This dissociation is not, however, egalitarian: it is meant to reaffirm the domination of men over women. And, however symbolic, this is always asserted violently.

For the Sara of Chad, as for most lineage societies, initiation is a second birth. The son born from a woman must die to be reborn as an accomplished man. The ritual often takes the form of a fable addressed to women. The dead ancestors of the lineage are supposed to come back to 'swallow' the young men. When they get nearer, at the sound of the *rhombe*, women and non-initiates have to hide in their cabins. Robert Jaulin astutely remarks that men themselves end up believing in these expressions of the beyond insofar as they manage to make women believe in them. The young men, 'swallowed' and then resuscitated by men, and men alone, during the initiation's 'second birth', come back to the village singing of the superiority of their new status. This they immediately put into practice through the ritual of the beating of the sisters. Robert Jaulin adds that 'later, the initiates will not hesitate to attack their own mothers.'[18] Among the Sara, initiation is an occasion for retaliation against women: men take advantage, as it were, of the presence of supreme authority at a symbolic level (that of dead ancestors). If a woman is found guilty of a misdeed, her cabin is broken on her back (literally) and all her belongings destroyed.

It is striking to observe that male initiation takes on the same meaning everywhere, even outside Africa. In New Guinea, among the Baruya studied by Maurice Godelier 'the making of a man is above all his initiation . . . .' 'To initiate is to separate brutally a ten-year-old boy from his family and from the realm of the feminine and confine him in the masculine world' . . . 'In this way the consciousness of belonging to a superior group is instilled in the boy, with the individual and collective pride of being a man and scorn for women . . .' Meanwhile a little girl is taught to respect men and all the duties she will owe her husband. Godelier insists that the 'explicit finalities' of initiation are 'to encourage the acceptance and reproduction of a given social order'.[19]

This order, as is apparent, cannot reproduce itself by itself without force of some kind. So little is natural about it, that everyone admits: 'women must be treated violently' (as the Baruya put it) or 'oppress them cheerfully' (as the Sara say), to make them accept their highly undesirable status.

Moreover, women by no means accept their subordination graciously. This is most apparent when we compare Western societies with lineage ones, for we quickly discover how little female oppression is internalized in the latter. On this point Robert Jaulin recounts an instructive anecdote: when women learned that a white man (Jaulin) was to be initiated, they demanded to be initiated themselves. The religious chiefs' response was 'to be particularly harsh with them. And to compensate for the fact that my initiation seemed to "open" these ceremonies to outsiders, the religious chiefs saw to it that everything took place as it should, with women and non-initiates

18. Robert Jaulin, p.116.
19. Maurice Godelier, 'Le sexe comme fondement ultime de l'ordre social et cosmique chez les Baruya', in *Sexualité et Pouvoir*, Paris 1976.

being subjected to all the customary ill-treatment.'[20] There is also the traditional feast of women, which is common to numerous lineage societies. On the occasion of this feast, which takes place once a year, it is as if all the rules of power are inverted. This is a compensatory practice or a safety valve, much like Carnival, at other historical periods.[21]

Thus men seem constantly haunted by the fear of a possible revolt by women. Indian stories about Latin American Amazons clearly betray an awareness of the reasons that might have driven women to secede. According to the traditions of the Indians of Guyana, 'Women are married without their consent, they have no choice and they are tired of working constantly.' Toeyza, wife of the Worisiana chief, when exhorting her women companions to leave, says: 'Some say that marriage is a protection, to me it is a vile subjection. We may as well be dead. For we have been given away by our parents and know nothing of love. Worries everyday. Work now, work tomorrow.' Men's response to their obsessive fear of a womens' revolt is a significant prohibition: women are forbidden to carry arms (we have already stressed how the memory of women warriors or huntresses has been obscured in all civilizations, including ours).

In most lineage societies, weapons are kept in the men's house and women are forbidden all access to it. Woe betide the woman who breaks this taboo. Among the Iatmul of Middle Sepik (New Guinea),[22] she is threatened with death. Not only weapons but also the insignia of power — sacred flutes, drums and so on — are kept away from women. Among the Bedik (Africa),[23] the drums of the father of the masks are stored in the little *Gandyarar,* the house of the young initiates, and its entrance is of course barred to women, who may not have any contact whatsoever with new initiates.

Among the Baruya (New Guinea), enforcement of this exclusion is even more absolute: 'Should a woman', writes Maurice Godelier, 'inadvertently come across men playing the sacred flute or sounding the *rhombes,* she is immediately put to death, without her lineage being able to oppose it or claim vengeance.'[24]

20. Jaulin, p.41.
21. This practice of the women's festival still survives in Europe. For example, the first day of the Cologne carnival concerns women.
22. Example reported by Margaret Mead.
23. Example reported by Pierre Smith, in his contribution to Paulme, ed., *Classes et d'Age Associations d'Age en Afrique de l'Ouest.*

Here again we can see how little such societies have 'internalized' the notion of women's natural inferiority before armed violence. African kingdoms (societies where the old lineage society has been eroded) have sometimes very cleverly taken advantage of women's capacities for war: the Amazons of Dahomey are actually the King of Benin's crack troops. They have even fought valiantly against French colonial troops (to the surprise of the French, one might add).This is why, in our view, it is highly significant that men in lineage societies are adamant that women should be disarmed. It is well known that differential access to arms always reflects class relations. Thus, in slave and feudal systems, neither slave nor serf could bear arms, since this was the privilege of 'free men', and subsequently of lords. Later it became the key question in workers' revolutions and bourgeoisies, traumatized by the Paris Commune and the fall of the Winter Palace, came to dread an arming of the workers. Likewise, in all historical periods women have been subjected to a set of class relations whose essential nature is betrayed by the fact that they invariably prevent women from bearing arms. In lineage societies, men forbid women to carry arms, whether for war or simply for hunting, and this demonstrates that their fundamental aim is to preserve the social edifice that rests on women's alienation and on the violence done to them.

No Alienation without Exchange

The nature of the violence directed against women in lineage societies refutes the idea of a freely accepted and egalitarian division of labour by sex. We have already noted the crucial part played by the exchange of women (exogamy combined with patrilocal residence) in making women work and in exploiting their labour-power. We want now to point out that the exchange of women is also a repressive mechanism. The precarious nature of women's status is reinforced by making them aliens in the lineage they joined through marriage ('one doesn't marry one's friends but one's enemies', say the Kavirondo of East Africa). Exchange also emphasizes the heterogeneity of the group of wives: with some exceptions, they come from different lineages or clans.[25] They are thereby atomized, and their subjection is

24. Godelier, p.286.
25. Some marriage rules require that the men of the group always take a wife from the same group. This system, however, is rare in Africa.

more easily guaranteed. Furthermore, as objects to be exchanged, they are subject to dual control: control by those who have parted with them and by those who have acquired them, and any rebellion on their part would run counter to the alliances and dealings carried out in relation to them and over their heads. In fact, such alliances can work against them, as when one of them runs away.

An example will serve to show how closely female status is linked to exchange, indeed to such an extent that a 'non-exchanged' woman may gradually acquire male status. Thus, among the Nuer, a woman of good birth may be accepted in her father's family for her entire life if she is sterile. She may then marry another woman (who is subject to matrimonial mobility) and she becomes the social father of the children born to this wife (these children's biological father is a poor foreigner, who 'doesn't count').

Lastly, the alienation and exchange of women would appear to be so intimately connected that the only known examples of societies in which women are not exploited are also societies without exchange. These are societies which may very well abide by the rule of exogamy (the obligation to marry outside a restricted and clearly prescribed kinship circle) but which have residence rules that are not patrilocal. The man goes away to live with his wife, who generally resides near her own mother's house: this residence rule is called 'matrilocal' or 'gynecostatic'. Among the Hopi Indians (Colorado), men have to prove that they too are good workers. Women are at home among their families. They may take the initiative in breaking off a marriage, simply by putting all their husbands' belongings out on their doorsteps. Relations between the sexes are marked by a reciprocity of a kind that contrasts quite dramatically with that known in patrilocal societies. The advice given by an uncle to some young grooms illustrates this point very well: 'Thank you my nephews. You are not very beautiful[26] and I thought you would never marry. I am glad you have chosen such remarkable women. You know that all women loathe a lazy man, and for that reason you must work hard and help your new fathers in the fields and look after the herds. When they see that you are willing to help, they will be happy and treat you as true sons.' There are, however, few obligations. Custom also requires that

26. This is a routine phrase. All newlyweds, men and women, will hear these same words spoken by their own parents.

the husband choose the moment when he settles with his wife. Before then he may very well visit her every night. And the gentleness that pervades these relations is clear in the advice given to young brides: 'Look for the good side of every day, treat your husbands well and make the most of your lives!' What a contrast when one thinks of the cries of revolt of the Indian women of Guyana ('married without love') or the African wedding songs that constantly evoke the sobs of the young bride, her anguish about living far away, her longing for her adolescence and its relative freedom.

The Hopi, along with various Polynesian islands, are one of the few societies which exhibit this kind of structure.[27] Aside from the fact that they present a rather pleasing image of male/female relations, they lead us to question the origins of patrilocal lineage societies, which are so alienating and so repressive toward women. Patrilocality, the exchange of women and alienation are closely interconnected. Indeed, patrilocality is the key to the alienation of women within lineage systems.

Matrilocality as an Earlier System than Patrilocality

Lineage societies are structured in accordance with kinship rules that display a wide range of variations, the most important being those that distinguish matrilineal from patrilineal descent. This does not mean, for instance, that in patrilineality the mother's kinship network is completely ignored, for it will always have some part to play in rules of descent. But in a lineage system with genealogical depth of thirty or forty generations, and one which can therefore form large clan groups, one rule of descent must prevail over the other.

In matrilineality, descent is traced from mother to daughter and enables the entire clan to refer itself back to a common woman ancestor. In patrilineality, descent is traced from father to son and enables everyone to refer to a common male ancestor. There are a few cases of bilineal societies also, in which matrilineal and patrilineal lineages and clans coexist. This complex system is frequently an indication of a period of considerable change.

27. It is estimated that nearly ninety per cent of the Indian population of the three Americas was decimated through contact with Europeans. The shock was so brutal that it may account for the persistence, among those who have survived, of social systems nearly impossible to find in other parts of the world.

In bilineal societies, the matrilineage and the patrilineage are never in perfect symmetry. An individual who belongs to two lineages — a matrilineage and a patrilineage — frequently does not inherit the same goods on both sides. An analysis of succession and inheritance enables one to date the relative age of these two rules of descent. In most cases, goods inherited matrilineally refer to very ancient social systems; whereas goods inherited patrilineally are more modern.

Thus, among the Tuareg, means of production and slaves ('modern' goods *par excellence*) are transmitted patrilineally, while political status and rights over conquered people (which have an earlier historical origin) are transmitted matrilineally. Such a system is, however, unstable. Around the eighteenth century, the Tuareg began to transmit a number of political and land rights down a paternal line; matrilineal inheritance became less important.

Most anthropologists therefore share the view that matrilineality is older than patrilineality. Thus, for all Akan peoples of the Ivory Coast, whether they have remained matrilineal (Alladian, Atie, Ebrie and Mbate) or become patrilineal (Ashanti, Agni), the primary legitimacy is matrilineality. The Baoulé also remained matrilineal until recently; their myths of origin are always the same and go back to a common female ancestor, who is said to have had two daughters and a son. The daughters are said to be their ancestors, one of the two being ancestor to the Atie and the other to the Baoulé (through segmentation) whereas Agni and Ashanti are descended from the female ancestor's son.

When the son died, a quarrel broke out: the dead man's son refused to let his uterine nephews (his cousins, legitimate heirs by virtue of matrilineal succession rules) have the sabre with the gold-covered handle, a sign of power. After an uncertain struggle, the nephews are said to have fled and separated after crossing the Comoe river. To the lagoon people of the Ivory Coast, the Agni are kin but they are also the descendants of a usurper. The legend describes how during the flight, the crossing of the Tano, then of the Comoe, required two sacrifices: the first was that of the son of Queen Poku, the Baoulé heroine; the second was that of the son of Chief Atie's sister (in their version the Alladian even indicate that the chief's wife refused her son's sacrifice).

This information suggests that matrilineality did in fact

precede patrilineality. But it also indicates that power within the lineage is passed on to men, the uterine nephews, by virtue of genealogical proximity to the common female ancestor. However some qualification is necessary: a woman may become chief (Queen Poku) in matrilineal societies, which is practically unthinkable under patrilineality. Being placed in the line of succession, some women (without brothers) were able to profit. In fact, this does not have much effect on the lineage system of production. The lagoon people of the Ivory Coast, too, consider that farming the land is a woman's or slave's duty (this addition comes later; see the essay in the present volume on slavery). In accordance with the patrilocal residence rule, women wives of matrilineal societies are also put to work on their husbands' land.

We are less concerned here with the standard common to both patri- and matrilineages (already extensively described above) than with the difficulty of exchanging women (patrilocality and its related alienation) in a matrilineal system. In our view, these complexities reveal that patrilocality is not straightforward, that it is caused by a 'rupture' within societies that were previously organized on the two-fold basis of matrilineality and matrilocality.

The term 'disharmony' has been, rightly, applied to societies that combine both matrilineality and patrilocality. In such societies, a man, for example an older brother, would have power: first, over a group made up of his sisters (his younger brothers are also below him in ranking order, unless through segmentation they leave and form their own lineage); then he has power over his sisters' children (uterine nieces and nephews) but not over his brothers' children who are counted as members of their mother's lineage, and so on; he has power over the children of his sisters' daughters, and so on.

However, with patrilocal residence rules, a daughter must marry outside her matrilineage or matri-clan (depending on the extent of rules of the exogamy). Under these conditions, the uterine uncle, oldest male relative, stands every chance of having his dependents widely distributed, according to the various alliances. Children of sisters and nieces will be born and reside in their fathers' families (patrilocality). On the other hand, it is in the father's interest to keep them as long as possible outside their uncle's and great-uncle's reach. Since the father's authority is very relative (a purely 'moral' authority, we would say), he is regarded by his children as a friendly male adult who helps them to counter their maternal uncle's claims. Consequently, patri-locality has a tendency to linger until the point when children never again return to the residence of their matrilineage (with the exception, however, of one male child: the oldest sister's son when he inherits the leadership of a matrilineage or a matri-clan). Within a production unit based on the rules of patrilocality relations of authority are complex: at the head is an uncle, then come all the households whose male element is 'son' to the uncle — over whom he has but a relative power. On the other hand, these sons are required to make certain payments (ob-tained mainly through their wives' work) to their own mothers' brothers.

Moreover, the head of a matrilineage has no direct control over the surplus produced by the labour of the women who depend on him (sisters, nieces, and possibly his mother). In this sense, his role is much less privileged than that of the head of a patri-lineage. The situations are not symmetrical: a brother, even in a matrilineage, does not directly exploit his sister. He may do so only through his brother-in-law, who has to hand him goods that have been accumulated thanks to, among other things, the work carried out by his sister, and his nephews and nieces.

Under these conditions, it is no wonder that matrilineality has trouble surviving. The advantages of patrilineality seem obvious. Hence, societies that maintained their matrilineal rules while reaching a relatively high level of economic development (flourishing agriculture, villages commonly engaged in exchange) introduced complex mechanisms to compensate for the disadvantages of matrilineality. When a village is made up of different matrilineages and matri-clans, people do their best to marry off girls inside the village. Thus, for an Ebrié woman, having one's first marriage take place 'outside' is tantamount to a sort of dishonour, an admission that no man wants her.

Another mechanism is that of prescribed marriages. Far from having only cultural origins (as some believed), such marriages correspond to specific economic goals. They rewrite the place of production and the matrilineage. Among the lagoon dwellers of the Ivory Coast, the problem of disharmony is all the more acute in that it concerns a settled population with a collective, rather than individual, notion of land ownership. The land belongs to the matrilineage and is held by the heads of the matrilineage, then portioned out among various male descendants, but a son is brought up at his father's until he receives land from one of his 'matri-ancestors'. The problem is solved through prescribed marriage between a man and his female patrilateral cross cousin. In this instance, the husband and wife each depend, in fact, on a different matri-clan: exogamy is respected. And the grandson will be entitled to claim the land of his paternal grandfather, since the latter is also his maternal grandfather. Sometimes a tacit arrangement may even enable the father (the one who married the cousin) to farm the land 'temporarily' as a guardian in the interests of his son, heir apparent.

Georges Balandier gives another example of prescribed marriage among the Bakongo, that of the maternal grandfather with his granddaughter. Exogamy is upheld since grandfather and granddaughter come from different clans. Such a marriage has the advantage of physically maintaining the granddaughter within the matrilineage and avoiding dispersal. In addition, through marriage with his granddaughter, the grandfather 'recovers' a descent which he was about to lose due to matrilineal rules.

Anthropologists have also observed that some compulsory class or age class systems[28] would seem to solve problems arising out of disharmony. According to Monique Gessain, in the matrilineal societies of Bassari and Coniagui this more than any other institution brings patrilineal elements to the fore. Furthermore, Denise Paulme says of her own research that the main role of the cyclic age group system[29] in the lagoon area of West Africa seems to be to enable young people to escape being entirely controlled by maternal kin, and to establish, through indirect channels, a tie between father and son. Where patrilocal filiation is recognized, this particular mode of recruitment disappears. At this point in her exposition, Denise Paulme embarks upon a comparative study within a limited geographical area, demonstrating that compulsory age group systems in patrilineal environments do exist in other African regions, particularly in East Africa, but that they play a different role. The interesting point about Denise Paulme's example is the fact that matrilineal

28. A system that regroups all children of a single residence unit according to age groups, and at each stage lays down ritual obligations that contribute to their education.

29. A system which adds a descent criterion to age, so that the 'copper' age group, for instance, is made up of the sons of the 'brass' age group (among the Suk of Kenya).

peoples are constantly aware of the disharmony and will use any means available to them to combat it.

We can see the extent to which matrilineality and patrilocality (and therefore the exchange of women) are contradictory. It is as though the exchange of women had been grafted onto a structure (matrilineage, matri-clan) which is incapable of integrating it. All the mechanisms that aim at consolidating the whole only serve to heighten this impression of original antagonism. The matrilineal family could function properly only if mothers and their children remained in their families (in short, if the principle of matrilocality was respected, as was the case among the Hopi). But the element which is primarily responsible for the organization of women's alienation would then be lost. Without the exchange of women, without patrilocality, the exploitation of women's labour would be impossible. Even if we were to assume that men had begun to oppress women in some way, women themselves would still remain in control of the organization of their labour and of the surpluses it provides. How could men maintain a form of oppression that was sufficiently persistent and uninterrupted to culminate in a stable exploitation of their sisters, if all the time they were 'sons' in the mothers' matri-clan? If they move out to live with a woman from another matri-clan, they come as foreigners.

Admittedly, such men might try, once in the matri-clan, to gain possession of goods that belong to women (mothers and sisters), but this could not take place continuously, in the main because the men would have to reckon with the combined opposition of all women who are of the clan, and who are bound together by stronger ties than the men are, since women are the ones who structure the group and the unit of residence.

Since matrilineality is prior to patrilineality, matrilocality would seem to have preceded all forms of kinship and even appears to have been the first stable form of human organization. Indeed, this hypothesis can be partially verified (although the rarity of matrilocal societies means that the evidence we have is very inadequate). There is, for instance, some correlation between the first forms of agriculture (by planting and grafting of tubers) and the survival of gynecostatism.

Patrilocality, which we have already found to be the major mechanism for the exploitation of female labour power, and thus of the lineage mode of production, now also appears, along with its corollary, the exchange of women, to be the key to women's alienation in lineage systems.

Yet, despite the views of many of those who have accepted the basic elements of Lévi-Strauss's theories of kinship, there is nothing self-evident about the exchange of women. In particular, we would emphasise that it cannot be mechanically derived from a preexistent sexual division of labour. Indeed, it looks as though patrilocality has been artificially grafted on to kinship structures (matrilineality) which are rather unfavourable to it, and as though it was preceded by a stable form of matrilocal and matrilineal organization (which may perhaps have been partially bilineal; the nearer one comes to the origins of a people, the shallower the genealogies and the easier it is therefore for individuals to take both parents' ancestors into account).

Before trying to determine how the change from one structure to another took place, we should characterize — as far as is possible — these first matrilocal structures. Indeed, by identifying the elements and the actors involved in their internal development, we can illuminate the history of this transformation. Did these matrilocal societies gradually adopt patrilocality? Or did they, or some of them, undergo a sudden break as might be expected from the violence done to women in lineage societies?

The Changeover from Matrilocal to Patrilocal Societies

Lineage societies, in the form in which we have known them, are undeniably more efficient, in terms of economy and warfare, than previous forms of organization. There is therefore no need to demonstrate that all matrilocal societies followed the same path before arriving at patrilocality. All that was required was that the exchange of women and the exploitation of women should have been discovered by some groups. No matter how these discoveries were made, such groups were subsequently bound to extend their model, either through force or through example. We will therefore not examine those cases in which the shift from matrilocality to patrilocality was the result of external influence. Rather, we will focus upon the internal factors in matrilocal societies which were liable to lead, in some cases, to the emergence of patrilocality.

The First Stable Forms of Human Organization

We know very little, of course, about the first social structures. All we can state is that knowledge of kinship through the mother was prior to knowledge of kinship through the father. In this sense the anteriority of matrilineality over patrilineality is not surprising.

Consequently, the first stable forms of social organization probably structured themselves around a simple concept of descent, which was essentially matrilineal and probably not very deep. A small number of women, bound by kinship ties (mothers — daughters — sisters) formed the core of such groups, with men (sons and brothers) possibly moving from one group to another, which does not imply that women were sedentary (social mobility — kinship — rather than physical mobility, is what is meant here). In other words, among a nomadic people, the core of the structure was where the 'mothers' were, given that the structure was organized around them.

Hunting, fishing or gathering were not in themselves capable of 'spontaneously' generating an efficient and lasting socialization process. Indeed, it was only when human beings had established a system of socialization and descent which could be extended to increasingly numerous human groups, that they were able to free themselves from merely taking from nature (as animals, whether singly or in groups, do) and enter upon a more developed social and economic process. Such taking from nature through hunting and gathering, which involves an immediate consumption of the product, is replaced by the accumulation of stocks. The creation of surplus corresponds to a higher level of efficiency (taking from nature is no longer limited by satiety but by an individual's capacity) and to new techniques (carrying, preserving). Making efficient tools (gathering and hunting implements, baskets, pottery) or inventing cooking (to guarantee the preservation of foodstuffs) would have no point if there was no readiness to defer consumption in order both to provide free time and to lay up stocks for the future.

The first economic act is both a gamble on the future and on relations between human beings. The accumulation of a surplus is a daring venture, for one cannot know for sure that the person involved will benefit from it: he is liable to lose it and, above all, it may be taken from him by others who are not 'playing the game'. The risk is so high that a rudimentary economy can work only within a human group which is already stable (where there is a network of stable ties). A stable social structure and the first economic acts go together. One has no effect without the other.

Social stability, however, directly affects the activities in which human beings are involved. Elgar Morin and Serge Moscovici are therefore quite justified in establishing a connection between the most advanced cybernetic techniques and the use of language, or the formation of groups that know how to transmit their experience from generation to generation. But Claude Meillassoux is equally justified in establishing a link between fathering and knowledge of sites, plants and wildlife. With one qualification: it is the stability of social ties that allows these new techniques to be developed and not the other way round, even though, in return, the effectiveness of invested techniques reinforces social ties by creating the 'common good', or heritage, of a human group.

Therefore, there is a dynamic interrelation between social stability and more developed forms of taking from nature, which in turn leads to the invention of breeding and agriculture. This 'social structure' allows for the development of the productive forces. But only up to a certain point. There is as yet no exploitation of the labour of some humans by others, and thus people work as they please, in 'free association'. Goodwill and laziness draw — in a rather pleasant way — the line these societies may not cross. On the other hand, in their ultimate stage, these societies manifest all the conditions necessary for social transformation.

The Conflict Mythologies Account for . . .

Most mythologies account for an ancestral conflict between gods and goddesses or men and women. The extent to which the myths gathered in Africa, Oceania and among American Indians broadly resemble the archaic texts found around the Mediterranean is actually quite surprising. We agree with Monique Saliou (see her article in the present volume) that psychoanalytic explanations cannot entirely account for this coincidence. In fact, it is interesting that the very few examples of matrilocal and matrilineal societies which have reached us have no men/women opposition myth in the arsenal — rich in all other respects — of their cosmology. We can therefore assume that these accounts bear witness, in their own way, to an ancient, fundamental historical fact.

Though analysis of mythology should be undertaken with the utmost caution, two major facts can be accepted:

— the great female divinities predate the male gods;

— an opposition between gods/goddesses or male/female ancestors (which is no contradiction since ancestors are assimilated to gods in lineage societies) that ended with the females' defeat.

It is in the oldest legends and the most primitive rites that male/female oppositions are found in which men are not necessarily shown in a good light. The examples found in New Guinea, Africa or India all tell the same story, under different guises: at some point in time, male ancestors got hold of the sacred objects discovered by female ancestors. They took them to the men's house and barred entrance to women. Since these sacred objects are also signs of power, the far-reaching significance of such accounts is very evident.

Thus Margaret Mead reports this legend of the Iatmul of the Middle Sepik (New Guinea): during the initiation rites that take place inside the men's house whose access is barred to women, new initiates are told how the sacred objects that make noise were originally discovered by women who let men in on the secret and went on to beg the men to kill them so as to preserve the secret forever!

Also in New Guinea, the Baruya not only believe in a primordial goddess mother of humankind, but also attribute most important discoveries to women: cultivated plants, sacred bows and flutes. According to one of these legends, men originated as tadpoles — which were transformed into men (and not into frogs) — for whom women made the first bows, which were merely toys. Then men appropriated the bow (another legend attempts to justify this appropriation: women who had invented bows did not know how to use them and killed too many people; consequently men took over the bow to turn it right side out). Sacred flutes, which to the Baruya are the voice of the spirits, are also said to be a female invention. But men, reports Maurice Godelier, stole the flutes from them by taking them from the menstrual houses where they were hidden beneath blood-stained skirts. Or at least, after discovering the flutes and transgressing the fundamental taboo of entering women's space, they played the flute; when the women returned and wanted to play, no sound was produced. They realized that men had come during their absence and that thereafter the flutes' voice would belong to men.

Another legend of this kind, from Africa this time: in *Les échelons d'âge dans l'organisation sociale et rituelle des Bedik*, Pierre Smith relates how boys' initiation is carried out under the protection of the father of masks; as a sign of authority the latter has drums which he beats during the village's ceremonial festivals. Yet, according to legend 'the drums of the father of masks were taken away from women to be entrusted to the new initiates.'[30] They keep the drums in the 'little *Gandyarar*' (house of the young initiates as opposed to the big *Gandyarar* of adult men). Of course entrance to the little *Gandyarar* is forbidden to women, who in fact are allowed no contact at all with the new initiates.

According to Bambara mythology, originally everything came from the void and the spirit (YO). The creation of the universe was achieved in stages. The initial couple was formed by Pemba, male divinity, and Muso Koroni, female divinity, the guardian of seed and knowledge. But, says the legend, Muso Koroni grew furious when Pemba was unfaithful. She introduced sorrow and death into the world. She also taught men the techniques of agriculture before she herself died.

The more recent the mythologies — revised or rewritten over successive periods — the more the account of the male/female conflict is watered down. The beneficial and powerful goddesses give way to rather baleful female divinities — whose knowledge and importance are minimized — and end up as mere 'shrews' (when you come down to it, Eve is a good example of the latter). Even the evil powers take on a masculine gender. All powers are virile and the male/female conflict takes on the appearance of domestic quarrels, even in the realm of ideology.

What can we infer from this? We can see how the account of a conflict between male and female principles could be so disturbing that it was gradually erased. If women had never held the slightest power, it would be hard to understand why such myths existed. It would seem more reasonable to assume that they reflect a very old and very unpleasant memory of humankind, a memory that had to be forgotten insofar as women themselves internalized their status.

30. Smith, in Paulme, ed., 'Classes d'Age', p. 201.

The Birth of Patriarchal Society

The examination of the violence done to women in lineage society and the analysis of myths leads one to posit a violent social upheaval, which could have taken place in societies with matrilineal and matrilocal structures. It is therefore by analyzing the features involved in these societies' internal evolution that one may hope to gain some understanding of this enigma. Eight features can be isolated.

1. Once the first human groups developed stable forms of organization, their methods of taking from nature improved. At the same time there is a tendency towards a seasonal sedentarization. Resources, modest though they may have been, were increasing. Life expectancy exceeded the initial twenty-year mark, even though infant mortality remained very high.

2. Under the impact of demographic growth, some stratification along age lines seems to have occurred. A population composed mainly of children and adolescents gave way to one that was more mature and more prepared to share tasks. A first 'division of labour', although still very flexible and restrictive, is likely to have emerged at that period.

3. With the formation of the first surplus, new contradictions arose, both between and within groups. The idea of collective property emerged from the ancient practices of sharing and reciprocity.

4. These stable matrilocal groups should not be regarded as ossified structures. A single population was made up of several core groups around which gravitated peripheral groups that recognized each other as kin. Logically we may assume that core groups were the ones that managed the newly established surplus. In other words, as production increased, so tasks were increasingly divided and the collective wealth began to be centralized in the hands of the 'mother-women' who provided the cohesion of the core groups.

5. Tending to settle in one place — relative though this may be — endowed with a material and cultural heritage (its knowledge, tools, surpluses), the first small human society was bound to strengthen its spatial and temporal cohesion. Relations between humans became codified, if only to ensure that experience was transmitted from one generation to the next. The most tangible ties were those of kinship through mothers, and matrilineal ties were strengthened. Previously, all those born in the

same group probably recognized each other more or less as brothers, visualizing adult men and women of the group as so many mothers and fathers, destined as a matter of fact to a very early death. With the increase in life expectancy, elders gained in importance. To define the group structure, genealogies (collective and not individual) were worked out; burial grounds enabled ancestors to be remembered. Matrilineality and matrilocality (which, as we have already seen, are logically interdependent) were the organizing principles behind the codification, as is demonstrated by examining current lineage societies, and by reconstructing early societies.

6.   Such a process should have evolved logically in the direction of a kind of supremacy of women, a matriarchate, where all their lives men would have appeared somewhat like overgrown children. However, since women did not have the power, despite everything, to exploit their companions' labour, such a society might in a way have become frozen.

7.   Within these embryonic societies, contradictions developed. The new division of labour increased male/female differences still further. But, contrary to what is often asserted, it did so mainly to the advantage of women. Long-lasting goods and techniques — those whose durability is most needed — were kept at the core of these essentially female groups. Conditions now existed for certain innovations — such as the development of a primitive agriculture — to be attempted. Given the matrilocal and matrilineal structure, such innovations could only reinforce the wealth and power of women.

8.   At certain moments these societies' internal contradictions may have led to clashes, perhaps not between the men and women of a single group but rather between the men of group A and the women of another group, B, since solidarity between men and women of the same group may itself have weakened. Any clash ending with a female victory, or simply one of group B, including both sexes, could only have led to a return to the previous situation. On the other hand, a male victory over group B's female core could have had very far-reaching consequences.

Women had nothing to gain from such clashes, since the evolution of these societies had been to their advantage. Certain men, on the other hand, could have realized what there was to gain by reversing the rules of the game, by trading matrilocality for patrilocality. Women were already producing surpluses, but were doing so freely. Certain men could well appreciate what they might win by forcing — for the first time in human history — certain human beings to work for others.

Lastly, it is enough for only one of these clashes to have had such an outcome for patriarchy to be established. The system could then demonstrate its efficiency. In fact, the analysis of many traditional societies suggests that they themselves did not experience this conflict but that it was imposed upon them by already patriarchal peoples. It is unlikely that at a given moment in human history *all* men were opposed to *all* women. Hence it seems difficult to regard *all* male individuals in the patrilocal lineage societies that resulted as part of the ruling class.

In these societies, male children and adolescents go through phases during which they are oppressed — like women — , during which they are not entirely identified with women but are not yet really part of the male group. Marriages and initiation will subsequently integrate them into the male group, which shows the very 'social' nature of this stratification.

To conclude, we do not believe that patrilocal societies emerged through continuous evolution but rather through a violent upheaval that took place within a small number of groups, which were efficient enough to transmit their experience to others. Men, who were the actors in such a transformation, formed a ruling class, access to which was subject to extremely strict rules. We have already noted that women were regarded as an exploitable labour force, and that all women in lineage societies could be regarded as an 'alienated social class'. Such societies are indeed the first class societies known to humankind. They are not transitional societies (even though, individually, some peoples may have gone through this historical period as a transition, under the influence of external factors).

We may note that the upheaval out of which patrilocal (and patriarchal, in the usual sense of the term) societies arose, did not institute equality between men. At the same time as they gained power over women, men entered strongly hierarchical relations. What is significant here, is that the true beginnings of a process of domination not only set man against woman, but ruling men against the rest of humankind. The exploitation of man by man did in fact begin as an exploitation of woman by man. But within this original exploitation lay the seeds of the exploitation of humans of both sexes by the ruling human (who is again male).

Property Forms, Political Power, and Female Labour in the Origins of Class and State Societies

Stephanie Coontz and Peta Henderson

Introduction

The introduction of this book disputes the assertion that males have always dominated women and cites some of the many instances of egalitarian relationships in simple foraging and horticultural societies. Indeed, a growing body of evidence supports the broad evolutionary perspective first suggested by Engels:[1] relations between the sexes seem to be most egalitarian in the simplest foraging societies and woman's position worsens with the emergence of social stratification, private property, and the state.

Despite its broad accuracy, however, this formulation leaves a number of problems unresolved. First, male dominance has been shown to exist in some pre-class, pre-state societies lacking true private property. Second, some of the evidence cited for high female status in the ancient world comes, not from communal foraging societies, but from complex West African kingdoms (which were more likely to be matrilineal than their politically more simple neighbours), the royal city states of ancient Sumer, or the prosperous trading centres of archaic Crete.[2] These two facts have led at least one author to conclude that the emergence of hierarchy may increase gender equality.[3]

A third problem is presented by the attribution of male domin-

---

1. Friedrich Engels, *The Origin of the Family, Private Property and the State*, New York 1972.
2. Denise Paulme, ed., *Women of Tropical Africa*, Berkeley 1971; R. Rohrlich, 'State formation in Sumer and the Subjugation of Women', *Feminist Studies*, vol. 6, no. 1, 1980; G. Glotz, *The Aegean Civilization*, London 1968.
3. Sherry Ortner, 'Gender and Sexuality in Hierarchical Society' in S. Ortner and H. Whitehead, eds., *Sexual Meanings: The Cultural Construction of Gender and Sexuality*, Cambridge 1981.

ance to class society, private property, *and* the state. Since these are clearly separate (though interconnected) phenomena arising at different points of time in various societies, there is a certain lack of analytical clarity in attributing male dominance to all three. It remains unclear whether female subordination was produced by something in class relations, in the nature of private property, in the state's codification of class rule, or only in the combination of the above. The precise contribution of each to the process is not spelled out.[4]

A fourth problem lies in understanding why, if we do not assume innate biological differences in temperament or capacity between men and women, it was men who became dominant over women once the processes of social stratification were set in motion. Most concrete studies of the effects of class stratification, private property, and state formation on male/female relations come from what we might call 'secondary' cases, where an egali-

4. Most anthropological theories of social stratification and state formation have ignored the question of sex inequality: see, for example, E. Service, *Origins of the State and Civilization*, New York 1975; K. Flannery, 'The Cultural Evolution of Civilizations', *Annual Review of Ecology and Systematics*, 3, 1972; J. Sabloff and C. Lamberg-Karlovsky (eds.) *The Rise and Fall of Civilizations*, California 1974; M. Fried, *The Evolution of Political Society*, New York 1967; R. Adams, *The Evolution of Urban Society: Early Mesopotamia and Pre-Hispanic Mexico*, Chicago 1966. Marxist theorists, following Engels, have corrected this by pointing to the association between processes of socioeconomic differentiation, leading to the development of classes and the state, and the institutionalization of female subordination. But in establishing the general correlation, the differential effects of property forms, classes and the state have been left somewhat vague. See Friedrich Engels, 1972; E. Leacock, 'Women in Egalitarian Societies', in R. Bridenthal and C. Koonz, eds., *Becoming Visible: Women in European History*, Boston 1977; E. Leacock, 'Women's Status in Egalitarian Society: Implications for Social Evolution', *Current Anthropology*, vol. 19, no. 2, 1978; R. Rapp Reiter, 'Men and Women in the South of France: Public and Private Domains', in R. Reiter, ed., *Toward an Anthropology of Women*, New York 1975; R. Reiter, 'The Search for Origins: Unravelling the Threads of Gender Hierarchy', *Critique of Anthropology*, vol. 3, nos. 9–10; R. Rapp (Reiter), 'Gender and Class: An Archaeology of Knowledge concerning the Origin of the State', *Dialectical Anthropology*, vol. 2, no. 4, 1977; K. Sacks, 'Engels Revisited: Women, the Organisation of Production, and Private Property', in R. Reiter, 1975; G. Rubin, 'The Traffic in Women: Notes on the "Political Economy" of Sex', in R. Reiter, 1975. For a discussion on the subordination of women by the stae, see M. Etienne and E. Leacock, eds., *Women and Colonization: Anthropological Perspectives*, New York 1980; R. Rohrlich-Leavitt, 'Women in Transition: Crete and Sumer', in R. Bridenthal and C. Koonz, 1977; M. Arthur, 'Liberated Women: The Classical Era', in R. Bridenthal and C. Koonz, 1977; J.McNamara and S. Wemple, 'Sanctity and Power: The Dual Pursuit of Medieval Women', in R. Bridenthal and C. Koonz, 1977; R. Reiter, 'The Search for Origins'; and R. Rapp (Reiter), 'Gender and Class'.

tarian society was transformed by contact with an already developed state or market system.[5] Here the mechanisms establishing female subordination often derived from the values of the intruders being imposed on the original society, or from male roles being transformed by the warfare, trade, or bureaucracy stimulated by contact with the new society. This leaves the 'pristine' development of male dominance and class stratification unexplained, causing us to wonder why it was men and not women who took advantage of changing property forms and social relations to establish their dominance.

This essay attempts to grapple with these problems by postulating an evolutionary dynamic in which the origins of male dominance were connected to processes of ranking internal to many primitive societies and to a type of property that historically preceded private property. We then distinguish between the effects of class relations and state formation on male-female relations. Our analysis should not be taken to imply a unilineal theory of evolution. The processes we will describe were not set in motion in all societies, and in many they took different forms because of interactions with other societies, variations in social relations, different ecological conditions and so on. We believe, however, that it is possible to suggest a (necessarily speculative) dynamic that can explain the rise of male dominance in prehistoric times without reference either to a *deus ex machina* in the form of external contact or a *deus in machina* such as a biological drive in men to endow their sons with property.

A starting point for such a project must be a recognition that the division of labour by sex developed in certain patterned ways, creating a predictable difference in male and female tasks and products in most early hunting and gathering societies. This division of labour, in and of itself, was not a sufficient condition to create male dominance, nor even male prestige, but in most societies it did lead to gender-linked differences in activities, especially as production was intensified, as with the domestication of plants. We will argue that the dynamic whereby a flexible, non-hierarchical division of labour became in many instances a rigid oppression of one sex by the other was related to the gradual emergence out of communal societies of a kind of property held by the corporate kin group,[6] accessible to all its members and inalienable by any individual, yet inaccessible to

5. Etienne and Leacock, 1980; P. R. Sanday, *Female Power and Male Dominance: On the Origins of Sexual Inequality*, Cambridge 1981.

non-members.

We suggest that the effect of kin corporate property on gender relations was tied to the elaboration of marriage systems and especially of residence rules in different societies. Preferential residence rules may have developed in communal foraging societies but they became of particular import in kin corporate societies because, for the first time, the possibility of a contradiction between the role of producer and of owner arose. When males moved to their wives' residences after marriage, they became producers within a kin corporate group in which they were not owners. When females moved, the same was true for them. We thus consider with Murdock[7] that residence was more significant in the origins of stratification (both gender and class) than descent.[8] Whoever moved, kin corporate marriage rules were organized originally in ways that maintained or re-established egalitarian relations within and among kin groups. But the very mechanisms designed to perpetuate equality carried the potential to create rank, and in some cases seem to have created distinct social classes. We contend that in patrilocal rather than matrilocal societies there was greater potential for corporate property relations to interact with the sexual division of labour to create internal stratification, both sexual and socio-economic.

This essay represents an initial attempt to synthesize some of the recent research on women's subordination by distinguishing the effects of property, class society and the state, rather than lumping them together. We will suggest that the roots of female subordination lie 1) in the growth of an incentive for property-owning kin corporations to privatize both female productive and reproductive capacities and 2) in the greater expansionary

6. K. Sacks, *Sisters and Wives: The Past and Future of Sexual Equality*, Westport, Connecticut 1979.

7. George P. Murdock, *Social Structure*, New York 1949, Ch. 8.

8. Marriage systems in which the husband moves to his wife's kin group's residence are known as uxorilocal or matrilocal. Those in which the wife moves to her husband's kin group's residence are called virilocal or patrilocal. Systems where the couple establishes a separate residence, independent of either kin group, are termed neolocal. In some matrilineal societies, the couple resides with the husband's mother's brother, in which case the residence rule is called avunculocal, or viri-avunculocal. For the sake of simplicity, our analysis will focus on the two polar opposites, matri- and patrilocal societies. We agree with Murdock, (1949), that avunculocal residence has a similar effect on women's status to patrilocal. In both, the woman is removed from her own kin group and is placed under the authority of males of her husband's kin group.

potential of kin corporations where women were the movable partners at marriage. When the point was reached at which social differentiation among kin corporations or subgroups was firm and permanent enough to constitute classes, new conditions came into play, and woman's role must be analyzed from the perspective of her class as well as her sex.

Without entering into detailed debates about ancient modes of production, we identify a broad category of class society in which production was appropriated directly by a ruling stratum relying on relations that still maintained the form of the kin corporation. We call such societies kinship-based kingdoms or states to differentiate them both from the kin corporate societies out of which they arose and from the civil states, based on absolute property rights, which in most cases supplanted them. These kingdoms, we will argue, had rather different effects on women than did the civil states that arose out of the decisive breakdown of kin corporate control over political, ideological and economic resources. We will argue 1) that the emergence of class society and the early kinship-based kingdom led to a rise in the prerogatives of aristocratic women even while womanhood as a social category was increasingly denigrated and 2) that the emergence of the civil state led to an attack on kinship modes of organization and hence on the prerogatives of aristocratic women, while it both institutionalized restrictions on all women and at the same time gave them protection against certain kinds of familial abuses.

The Development of a Sexual Division of Labour

The earliest human societies were undoubtedly small, loosely organized groups whose survival depended upon generalized sharing and cooperation as well as on flexible living and work arrangements.[9] As Leibowitz argues in her contribution to this volume, an informal division of labour by sex probably developed in populations that adopted projectile weapons, or any other technology allowing specialization between hunting of big game and collecting. With smaller numbers of hunters pursuing game over long distances, and with the possibility of spon-

9. N. Tanner, *On Becoming Human*, Cambridge 1981. R. Leakey and R. Levin, *Origins*, New York 1977.

taneous hunting as soon as animal tracks were sighted (without the time-consuming collective preparation required by the 'surround'), it was more convenient, usually, for hunters to be males. This was not due to differences in size, strength or aggressive capacity but to the inadvisability of risking childbearers in such ventures or of requiring mothers, who were likely to have a nursing child beside them for a period of up to four years,[10] to drop the child, without prior arrangement, in the interests of a speedy pursuit of game. Despite the wide variability in the sexual division of labour and in the valuation of male and female tasks, there is a clear cross-cultural pattern in primitive societies whereby women perform subsistence, manufacturing and processing tasks that are closer to home base, while males take on more long-distance and risky pursuits that require sudden, sustained and unplanned periods of activity and are thus difficult to reconcile with pregnancy or nursing.[11]

We want to be very clear about what this division of labour did and did not imply. It did not mean that men were more aggressive or powerful than women, since hunting is not normally an aggressive act in foraging societies,[12] and disputes are rarely settled by the use of weapons but rather by individual fission[13] or by involving the whole community in the argument until a solution is reached.[14] Indeed, women frequently show themselves every bit as capable of aggressive behaviour as men[15]. Contrary to Brown and Parker and Parker,[16] moreover, it did not mean that women's tasks were dull or, because compatible with frequent breaks for nursing, less skilled than men's, nor that they were considered so by members of society. Draper[17] has shown that the gathering expeditions of !Kung women require

10. R. Lee, *The !Kung San: Men, Women and Work in a Foraging Society*, Cambridge 1979.

11. S. and H. Parker, 'The Myth of Male Superiority: Rise and Demise', *American Anthropologist*, 81, 1979.

12. R. Rohrlich-Leavitt, 'Peaceable Primates and Gentle People: Anthropological Approaches to Women's Studies', in B. Watson, ed., *Women's Studies: The Social Realities*, New York 1976.

13. Lee, 1979, p. 397.

14. Colin M. Turnbull, *The Forest People: A Study of the Pygmies of the Congo*, New York 1962, p. 125.

15. Margaret Mead, *Sex and Temperament in Three Primitive Societies*, New York 1963; Lorna K. Marshall, 'The !Kung Bushmen of the Kalahari Desert', in J. Gibbs, ed., *Peoples of Africa*, New York, 1965.

16. J. Brown, 'A Note on the Division of Labour by Sex', *American Anthropologist*, 72, 1970; Parker and Parker, 1979.

great skill and are eagerly greeted by the entire camp on their completion. Briggs[18] has argued that even among the Eskimo, where the division of labour results in a preponderantly male contribution to the diet, female work is not devalued. In most gathering societies, both male and female tasks are celebrated, and individuals of both sexes gain respect by excelling in their work. The frequency of female representations in Palaeolithic and Neolithic art work suggests that this was the case then as well.

Nor did the division of labour make women immobile or sedentary. In some West African societies women have carried on trade over considerable distances, in many hunting-gathering societies childless women may accompany men on the hunt, and in nomadic groups women move readily along with the men and do their fair share of the work. Gathering activities often cover wide territorial areas, and a woman simply puts her child in a sling, where it may remain for hours, nursing and dozing as the woman walks. It does seem clear, however, that where a society developed a division of labour that required some members to be more frequently near home (as with gathering or plant cultivation) and others to engage in unpredictable, long distance pursuits, the tendency was to assign the former tasks to women and the latter to men. This was not, we repeat, a biologically determined division of labour indicating that males were more capable of hunting than females, but a matter of social convenience. Individual women have hunted and even made war in some societies, but when any group of women system-atically engages in such pursuits, it is made up of women who, by choice or decree, are not playing a maternal role. Canadian Indian males were accompanied on the hunt by childless women who declared themselves unwilling to marry, while the famous female warriors of Dahomey were required by the king to remain celibate.[19]

While the division of labour by sex may vary considerably and be very flexible in some cultures, there is a general pattern. Murdock, Heath, and Murdock and Provost[20] have found that

17. P. Draper, '!Kung Women: Contrasts in Sexual Egalitarianism in Foraging and Sedentary Contexts', in R. Reiter, 1975.

18. J. Briggs, 'Eskimo Women: Makers of Men', in C. J. Matthiasson, ed., *Many Sisters: Women in Cross Cultural Perspective*, New York 1974.

19. B. La Hontan, *New Voyages to North America*, vol. 2, New York 1970 [1703], p. 463; Karl Polanyi, *Dahomey and the Slave Trade: An Analysis of an Archaic Economy*, Seattle 1966.

most societies tend to assign the following tasks predominantly to women: the gathering of food and fuel, grain-grinding, water-carrying, food preservation, cooking, pottery-making, weaving, cloth and basket manufacture, dairy production, and laundering. Males, on the other hand, predominate in herding, fishing and hunting for large game, lumbering, trapping, mining and quarrying, and warfare. Although men tend to take over agricultural work in societies using the plow, women have large responsibilities for horticultural production in systems of less intensive agriculture. Childe[21] suggests that the division of labour in the Neolithic was one in which women were associated with cultivation and daily subsistence manufacture, and men with herding, hunting and, where it occurred (infrequently), warfare.

It does not follow from this that males were associated with 'prestige' goods and women with 'mere subsistence'.[22] Where such a valuation exists it needs explaining, since many societies value female activities highly and ancient fertility symbols suggest a particular reverence for women's association with cultivation. It does follow, however, that Palaeolithic and early Neolithic societies had a division of labour in which females were associated with the tools or products of the land and males with those of hunting, herding and exchange. The labour of women tended to be the stuff of daily subsistence. Female activities were required every day, and female labour was necessary both to support the community when men failed to bring home goods and to process products that men did bring home. Female manufactured goods were available to any household with a woman, while all female work groups could also usually count on roughly similar returns to gathering and horticultural activities. Hunting, trade, and warfare, however, could produce either big windfalls or nothing at all for a work party. Male goods, therefore, were more likely to require elaborate rules for redistribution, while female goods could be consumed at the family level or distributed through personal networks without fear that other families would go wanting.

20. George P. Murdock, 'Comparative Data on the Division of Labor by Sex', *Social Forces*, 15, 1937; D. B. Heath, 'Sexual Division of Labor and Cross-Cultural Research', *Social Forces*, 37, 1958; George P. Murdock and C. Provost, 'Factors in the Division of Labor by Sex: A Cross-Cultural Analysis', *Ethnology*, 12, 1973.

21. Gordon V. Childe, *What Happened in History*, Harmondsworth 1964, p. 67.

22. Chet S. Lancaster 'Women, Horticulture and Society in Sub-Saharan Africa', *American Anthropologist* 78, 1976, pp. 539–64.

There is nothing about such a division of labour that would necessarily create inequality. The most technologically simple communal societies known exhibit, in general, a flexible division of labour by sex and age, with balanced spheres of autonomy, influence and respect for both sexes, and many horticultural societies in history have combined a firm division of labour with unmistakable guarantees of female autonomy. We believe that the emergence of processes that could transform the flexible division of labour among communal peoples into an exploitation of female labour flowed from the development of kin corporate property and the social relations that this represented.

Kin Corporate Societies and Gender Relations

A. The Development of Kin Corporate Property

Although many band-level, communal societies associate certain groups with particular territories or resources, this simply gives group members the right to be consulted by other users or to have the honour of distributing 'their' products; it is inconceivable that permission to use the resources would be refused or that the products would not be shared. Moreover such honorary 'ownership' is more closely connected with local residence than with filiation. Kinship is not the only, nor even necessarily the primary, means of establishing interconnections between people. The Australian aborigines use complementary sections and subsections to do this, and the !Kung Bushmen of the Kalahari Desert use 'name connections'. Although, according to Lee,[23] Bushmen bands are associated with particular territories and water holes, in fact there is much seasonal mobility among individuals and whole bands due to ecological imperatives. 'Strangers' and 'visitors' are never refused access to resources by the 'owners' of a water hole or particular territory. Similarly, among the Hadza, 'People are entitled to a share of meat simply by being in a particular camp at a time when a large animal is killed there and do not have to rely on specific categories of kin or other specific individuals to supply them.'[24] We

23. Lee, 1979.
24. James Woodburn, 'Stability and Flexibility in Hadza Residential Groupings', in R. Lee and I. DeVore, eds., *Man the Hunter*, Chicago 1968, p. 107.

suggest that the earliest human societies were organized in this flexible and communal way.[25]

A qualitative change occurs when the local kin group can and does exclude unrelated residents from use of resources and when spatially distant kin have a call upon resources by virtue of their kinship alone. The gradation from communal to kin corporate society is gradual, for as Engels[26] recognized, the germ of property is present in primitive communism, but the distinction is clear at both ends: in the one, people share and consider themselves related because they live together, with both strangers and visitors having the right to resources and the duty to work; in the other, people live together and share because they are related, and strangers and visitors must make special arrangements to either consume or produce in the territory of the

25. The question of whether women may be ideologically devalued to some extent in communal society has not been definitely settled. Leacock, 1977, 1978, Rohrlich-Leavitt, 1976, and M. Caulfield, 'Universal Sex Oppression? A Critique from Marxist Anthropology', *Catalyst*, 10–11, 1977, adduce evidence of equal relationships in a whole number of primitive societies. Turnbull's analysis of sexual relations among the pygmies is striking in its revelation of fully egalitarian sexual relations, (Colin M. Turnbull, 'Mbuti Womanhood', in F. Dahlberg, *Woman the Gatherer*, New Haven 1981). But Maurice Godelier, in 'The Origins of Male Domination', *New Left Review*, 127, 1981, emphasizes the superiority enjoyed by males among the Mbuti, as well as among Australian foragers, and E. Friedl, in *Women and Men: An Anthropologist's View*, New York 1975, finds varying degrees of male superiority in some band societies and relative equality in others. In many otherwise egalitarian South American groups, moreover, there is clear female subordination. Perhaps special prestige is assigned to male tasks in some ecological settings, such as those where male hunting provides the overwhelming majority of the food and is the main productive activity (H. Sharp, 'The Null Case: The Chipewyan', in Dahlberg 1981) but most of the examples of male dominance in communal societies are suspect. The South American groups, for example, are devolved tribes distorted by years of warfare (K. Martin, 'South American Foragers: A Case Study in Devolution', *American Anthropologist*, 71, 1969; L. Dube, E. Leacock, Shirley Ardener, eds., *Visibility and Power: Essays on Women in Society and Development*, Delhi, forthcoming.) Whereas most hunting and gathering peoples practice infanticide, an indication that they face no serious population shortage, the Australian aborigines frequently confront demographic crises, and it is possible that this has led to an attempt to control women for reproductive purposes. It is interesting, though, that some observers stress the important role played by older women in Australian society, despite the general control over women as spouses and potential mothers. See C. Berndt, 'Interpretations and "Facts" in Aboriginal Australia', in F. Dahlberg, 1981; D. Bell, 'Desert Politics: Choices in the "Marriage Market" ', in Etienne and Leacock, 1980. The best generalization to be made about communal societies remains that they lack the institutionalized subordination of women or the consistent denial of social adulthood to the female sex.

corporate owners. The key difference is the existence or non-existence of discrete lineal corporate groups exercising exclusive control over particular subsistence resources within a given territory, or over the territory itself, and systematically restricting the access of non-kin.

Clearly, the transition to food production, which created the need for continuity in work and storage, stimulated the more formal assignment of particular rights, obligations and use of resources to distinct kin groups. The kin corporate mode of production is identified by both Sacks and Meillassoux[27] as the mode of production of food growers. Herding, of course, would have had similar effects where cattle were the property not of individuals but of a descent group. Thus kin corporate societies would have emerged with the series of transformations known as the Neolithic Revolution.

It is also possible, however, that kin corporate ownership may have appeared among certain foragers where there were rich and diverse resources which allowed a sedentary lifestyle,[28] especially if accompanied by fluctuations in supply which required some planning of resource use. Corporate ownership, for example, is found among some foraging Indian tribes of the Northwest Coast.[29] The emergence of such kin corporate groups from natural variations in the production of surplus may even have been the stimulus to food production in some early Neolithic societies.[30]

At any rate, in kin corporate societies specific resources are assigned to distinct kin group units, and kinship organizes the tasks and mutual obligations that can no longer be left to informal good will. Formalized 'balanced' reciprocity in gift-giving and the strategically regulated circulation of spouses become part of the mode of production itself, achieving the balancing out of goods and labour that informal sharing and individual mobility effected in communal bands.

The emergence of corporate property-owning groups, we stress, represented not some instinctual drive to possess but a

26. Friedrich Engels, *Anti-Dühring*, Moscow 1954.

27. Sacks, 1979; Claude Meillassoux, *Maidens, Meal and Money: Capitalism and the Domestic Community*, Cambridge 1981.

28. L. R. Binford, 'Post-Pleistocene Adaptations', in Struever, ed., *Prehistoric Agriculture*, Garden City 1971, pp. 22-49.

29. Fried, 1967.

30. R. L. Blumberg, *Stratification: Socioeconomic and Sexual Inequality*, Iowa 1978.

logical formalization of communal sharing when it became necessary to regularize resource management and the deployment of labour. But it had a number of consequences that could create momentous transformations in social relations. These consequences did not in and of themselves create inequality, but they laid the basis for further differences in age and sex roles that could, under certain conditions, be transformed into institutionalized ranking and male dominance.

B. *The Social Consequences of Kin Corporate Property Relations*

The development of kin corporate property leads to a greater emphasis on continuity and hence on unilineal descent. Unilineal ties of descent are increasingly emphasized over collateral kinship ties, and seniority becomes in a very real sense a relation of production rather than a mere mark of respect. Age and proximity to ancestors come to organize and identify rights and duties in production and distribution, while respect for seniority is further fostered by the longer periods of training necessary for people to learn their tasks. No longer does each producer completely control his or her own labour and products; ultimate control passes to an intermediary — the lineage head. This does not, however, explain male dominance, since both men and women can gain status with age, and seniority elevates certain matrilineages in some societies as well as certain patrilineages in others.

Second, the sexual division of labour becomes incorporated into the institutions of kin corporate society. Male and female spheres are spelled out more clearly, as the once flexible division of tasks by convenience becomes an institutionalized way of organizing labour, and sexual metaphors help people to conceptualize all social relationships. The existence of separate sexual spheres can certainly lead to male dominance if the male sphere expands at the expense of the female, but most recorded instances of such a disruption — from warfare, migration, trade, or cultural stress — are the result of contact with already unequal and aggressive societies.[31] Again, therefore, the formalization of separate sexual spheres does not in and of itself

31. Sanday, 1981; Etienne and Leacock, 1980.
32. J. Brown, 'Iroquois Women: An Ethnohistoric Note', in R. Reiter, 1975; A. Schlegel, ed., *Sexual Stratification: A Cross-Cultural View*, New York 1977.

determine unequal valuation for those spheres. Numerous examples exist, indeed, that show complementarity, from the informal balance of the Iroquois and Hopi[32] to the elaborate dual sex systems in West Africa and elsewhere.[33]

A third consequence of kin corporate property is greater concern among distinct kin groups for their biological perpetuation. It is a matter of complete economic indifference to members of a communal society whether any particular kin group expands or dies out. So long as a minimum population is maintained, the distribution of families across bands is unimportant, since everyone has access to the products of all and inter-band mobility is always possible. But when access to resources is mediated through a kin corporate owner, group boundary maintenance becomes vital. The kin corporation, including each local segment, must perpetuate itself biologically in order to maintain its social existence.[34] All kin corporate societies, whatever their residence and marriage rules, need to control and regulate repro-

33. Sanday, 1981; W. Leis, 'Women in Groups: Ijaw Women's Associations', in M. Rosaldo and L. Lamphere, eds., *Woman, Culture and Society*, Stanford 1974; Paulme, 1971; K. Okonjo, 'The Dual Sex Political System in Operation: Igbo Women and Community Politics in Midwestern Nigeria', in H. Hafkin and E. G. Bay, eds., *Women in Africa*, Stanford 1976.

34. We should distinguish our position from that of Meillassoux, 1981. Meillassoux argues that the emphasis on descent and marriage among food producers is simply a consequence of new productive techniques requiring continuity and storage, and that women's subordination arose as a consequence of the danger of demographic nonviability in matrilineal/matrilocal society. Such demographic crisis, he argues, resulted in a chronic tendency to social instability as men sought wives through capture. The solution to this instability was patrilineality and circulation of women who, having been the victims of violence, acquired the habit of submissiveness and acquiesced in this arrangement. Meillassoux's explanation is unsatisfactory because it emphasizes technical, not social, reasons for the new emphasis on descent and marriage rules, and because it puts biological rather than social reproduction in central place. His argument that groups must circulate women in order to survive contradicts the evidence of existing matrilineal matrilocal societies. Moreover, it seems likely that environmental conditions were more, rather than less, favourable for the survival of primitive groups in the prehistoric era (see Marshal Sahlins, *Stone Age Economics*, Chicago 1972, pp. 1—40; Lee and Devore 1968), a point which calls into question Meillassoux's basic premise that the threat of demographic extinction explains patrilineality, male dominance and marriage prestation systems in which women circulate. We suggest that in general the increased emphasis on descent and marriage were the result of a social, rather than a demographic imperative, an imperative flowing from property relations in the kin corporation. See Olivia Harris and Kate Young, 'Engendered Structures: Some Problems in the Analysis of Reproduction', in Joel Kahn and Josep Llobera, *The Anthropology of Pre-Capitalist Societies*, London, 1981.

duction in a manner different from communal societies. And the need to control reproduction has different implications for women than for men, since the genitor requires less corporate control than the childbearer. Thus kin corporate societies exhibit more concern and exert more control over fertile women than do communal societies. Again, though, this fact in and of itself cannot explain male dominance. Young women could certainly be controlled by older women as well as by men, and indeed they were and are in some societies.[35]

Fourth, the development of corporate property rights increases the potential sources of conflict between communities, whether over resources or labour. This may increase the importance of the male role as warrior. But aside from exceptional circumstances (such as colonialism) that transform warfare into the main activity of a group, even this does not necessarily lead to male dominance. Warfare remains sporadic and minor among most egalitarian kin corporate societies,[36] and a strong emphasis on male military prowess, as the Iroquois show, is perfectly compatible with an equal regard for the female role.

Fifth, the existence of distinct property-owning groups increases the possibility of differences at the local level in access to resources, or, perhaps even more important, in household membership, which means access to labour for processing resources. To balance out the unequal accumulation of labour and/or goods at the local level, kin corporate societies must develop more formalized exchange networks for people and for goods. Goods may be exchanged through elaborate feasting and gift-giving or through complex exchange networks such as those of the Trobrianders.[37] People may be exchanged through more formal marriage rules and through adoption.

Again, however, exchange does not on its own explain male dominance. Both men and women may take part in exchange networks of goods[38] and in adoption procedures, and receive equal benefits from them. (Males, however, may have more constraints on them to redistribute goods gained through

35. Brown, 1975; B. Quain, 'The Iroquois', in Margaret Mead, ed., *Cooperation and Competition among Primitive Peoples*, Boston 1961; D. Schneider and K. Gough, *Matrilineal Kinship*, Berkeley 1961, p. 211; K. Martin and B. Voorhies, *Female of the Species*, New York 1975, p. 225; Schlegel, 1977.
36. Fried, 1967.
37. Bronislaw Malinowski, *Argonauts of the Western Pacific*, New York 1961.
38. A. B. Weiner, *Women of Value, Men of Renown: New Perspectives on Trobriand Exchange*, Austin 1976.

hunting, warfare, or exchange, and may engage in this more frequently than women).

More problematic is the elaboration of marriage rules, since the spouse that moves at marriage does face some advantages. Indeed, Sacks[39] suggests that the defining dynamic of the kin corporate mode of production is the potential for conflict between owners and producers, often expressed in the marriage relation. Siblings share the same relationship to the means of production, but spouses do not. The sex that moves at marriage is, therefore, separated from direct control over his or her natal group property and becomes a producer but non-owner in the household of another kin corporation. The loss of access to one's natal group's property would increase as the scale of society increases and with it the depth and spatial separation of corporate groups. The in-coming spouse could lose considerable domestic authority and even manoeuvering room at the same time.

Nevertheless, in small societies these disadvantages would not be decisive on their own. Thus, for instance, among the patrilineal patrilocal Lovedu, marriage takes place within a small area, and women retain important rights in their natal group property.[40] Moreover, contrary to Meillassoux,[41] there is nothing inherent in the structure of primitive societies that determines it should be women rather than men who circulate in marriage exchanges. There are kin corporate societies in which men move, facing similar disadvantages,[42] and there are sound historical reasons for believing that there were more such societies in the past.[43]

We would argue that in their original simplest forms, matrilocal and patrilocal kin corporate societies were functionally equivalent, presenting the in-marrying spouses with some disadvantages but not destroying their independence.[44] In the most simple societies where women move, the male owes brideservice or a very small bride-wealth to the woman's family. This confers no rights over the female's person, and contrary to many

39. Sacks, 1979.
40. Ibid, p. 147.
41. Meillassoux, 1981.
42. C. Lancaster, 'Brideservice, Residence and Authority among the Goba of the Zambesi Valley', *Africa*, 4, 1974; 1976: Audrey I. Richards, 'Mother-Right among the Central Bantu', in Edward E. Evans-Pritchard and others, eds., *Essays Presented to C. G. Seligman*, Westport 1970.

authors[45] it is not unique to the circulation of women. Where men move, there may also be groom service or groom price. Thus among the matrilocal Hopi, where women initiate marriage, 'the transfer of labor and loyalty to the wife's household is symbolized by a ceremonial presentation of cornmeal to the groom's household, conceptualized by the Hopi as "paying for him", and by the short period of groom service that the bride performs by grinding corn and cooking for her husband's household while her wedding robes are being woven.'[46] Jill Nash[47] has also shown the existence of groom-price among the Nagovisi of New Guinea, while Singer[48] reports that among non-aristocratic Nuer, where matrilocality is common: 'A woman's family often gives cattle to the groom, and hence to his lineage, who have the right to place claims upon his herd; the groom then goes to live in his wife's village.'

Again then, the explanation of male dominance must not lie in the exchange of spouses *per se* but in some elaboration of that exchange. We must look for something that explains why patrilocal societies, which circulate female spouses, moved toward a situation where women became objects rather than actors in the exchange and increasingly lost their independence, and why the

43. On the historical trend away from matrilocality and matrilineality, see Kathleen Gough, 'Variation in Residence', in David Schneider and Kathleen Gough, *Matrilineal Kinship*, Berkeley 1961, pp. 631-54; Karla Poewe, 'Matriliny in the Throes of Change', *Africa*, vol. 48, no. 4, 1978; Karla Poewe, *Matrilineal Ideology*, London 1979; Karla Poewe and P. Lovell, 'Marriage, Descent and Kinship', *Africa*, vol. 49, 1979; Lancaster, 1974, 1976; C. Lancaster, 'Gwembe Valley Marriage Prestations in Historical Perspective: A Rejoinder to Colson and Scudder', *American Anthropologist*, 83, 1981; Chet S. Lancaster, *The Zambezi Goba: Sex Roles, Agriculture, and Change*, Norman 1981; Elizabeth Colson, *The Social Consequences of Resettlement*, Manchester 1971; Elizabeth Colson and T. Scudder, 'Valley Tonga Residential Patterns: Comment relating to Letters of Karla Poewe and Chet S. Lancaster', *American Anthropologist*, 82, 1980; Elizabeth Colson and T. Scudder, 'Comment on Lancaster's Response: Gwembe Tonga Virilocality', *American Anthropologist*, 83, 1981; Martin and Voorhies, 1975, pp. 220–29.

44. We do not discuss here the original reasons for matrilocal versus patrilocal residence. Some authors, such as Murdock, 1949, and H. E. Driver and W. Massey, *Comparative Studies of North American Indians*, Philadelphia 1957, have argued that this is affected by the interaction of the division of labour with a particular subsistence pattern. H. Ember and C. Ember, in 'The Conditions favouring Matrilocal versus Patrilocal Residence', *American Anthropologist*, 73, 1971, dispute this, and relate matrilocality to external (as opposed to internal) warfare. The heavy reliance of their work upon data from devolved South American tribes makes it suspect for explaining residence rules in the early Neolithic, where warfare was not a widespread phenomenon.

124

reverse did not happen in matrilocal societies.

Sixth and finally, kin corporate societies introduce another institution that has relevance for our analysis. They tend to develop formal standards of balanced reciprocity and redistribution, involving structured exchange between groups rather than the generalized and informal reciprocity among individuals that characterized communal society. Balanced reciprocity implies the existence of discrete social units and reinforces their separate existence even as it compensates for their differences.[49] Redistribution is a logical extension of balanced reciprocity when immediate, one-to-one, exchanges cannot be effected between kin groups. In kin corporate societies, chiefs or village heads may become necessary to coordinate the redistribution of goods through feasts and ceremonies, or even the redistribution of feelings. Thus the main functions of chiefs in North America were to redistribute goods through generosity and to mediate and settle quarrels,[50] and Fried[51] confirms this for other areas of the world. As Sahlins[52] points out: 'The economic role of the headman is only a differentiation of kinship morality. Leadership is here a higher form of kinship, hence a higher form of reciprocity and liberality.'

The increasing need for redistribution (both within local groups and between them) and the political tasks this creates have consequences for sex roles in that these political roles are often filled by males, even in matrilineal/matrilocal societies.

45. Friedl, 1975, p. 523.

46. Schlegel, 1977, p. 248.

47. Jill Nash, 'A Note on Groomprice', *American Anthropologist*, 80, 1978.

48. A. Singer, 'Marriage Payments and Exchange of People', *Man*, 8, 1973, p. 87.

49. An understanding of this does more to explain the tensions associated with gift giving in many societies than does the assumption (for example, in Marcel Mauss, *The Gift*, New York 1967) that the gift is all that stands between these societies and a state of war. The tensions around gift giving testify to the importance of the relationships that gifts perpetuate and to the fear that those relationships might be ruptured. See Van Baal, *Reciprocity and the Position of Women*, New Jersey 1975, pp. 30–69, for a good critique of analyses which assume that gift giving is a way of staving off some more 'natural' enmity. It would be more appropriate to see reciprocity as the natural state and war as the consequence of its breakdown.

50. Robert Lowie, 'Some Aspects of Political Organization among the American Aborigines', in R. Cohen and John Middleton, eds., *Comparative Political Systems*, New York 1967.

51. Fried, 1975.

52. Sahlins, 1972, p. 132.

Presumably this flows from the division of labour that associates males with long distance activities, external affairs, and products requiring group-wide redistribution, while females are more occupied with daily productive tasks from which they cannot be absented. The consequences of male political leadership roles, however, have been greatly overestimated. There are notable historical exceptions where females have wielded political power,[53] the data is skewed by the impact of colonization,[54] and even in many societies where village heads or chiefs are normally male there are channels for women to exercise a commensurate amount of political power in other ways.[55] Furthermore, in their simplest forms, the offices of headman or chief have been more onerous than powerful, and have conferred no ability to command others. Chiefs were traditionally expected to give more than they received, as William Penn[56] marvelled when he remarked that the Indian 'Kings' hardly leave 'themselves an Equal share with one of their subjects: and be it . . . at Festivals, or at their Common Meals, the Kings distribute, and to themselves last.' They were also expected to work harder than anyone else, all in return for an amorphous prestige that gave them no control over the lives of others aside from that they exerted through their persuasive powers.[57] (When European colonists attempted to appoint Bari chiefs to organize the native work force, the unfortunate individual so designated 'ended up doing almost everything himself, for the Bari do not give or take orders.'[58]) Thus the institutionalization of a political office, even when filled by a male, cannot be equated with male dominance in general.

53. A. Lebeuf, 'The Role of Women in the Political Organization of African Societies', in Paulme, 1971; C. Hoffer, 'Madam Yoko: Ruler of the Kpa Mende Confederacy', in Rosaldo and Lamphere, 1973.

54. Schlegel, 1977, p. 121; Brown, 1970; P. Sanday, 'Female Status in the Public Domain', in Rosaldo and Lamphere, 1974; Paulme, 1971.

55. Contact with expanding European societies invariably destroyed the balance of political power between the sexes and has left us a greatly distorted view of female political roles, for the Europeans chose to deal with the males within the system and often refused to recognize women's roles. (R. S. Grumet, 'Sunksquaws, Shamans, and Tradeswomen: Middle Atlantic Coastal Algonkian Women During the 17th and 18th Centuries', in Etienne and Leacock, eds., 1980.) It is significant that most of the societies in which Sanday found political power for women were those described prior to 1925, whereas most of those that lacked female economic or political power were societies described later, and therefore more likely to have been influenced by Europeans for a longer period (Sanday, 1981, p. 158).

If the earliest kin corporate societies emerged during the Neolithic, it is likely that they exhibited many of the above characteristics. We would expect to find a firm division of labour, a heightened concern with female reproduction, and an elaboration of political and military roles filled by males. The archaeological record supports such inferences. But we would not equate this with male dominance. Rather, we would expect to find a balance between male and female spheres and a high regard for women's ability to create life, both in reproduction and cultivation. Analysis of religious symbols from the Neolithic world suggests that this was indeed the case.[59]

Though the sex that moved at marriage in Neolithic kin corporate societies would have faced some disadvantages, these would not have been decisive in small-scale societies, and there are also good reasons for believing that matrilocal societies were more numerous then.[60] Two questions logically follow: 1) Why is there no evidence that matrilocal societies institutionalized female dominance? 2) Why did those patrilocal societies that institutionalized male dominance expand successfully? To answer these questions it is necessary to examine the intersection between the sexual division of labour and the development of social differentiation among kin corporations.

C. The Evolution of Social Differentiation in Kin Corporate Societies

As Friedman and Rowlands point out,[61] all lineage societies have the structural potential for ranking built into their originally egalitarian social relationships. In kin corporate society, as we have seen, the marriage alliance network 'may be a funda-

56. William Penn, *William Penn's Own Account of the Lenni Lenape or Delaware Indians*, edited by A. Meyers, New Jersey 1970 [1683], p. 31.

57. Sahlins, 1972; Lowie, 1967.

58. E. Buenaventura-Posso and S. E. Brown, 'Forced Transition from Egalitarianism to Male Dominance: The Bari of Columbia', in Etienne and Leacock, 1980, p. 116.

59. A. Barstow, 'The Uses of Neolithic Archaeology for Women's Prehistory', *Feminist Studies*, 4, 1978; Joseph Campbell, *The Masks of God: Occidental Mythology*, New York 1964.

60. Barstow, 1978; Campbell, 1964; Martin and Voorhies, 1975; Rohrlich-Leavitt, 1977; George Thomson, *Studies in Ancient Greek Society: The Prehistoric Aegean*, New York 1965.

61. J. Friedman and M. J. Rowlands, 'Notes Towards an Epigenetic Model of the Evolution of "Civilization" ', in J. Friedman and M. J. Rowlands, eds., *The Evolution of Social Systems*, Pittsburg 1977.

mental or even dominant relation of production . . . since it is . . . a major factor in the distribution of total social labor.' (p. 206). Similarly, the ideology of seniority and ancestor worship is not just an epiphenomenon but part of the total system of productive relations. The supernatural, argue Friedman and Rowlands, 'is an extension of the lineage structure so that ancestors are spirits whose function it is to communicate with higher spirits in order to bring wealth to the group. . . . The logic of the structure is one in which all local lineages are linked in a single segmentary hierarchy in which wealth produced at the lowest level appears to be the "work of the gods" ' (p. 207).

By the egalitarian principles of reciprocity, such wealth, given by the ancestors/gods to a local lineage, must be redistributed through feasting. But if one or another lineage consistently feasts the rest of the community, it acquires quite naturally and even without self-enhancement a reputation for special proximity to the ancestors and to the supernatural. 'Insofar as the society is socially committed to kin relationships, morally it is committed to generosity; whoever, therefore, is liberal automatically merits the general esteem.'[62] When it is a lineage, not just an individual, that is regularly liberal, that lineage gains special esteem: 'Within the local community, such a lineage would be an older lineage, a direct descendant of the territorial ancestor spirit of that larger group . . . '[63]

So far, this description of the emergence of ranking applies equally well to matrilocal and patrilocal societies, and among many matrilocal societies there are indeed lineages that are considered senior and have ritual and political primacy. But when Friedman and Rowlands go on to describe the next step in the development of ranking, they ignore the existence of matrilocal societies and simply assume patrilocality. Once a lineage has become senior, they argue, it may give wives

'to other low status groups in exchange for a bride-price which measures the social value of the wife-giver. The relation is one where a given quantity of real wealth is exchanged for a kinship connection (matrilateral link) to the source of wealth. In such a system marriage will tend not to be reciprocal so that differences in prestige are continually converted into the relative ranking of lineages . . . The lack of reciprocity implies that bride-wealth goods must enter into

62. Sahlins, 1972, p. 133.
63. Friedman and Rowlands, p. 207.

the circuit, flowing in a direction opposite to that of women. The asymmetry of this form of exchange permits the differential "social valuation" of local groups in such a way that interlineage rank is expressed by the differentials in bride-price'(pp 207-8).

The leading lineage, then, feasts the community and, by the rules of reciprocity, gains back more gifts and bridewealth from the rest of the community. These in turn are recirculated, pulling in more wives, children, and obligations of aid to supplement the senior lineage's family labour force. The notion that a return gift must be equal or even greater, a concept that once perpetuated egalitarian social relationships, now transforms them. More and more surplus flows to the leading lineage, and when other groups cannot repay the lineage's recirculation of that surplus they begin to pledge labour instead. Goods and labour, however, are not equivalent, and a structural inequality begins to emerge when the senior lineage gains control over dependent labour. The 'conical clan', argue Friedman and Rowlands, represents a transformation from relative to absolute rank:

'In the more "egalitarian" period the community makes offerings to the local ancestor-deities who in return maintain and increase the group's wealth. As a living lineage comes to occupy the position of mediator in this activity it is entitled to tribute and *corvee* as the cost of performing the necessary function of seeing to the welfare of the community. . . . This is a new vertical relation of production between a lineage and the community as a whole . . . ' (p. 211).

The transformation of the role of the headman, or chief hereditary position within the senior lineage, is furthered by the way that chiefly lineages get more access to long distance exchange and valuables from outside the region through their preferential role in the alliance network: 'Because the nature of the payments is a function of rank, the development of chiefly hierarchies is linked to an inflation that enables powerful aristocratic lineages to accumulate increasing control over the total wealth in circulation at the same time as they gain more direct control over the total labour of the community, all of which is used in the expanding external exchange network' (p. 213).

But this expansion of external exchange calls for more surplus and hence creates a tendency to bring in new labour, such as captive slaves. As labour is brought in from outside the community, a regional pattern emerges 'in which centers of power expand at the expense of surrounding societies which may have had similar structures but which are reduced in the process to acephalous societies' (p. 213). The way has been paved for the leading lineage or lineages to acquire a source of labour and goods that is independent of kin relations and reciprocity, and hence to establish class rule.

The above analysis suggests the possibility that the nature of the alliance network — matrilocal or patrilocal — plays a crucial role in determining whether a society will develop or utilize such differentials in lineage surplus in a way that leads to social stratification. We suggest that the source of female subordination lies not in an attack on women by men but in the attempt by both female and male members of specific kin corporations, under conditions of competition with others, to accumulate and control labour. Patrilocal societies had both more incentive and more opportunity to exert such control, and their efforts were directed at the in-marrying wives, with eventual repercussions on all women.

Wealth Accumulation, Residence Rules, and the Sexual Division of Labour: The Advantages of Patrilocality in Kin Corporate Society.

Once the development of kin corporate property and ranking of lineages developed, the sexual division of labour that had once been a social convenience could become a means of accelerating differences among local lineages and/or households. A critical factor in the development of ranking into social stratification is the concentration of wealth and authority within a local lineage, as opposed to its distribution among dispersed (lineal or collateral) kindred. Such a concentration allows for the maximization of household production, which is identified by Sahlins[64] as the key element in the development of surplus production and economic differentiation. It also undermines the constraints on accumulation imposed by the obligations of the local lineage to the larger (dispersed) kin corporation. As we shall see, patrilocality offered more opportunities for a local lineage to concentrate labour, wealth, and power than did matrilocality.

First, patrilocal societies concentrated related males — the

64. Sahlins, 1972, pp. 101–148.

people bringing in more variable wealth — in the same local lineages, where they lived together, subject to the authority of the ancestors and their living representatives, usually senior men.[65] The obligations of these men were thus to spatially close relatives (and ancestors), rather than, as in matrilocal societies, being divided between their wives', their sisters' and their ancestors' households. In both matrilocal and patrilocal societies, male products tended to be the subject of more elaborate redistribution ceremonies than female ones. In patrilocal situations, then, the concentration of males at the local level provided the means and incentive for accumulation of a surplus in male products as well as for greater variability in the amount available for redistribution. Even in the absence of polygyny, male activities were more likely to result in differences in formal redistributive occasions between local lineages than female ones. Yet wives' services and products were necessary for the feasts that local patrilineages could host at redistribution ceremonies. Because women tended to produce for the household rather than for wider kin networks,[66] their products could be added to the male surpluses and used for feasting, eventually producing the 'big man' phenomenon.

Matrilocal kin corporations on the other hand concentrated related females, while males were dispersed among the kin corporations into which they were married. Women's products, produced by matrilineally-related women who lived together, were likely to be shared immediately among members of the household or local groups, rather than being subject to elaborate redistribution, while male products had to be shared more widely, at the very least between their sisters and their wives.[67] This need for broader distribution of male products between his wife's household and his own provided less opportunity for the local matrilineage to concentrate male wealth, or for differentials to emerge among lineages in the amounts accumulated. Occa-

65. J. Friedman, 'Tribes, States and Transformations', in M. Bloch, ed., *Marxist Analyses and Social Anthropology*, New York 1975; Friedman and Rowlands, 1978; D. Jewsiewicki, 'Lineage Mode of Production: Social Inequalities in Equatorial Africa', in D. Crummey and C. C. Stewart, *Modes of Production in Africa: The Precolonial Era*, Beverley Hills 1981; Joel Kahn, *Minangkabau Social Formations*, Cambridge 1981.
66. J. F. Collier and M. Z. Rosaldo, 'Politics and Gender in Simple Societies', in Ortner and Whitehead, 1981, p. 282; Douglas, 1967, pp. 129–30.
67. M. Douglas, 'Is Matriliny Doomed in Africa?' in Mary Douglas and Phyllis M. Kaberry, eds., *Man in Africa*, London 1969, pp. 125–30.

sions for formal redistributive feasts were therefore less frequent.

Secondly, patrilocal kin corporations could make better use of the household production needed to transform male or female surpluses into feasts than could matrilocal societies, because lines of authority in external exchange were reinforced by domestic lines of authority. In patrilocal societies the people who provided the labour necessary for transforming surpluses into feasts (wives), were not owners within the kin corporation and therefore had less say over the allocation of food and other goods for consumption versus redistribution. This left them vulnerable to demands that they increase their household production of articles for redistribution by male household heads.[68] Those with an interest in increasing redistributive activities (male lineage heads responsible for external relations and political functions) also had domestic authority over household production, and could thus use household and lineage production more readily for exchanges among lineages.

In matrilocal societies, by contrast, less coordination of lines of authority and power was possible. Males who sent wealth home to sisters were less easily able to exercise authoritative control over the allocation and distribution of this property, while their wives and children lacked incentive to increase household production, since to the extent that males had a call on this it would be at least partly diverted to a different lineage. Male political authority in external relations of the lineage was balanced by strong female authority within the local lineage.[69] Indeed, Schlegel found that, even today, three-fourths of the matrilocal societies for which she had descriptions had either 'wife control' or shared female-male (brother or husband) control over domestic group property.[70] Johnson and Hendrix,[71] in a test of the cross-cultural data, found that male control is less likely to be associated with matrilocal societies than any other single political or economic variable. They also found that 'marital residence rather than type of economy is the most important

68. Friedman, 1975; Friedman and Rowlands, 1978.

69. Brown, 1975; Fred Eggan, *Social Organization of the Western Pueblos*, Chicago 1950; Schlegel, 1977; E. P. Dozier, *Hano: A Tewa Indian Community in Arizona*, New York 1966, p. 40.

70. A. Schlegel, *Male Dominance and Female Authority: Domestic Authority in Matrilineal Societies*, New Haven 1972, p. 192.

71. Johnson and Hendrix, 'A Cross-Cultural Test of Collins's Theory of Sexual Stratification', *Journal of Marriage and the Family*, 2, 1982.

variable' in explaining sexual dominance.[72] Even in matrilocal groups having (at least in recent times) a general subordination of sisters to brothers, such as the Yao, internal lineage affairs are still strongly influenced by women in ways that significantly limit the rights of men over external affairs. Among the Yao a man could not go off to found a new hamlet or village without the consent of his sisters and without this he could not become a headman.[73] Among the Iroquois, external actions of males, such as the decision to go to war, could be effectively vetoed by a decision of the women not to supply them through household production.[74]

The domestic authority of women in matrilocal societies did not produce the mirror-image of the domestic authority of men in patrilocal societies for two reasons. First, it was not reinforced by female control over external affairs. Second, women had less incentive to make demands of husbands than males did to make demands of wives. Ironically, the fact that male goods are more likely to be redistributed than female goods means that women need husbands far less than men need wives.[75] A woman is entitled to male redistributed goods simply by being a member of a kin group. An adult male is entitled to female products only by being married to a woman. Women in communal or kin corporate societies may pressure men as a group to go hunting,[76] but a woman is not entirely dependent on the actions of her own husband. A man whose wife refuses to garden, gather, or cook, however, could well go hungry. Thus husbands in patrilocal lineages have more need of domestic authority than wives in matrilocal ones, a fact which may account for the lack of pressure towards household cohesion in the latter.

There was, in short, an important difference in the authoritative control of household labour in the two types of Neolithic kin corporate society. In the patrilocal case the political authority of males in exchanges with other groups was coordinated with and reinforced by their authority over internal lineage affairs, especially the production of both women and junior men. Patrilocal societies were more likely to develop cohesive household

72. Johnson and Hendrix, 1982, p. 681.
73. J. C. Mitchell, *The Yao Village: A Study in the Social Structure of a Nyasaland Tribe*, Manchester 1966, p. 181.
74. Brown, 1975.
75. Collier and Rosaldo, 1981.
76. J. Siskind, *To Hunt in the Morning*, Oxford 1973.

units producing for redistribution by senior males.

Third, the differing structural characteristics of the two types of kin corporate society were reinforced by contrasting ideologies, one tending to hierarchy, the other to a more egalitarian social outlook. In all kin corporate societies, the implicit seniority principles of the kinship structure, such as belief in a divine ancestor, or the primacy of the group who first settled the land, contain the seeds of hierarchy.[77] In patrilocal/patrilineal societies the concentration of related males resulted in a mutual reinforcement of the ideology of seniority and relations of production such that the success of a local lineage could be perceived as enhancing the welfare of the total society even while it threatened the egalitarian premises on which that social organization originally rested. The greater emphasis on redistribution in patrilocal societies would have heightened the social perception of seniority as the source of good fortune, and simultaneously justified the accumulation of goods by senior lineages. As Jewsiewicki has observed: 'Throughout Central Africa, seniority seems to have formed the main principle justifying an unequal division of those goods which for various reasons fell within the common domain.'[78]

Matrilineal/matrilocal societies had different structural and ideological characteristics, many of which militated against the development of hierarchy. Work was more likely to be carried out cooperatively among collaterally-related kin. Same sex sibling groups acted collectively (for instance, Trukese sister and brother work teams),[79] while unilineal principles were less likely to be emphasized in the establishment of relations of authority both between and within local lineages and kin corporations. Matrilocal societies also had to depend on more flexible and open methods of recruitment than strict unilineal descent to ensure their demographic viability, because they were otherwise limited to the women born into them and hence vulnerable to depopulation. There was consequently much less possibility than in their patrilocal counterparts of restricting access to labour and spouses within separate local lineages.

Corresponding to these structural and demographic imperatives, matrilocal/matrilineal ideology in its pure form tended to

77. H. K. Schneider, *Livestock and Equality in East Africa*, Bloomington 1979.
78. Jewsiewicki, 1981, p. 99.
79. W. M. Goodenough, *Property, Kin and Community on Truk*, Hamden, Connecticut 1966.

be inclusive and egalitarian.[80] It emphasized the one-ness of the group that was of 'one womb' or one blood, and such a group could extend to all the members of a dispersed clan. Thus there was less emphasis on territorial association or on the exclusivity of the local lineage. Matrilineal ideology justified and necessitated sharing and cooperation to the same extent that patrilineal ideology stressed the authority of seniors, the ideology of conical (lineal, hierarchical) clanship, and the territorial association of related males. It would not be surprising if matrilocal societies in the Neolithic world had ideological systems that corresponded to their more stable, flexible interlineage relations and which therefore militated against the development of competitive redistributive and exchange systems. For example, an analysis of the religion of Catal Huyuk, a city in ancient Anatolia which was almost certainly matrilocal, shows that there were no sacrifices or burnt offerings of any kind, while its major themes were the products of human ingenuity — agriculture and pottery — and the birth of humans and animals. It seems to have been 'a religion devoted to the conservation of life in all forms, devoted to the mysteries of birth and nourishment and life after death.'[81]

Fourth, patrilocal lineages had an advantage in the utilization of surpluses for redistribution because they were able to rapidly expand their supply of female labour — the key labour in feasting and preparation for redistribution — through marriage and polygyny. It is easier and faster to find a marriageable woman than to rear a daughter to maturity. Since the labour of women in Neolithic society was a more constant requirement than that of men, this was a significant advantage. Any increase in the time men spent in wealth-getting expeditions, the amount of goods brought back, or the number of men involved would require a proportionate increase in the amount of subsistence and/or processing work for women. Women were needed to free up male labour, to produce the food and other consumables necessary in feasting, or simply to process any new products. Where the same amount of male labour might on occasion bring in an unforeseen amount of goods, as with a lucky hunt or raid, or a successful trading expedition, the returns to female labour were less variable from lineage to lineage. A big advantage for

80. Poewe, 1979.
81. Barstow, 1978, p. 15; J. Mellaart, *Catal Huyuk: A Neolithic Town in Anatolia*, New York 1967; Campbell, 1964.

the accumulation of wealth by local patrilineages, then, was their ability to take advantage of surpluses or trading opportunities by increasing their female labour supply, especially through polygyny. Among the Plains Indians, for example, the introduction of the horse provided the possibility for a man to get many more buffalo than one wife could process, while the introduction of the fur trade provided the incentive for him to do so. The result of the upsurge in buffalo killing was a sharp increase in polygyny and a fall in the age at marriage for women.[82]

Patrilocal kin corporations were best able to take advantage of the possibilities of plural marriage. In patrilineal/patrilocal societies, polygyny both increased the labour force of particular men (often senior men) and the overall membership of the local lineage. This explains the association of polygyny with increased production in farming societies practising extensive forms of shifting cultivation, as would have been the norm in Neolithic societies. The adaptability of this method of increasing productivity is shown by the fact that even in some areas of the modern world, polygyny is known to have provided a substitute for the adoption of new, more intensive (and expensive) agricultural technologies.[83]

Lineages in which, for whatever reason, women moved at marriage, and which therefore had the opportunity rapidly to increase the supply of subsistence or processing workers through polygyny, were better able to take advantage of regular or periodic increases in the supply of goods to establish redistribution networks; lineages that did not circulate women had an incentive to do so. As Martin and Voorhies point out: 'Polygyny is typically a mechanism for increasing the yield of one-male households.' Thus 'patrilineal organization provides a labor structure for increased productivity.'[84] In its early forms at least, as Poewe suggests, 'polygyny is not about male dominance (except as a male justification); rather it is about the individuation of access to resources. From the perspective of men, [and even many women, we will argue] polygyny may be about the potential of maximizing wealth, reproduction, or family

82. Oscar Lewis, *Effects of White Contact upon Blackfoot Culture*, Monographs of the American Ethnological Society, 6, Seattle 1942; A. Klein, 'Adaptive Strategies and Process on the Plains: the 19th Century Cultural Sink', Ph.D. dissertion, State University of New York at Buffalo, 1976.

83. Audrey I. Richards, *Economic Development and Tribal Change*, Cambridge 1952.

84. Martin and Voorhies, 1975, p. 236.

136

personnel.'[85] We suggest that this kind of consideration, which gives explicit recognition to the value of women's work as well as their reproductive power, better explains the relationship between wealth, patrilocality, and patrilineality in kin corporate societies than some innate desire of fathers to endow their sons with goods.

Plural marriage simply offered fewer advantages to matrilocal groups.[86] Polyandry (plural husbands) would have been more of a drain than a benefit to local lineages in societies where women did the bulk of subsistence farming, and where male wealth was owed to sisters as well as to wives, while it would not have increased future generations of labourers born to a lineage. Poewe suggests that polyandry 'is usually about communal (non-individuated) access to resources, women, and off-spring.'[87] In the rare cases where it occurs in any significant form, this is in societies where the female contribution to subsistence is 'insignificant'.[88]

Polygyny (plural wives) does occur in some matrilocal societies, but its contribution to the accumulation of wealth within a matrilineage is far more limited than in patrilocal societies. With the exception of sororal polygyny (where one man marries two or more sisters), there is a structural contradiction between the out-marriage of men and their ability to acquire more than one wife, for the man can not accumulate a permanent labour force in one domestic unit.[89] Either he must circulate between wives, thus diffusing his energies and

85. Poewe 1981, p. 40.
86. The World Ethnographic Sample reveals that polygyny occurs in 56% of the matrilineal societies (Murdoch 1965). However, general polygyny occurs in only three of twenty-four matrilocal societies (one-eighth) coded by Schlegel (1972), although it occurs in limited form in the majority (it was totally absent from five of the twenty-four cases). It is also possible that polygyny was a later addition in matrilocal societies where the market had penetrated and where colonialism fostered or encouraged male dominance. For, as noted earlier, polygyny concerns 'the individuation of access to resources' (Poewe 1981, p. 40). Be that as it may, there are sound structural reasons why general polygyny would be less developed in the matrilocal context. Polyandry (plural husbands), likewise, offered only limited advantages to the matrilocal group. David Aberle's 'Matrilineal Descent in Cross-Cultured Perspective', in Schneider and Gough, 1961, p. 721, reveals only one case, and that was in a duolocal society. Murdoch, 1949, p. 261, cites two cases, the Marquesans and the Toda (fraternal polyandry); Goodenough found one case on Truk; Schlegel counted one case.
87. Poewe, 1981, p. 87.
88. Heath, 1958, p. 79.
89. Eric Wolf, *Peasants*, New Jersey 1966, p. 65.

authority within any single lineage; or he must live uxorilocally with one wife and his other wives must come for visits — a situation fraught with potential for domestic disputes; or he must shift to virilocality (which, historically, was undoubtedly a common solution once the advantages of polygyny were apparent). Sororal polygyny may have solved the difficulty for some matrilocal lineages, but the possibility of expansion of the female labour force is limited here by demography, and sororal polygyny seems to have been generally associated with forcing a man to provide for more women[90] rather than with helping the lineage to accumulate wealth. Polygyny, then, was less beneficial to lineages in matrilocal than in patrilocal societies, and of far more limited occurrence.

Fifth, and finally, the circulation of women in marriage exchange systems, especially in conjunction with polygyny, had a further important implication for the elaboration of wealth and power differentials among lineages different from the circulation of men. Because women created a new generation of labourers in addition to contributing their own work, societies in which women moved and multiple wives could be brought in had more potential for a long-term, uneven accumulation of labour. This in turn would have greatly accelerated the process of socio-economic differentiation: the more labour a lineage had, the more bridewealth it could produce and the more feasts it could host, calling forth even more in labour and obligations. Again, though, it is worth noting that the advantage of patrilocal lineages in the accumulation of labour is not a 'natural' demographic one. While it is true that dependence upon the women of one's natal group for reproduction makes a lineage more susceptible to demographic accident,[91] there is no reason, as Poewe[92] notes, that matrilocal or matrilineal groups cannot compensate for demographic reverses simply by emphasizing collateral (horizontal) ties over lineal (vertical) ones, thus finding recruits to offset a short-term imbalance in their own births. By going outside the strictly defined local lineage group for recruits, however, the accumulation and concentration of wealth, power, and obligations within the local descent group are offset. Broader alliances are established and obligations are diffused

90. H. E. Driver and W. Massey, *Comparative Studies of North American Indians*, Philadelphia 1957.

91. Meillassoux, 1981, p. 44.

92. Poewe, 1981.

more widely. Thus in yet another sense, matrilocal societies would have offered less independent scope for action and accumulation on the part of particular local lineages.

We suggest that the modern concentration of matrilineal/matrilocal societies at the low end of a continuum of social complexity, wealth, and productivity[93] is a consequence of social relations that offered less opportunity or incentive for the independent self-enrichment of the local lineage. Without such unequal enrichment and consequent competition at the lineage level, there is no social incentive for a population to forego leisure and increase production above the subsistence level. Such societies remain stable and non-expansionary. Ancient matrilocal societies would probably have been similarly non-expansionary. Thus Catal Huyuk was remarkable in its lack of stratification, community surplus, or military expansion.[94] But such communities would have been very vulnerable to expansionary patrilocal neighbours. Where they did overcome the diffusionary effects of matrilocality and develop wealth differentials at the local lineage or household level there was probably a tendency then, as there has been in recent history, toward a shift to virilocal or neolocal residence.[95]

In summary, we are arguing that the social relations inherent in patrilocality could have served as a starting mechanism for ranking and eventually for social stratification in the Neolithic world through their greater ability to channel labour and prestige into a single local lineage, thus creating the potential for development of inter-lineage inequality. Alternatively, as wealth and surpluses increased in matrilocal society, local lineages would have had an incentive to shift to virilocality (either avunculocality or patrilineal/patrilocality). Men who acquired movable property could offer a brideprice to induce other lineages to shift from brother- to sister-exchange,[96] while women would have had an interest in agreeing to marry out so as to gain wealth and prestige for their natal kin group, in which

93. Aberle, 1961, p. 717 and Table, p. 723; M. Whyte, *The Status of Women in Preindustrial Societies*, Princeton 1979; E. Boserup, *The Conditions of Agricultural Growth: The Economics of Agrarian Change under Population Pressure*, Chicago 1965; Boserup, *Woman's Role in Economic Development*, London 1970; Lancaster, 1976.

94. Mellaart, 1967; Barstow, 1978.

95. Schneider and Gough 1961, p. 585; Murdoch, 1965, pp. 207–12; Thomsen, 1965.

96. Murdoch, 1949.

they remained co-owners even after they had moved to their husbands' locality.[97]

Rank differences between local lineages emerged from a situation where successful large-scale feasting enhanced the prestige and welfare of the feast-giving group.[98] But the ability to feast and redistribute generously depended upon the ability of the successful group to control the labour necessary for feasting. It is in this sense that we believe the subordination of female labour and reproductive power in marriage was a precondition for the emergence of other forms of stratification. The fact that men required the services of wives more than women required the services of husbands made control over marriage a greater source of power in patrilocal societies than in matrilocal ones, enabling senior men to use the threat of withholding a wife to control junior men. The intersection between wealth accumulation and polygyny restricted the access of some groups, and of some men within groups (juniors), to wives, and thus to future as well as present labour. Polygyny created a potential scarcity of women because it allowed some men to monopolize many women. The power of some men over other men thus increased as a result of the increase in the power of all men over their wives. Once women's valuable labour and reproductive power could be restricted and manipulated by different lineages, the marriage exchange system that had originally emerged to maintain equality among groups could become transformed into a system that expressed rank differences in society through an inflation of bridewealth.[99]

The social relations of matrilocal kin corporations offered less opportunity or incentive for the independent development of the local lineage segment. The triggers for emergence of rank differentials through polygyny, feasting, and effective exploitation of inter-group marriage exchange were absent, or present only in limited and diffuse form. The division of labour by sex offered less necessity and less incentive for effective exploitation of the labour of in-marrying husbands than for that of in-marrying wives. The surplus produced in matrilocal societies was more likely to be consumed than accumulated for purposes of exchange, while the labour of an in-marrying husband did not reproduce itself. Therefore matrilocality did not have the poten-

97. Sacks, 1979.
98. Friedman, 1975.
99. Ibid; Meillassoux 1981.

tial for groom price that patrilocality had for inflated bride price. Consequently, such rank differences as did emerge from the development of the forces of production in matrilineal/matrilocal societies were not as easily translated into institutionalized relations of dominance and subordination through the marriage exchange system. Among matrilocal societies in the recent past, where substantial transfers of bridewealth did occur in the context of a general market system, the residence rule was likely to shift to viri-avunculocality.[100]

From Patrilocality to Male Dominance

In its original form, the circulation of spouses was undoubtedly an egalitarian process in which both men and women willingly participated. Where a rapid transition was made to patrilocality, under pressure from outside sources or as a response to the needs of corporate groups to mobilize female labour, it is possible to speculate that women would still have had an incentive to acquiesce in this.[101] In some cases, alternatively, they may have resisted. But it is not really necessary to postulate, in most cases, a forcible imposition of patrilocality on women by men. The variability in patrilocal societies — from relative egalitarianism to extreme subordination — argues against any such universal catastrophic explanation, as does the fact that older women often actively sought the submission of young wives in order to use their services as daughters-in-law. While some patrilocal societies have myths about an ancient male overthrow of female rule, many others do not. Such myths, which typically suggest that female rule caused chaos and had to be overthrown, often simply seem to be attempts to justify male control by men who were well aware that women are not naturally mentally or physically inferior. In other cases, such myths may have historical origins in the expansion of patrilineal chiefdoms and their extortion of tribute and female labour from conquered neighbours. We see them, however, as testimony to a social conflict in which sex became entwined, not as a conflict between men and women *per se*. Another reason for rejecting any characterization of developing patrilocality simply as a war between the sexes lies in the ways that restrictions against women were also restric-

100. Murdock, 1949; Gough, 1961, p. 565.
101. Sacks, 1979.

tions against some men. Even the imposition of female chastity can be seen as a way of also controlling men, for its essence is to deny women the right to make a free marital choice. This means that a man cannot gain a wife simply by winning a woman's favour; he must also satisfy the woman's father and brothers.

The fact remains that, as soon as a distinction was made between sister and wife, the woman, as the in-marrying spouse in societies practising some form of virilocality, was at a disadvantage for at least part of her life cycle. The fact that she married out tended to separate her from direct control over the kin corporate property, and this separation would increase as the scale of the society, the depth and spatial separation of corporate groups, increased. These disadvantages would have been multiplied as the incentive and ability of lineages to maximize domestic production grew. As wives' productive and reproductive powers became part of a lineage's own particular resources, to be utilized in competitive redistribution, lineage heads would have increasingly yielded control over the lineage's own sisters and daughters in exchange for greater control over in-marrying wives. It is thus no historical accident that the more substantial the bridewealth payments, the more complete the transfer of rights in a woman to her husband's lineage[102] and the more emphasis on the wifely status of women over their sisterly status.[103]

At the same time, the interconnections between interlineage ranking and the competitive utilization of women's reproductive and productive powers would have led to a number of tensions about women. In Hagan society, for example, 'Women, who at marriage normally change residence, are thought by men as more prey than themselves to conflicting interests',[104] which leads women to be categorized as fragmenting or individualistic. Women are thus conceptually opposed to males, who are identified as 'social' actors — 'social' being defined as those who put clan interest first. Yet men's dependence on women for success in redistributive feasting means that women are seen as a

102. Jack Goody and S. Tambiah, *Bridewealth and Dowry*, Cambridge 1973, p. 3; Audrey I. Richards, 'Some Types of Family Structure amongst the Central Bantu', in A. R. Radcliffe-Brown and D. Forde, *African Systems of Kinship and Marriage*, London 1950.
103. Sacks, 1979, p. 183.
104. Marilyn Strathern, 'No Nature, No Culture: The Hagan Case', in C. MacCormack and Marilyn Strathern, eds., *Nature, Culture and Gender*, Cambridge 1980, p. 208.

constant source of danger rather than being contemptuously dismissed. This would certainly have increased fears of female pollution. Indeed, Raymond Kelly has argued that, in New Guinea at least, the elaboration of pollution beliefs occurs in areas where 'male prestige depends heavily upon female productive labour.'[105] This kind of tension would have been exacerbated by the ways in which senior men controlled junior men through restricting their access to women, a practice which would be threatened by women's free sexual choice, and could well explain the common association in patrilocal societies of female sexuality with social chaos. While male prestige and power would rest on the direction of women's work activities, male competition for resources and labour would come to be expressed in control over female sexuality and reproduction. Thus patrilocality, with its greater possibilities for the appropriation of wives' labour, could more easily set into motion the kind of social, political, and psychological processes that could culminate in the full-fledged control of all women's lives and bodies.

Women in Early Class Societies: The Kinship-Based Kingdom or State

The development of kin corporations out of communal society, as we have seen, greatly increases the potential for social inequality, setting in motion processes and conflicts that may culminate in the establishment of a true class structure. These early class systems, which we call kinship-based kingdoms or states, retained many of the prior forms of kinship organization, even while social relations were transformed and class differences were institutionalized in the social, political, economic and religious spheres. Our historical referents for such societies include Sumer from the Uruk through the Early Dynastic period, the aristocratic kingdoms of Homeric Greece, early Minoan Crete, Aztec society in its initial conquest period, and the early Inca Empire. Many West African kingdoms observed in the eighteen and nineteenth centuries, we believe, also come under this category.[106]

While most accounts of early class societies tend to view them either as simply intensifying the female subordination begun in

105. Ortner and Whitehead, 1981, p. 20.

kin corporate society or as actually initiating female subordination, we believe the actual effects on women were more complex. It is certainly true that in early class societies we tend to see a hardening of prejudices and restrictions regarding women as a sex. However, the institutionalization of class relations often resulted in an elevation in the status of elite women who, in the absence of the civil state, performed the function of linking aristocratic clans in political and economic alliances.

Although the dynamic by which classes emerged out of kin society is as variable as the social relations and forces within the kin corporate mode of production itself,[107] the development of social stratification typically stemmed from social processes emphasizing relations between men, as with warfare or trade. A critical factor often seems to have been the development of patron-client relations. While originally these were probably a means of redistributing strangers such as refugees and/or whole kin groups in a way that was consistent with egalitarian principles of social organization, permanent forms of clientage developed under certain historical conditions which could be manipulated by aspiring strong men or lineage heads to ensure their political and economic supremacy.[108] The relations between the 'senior' clan and the new arrivals were expressed as relations of patron-clientage. In return for allowing the stranger group(s) to settle and inter-marry, the chief of the senior clan or

106. Without implying any necessary uniformity of mode of production, we do suggest that there were similar processes at work affecting women in transitional class societies where, in the absence of the political forms through which state power and authority could be exercised, kinship funtioned as political relations among aristocratic groups. Lebeuf, 1971, has described several cases of this type of society in Africa. Dahomey, as analysed by Polanyi, in *Dahomey and the Slave Trade: An Analysis of an Archaic Economy*, Seattle, 1966, seems to us to epitomise a class society in which kinship is still of extreme importance to the ruling class, and in which the daughters of the king functioned as his emissaries throughout the kingdom. Goldman (1967) and Sahlins (1961) have discussed kinship-ordered class societies in Polynesia (I. Goldman, 'Status Rivalry and Cultural Evolution in Polynesia', in Cohen and Middleton, eds., 1967; Marshall Sahlins, 'The Segmentary Lineage: An Organization of Predatory Expansion', *American Anthropologist*, 63, No. 2, 1961, pp. 332–45).

107. Sacks, 1979, p. 115.

108. On African systems of patron clientage see Lucy Mair, 'Clientship in East Africa', *Cahiers d'Etudes Africaines*, 2, 6, 1961; Lucy Mair, *Primitive Government*, Bloomington, 1977; Jean Buxton, *Chiefs and Strangers*, Oxford 1963; and the special edition of *Cahiers d'Etudes Africaines*, 9, 1969. See also Frederick Barth, *Political Leadership among the Swat Pathans*, London 1965, on the functioning of patronage among the Swat Pathans; Goldman (1967) and Sahlins (1961) discuss its contribution to political evolution in the South Pacific.

144

lineage could claim rights to tribute payments and/or service obligations.[109]

Clientage systems, where they developed, had the effect of transforming kin corporate relations of production by freezing them into relations of permanent seniority/juniority. The junior could no longer expect eventually to become an elder and thus to escape exploitation.[110] To the extent that it involved permanent, asymmetrical, institutionalized economic and social superiority/ disability, the patron-client relationship had the potential for transcending rank differences, based on differential prestige or ritual, and thus of becoming the basis for assignment of people to true classes. The patron's claim of a right to his client's tribute and services could be the seed of a true class relationship between aristocrat and commoner.

Lucy Mair suggests that 'clientship can develop in the presence of quite small inequalities of wealth, and that the loyalty of a client to his patron gives the latter the power, independent of entanglements with competing structural groups, which is essential to the appearance of an authority overriding all of these.'[111] She views patron-client relations as 'the basis of the development of the kind of power which we associate with the office of chief, and, as the organization of government becomes more complex, with the type of political system that we call the state.'[112] As with war and trading, this kind of dynamic typically favoured only certain males. Women only rarely participated in relations of patron-clientage, being more commonly added to lineages as household slaves, unless they were acting in the capacity of men — that is, as female husbands.

The growth of social stratification, then, not only heightened the incentive for households to privatize the subsistence labour and reproductive functions of women, but it attached prestige to wealth- or power-getting mechanisms which were associated with the male side of the division of labour. Hence womanhood, as a social category derived from the sexual division of labour, was devalued. This devaluation of women would also have been associated with the expansion of patrilineal chiefdoms. Even where the conquered groups were not actually matrilineal, they would have been conceptualized as female

109. Service, 1975.
110. Meillassoux, 1981, pp. 78–81.
111. Mair, 1961, p. 316.
112. Ibid. p. 315.

because their obligations to the patrilineal central powers were so like those of the wives within its lineages. Thus among the Aztecs of the fifteenth century 'the tools and raw materials used by women became a metaphor for subordination and humility',[113] and in most aristocratic kingdoms femaleness was associated with dependence if not outright servility. Among pre-Conquest Andeans, though noble women played far more important roles than they did in the Inca empire, maleness was associated with conquest and femaleness with defeat.[114]

Nevertheless, despite the tendency of class societies and early kinship-based states to devalue women as part of a social category, there was not a unilineal decline in the influence and personal autonomy of all women as individuals. Indeed, as the ruling class was able to command female slave labour or draftee male labour, the need for the labour of upper-class wives was greatly lessened, leading to a loosening of control over them, while the need to marry off daughters to gain bridewealth was also obviated. Though sometimes the desire for legitimate heirs contributed to a sexual double standard, this did not necessarily occur with an aristocracy secure in its social, economic, and political position. Indeed, ideologies of purity and virginity may have been more common among the lower and middle classes, anxious to improve their status, than among the elites.[115]

As the institutionalization of classes allowed the upper strata to look beyond their own family and kin for labour, elite women typically took on important roles as links between upper-class families and as agents for their kin groups within a society increasingly characterized by class endogamy.[116] With marriage alliances becoming an instrument of ruling-class solidarity and

113. J. Nash, 'The Aztecs and the Ideology of Male Dominance', *Signs*, 4, 1978, p. 356.

114. I. Silverblatt, 'Andean Women: Gender and the Origin of the State', *Feminist Studies*, vol. 4, 1978, p. 47.

115. Sherry Ortner, 'The Virgin and the State', *Michigan Discussions in Anthropology*, 2, 1976; J. Schneider, 'Of Vigilance and Virgins: Honor, Shame, and Access to Resources in Mediterranean Society', *Ethnology*, 10, 1, 1971; Silverblatt, 1978. In European history, insistence on female virginity and chastity was closely connected to a rising middle class that also stressed conjugal love and cooperation. See Eli Zaretsky, *Capitalism, The Family, and Personal Life*, New York 1976; Lawrence Stone, *The Family, Sex, and Marriage in England, 1500-1800*, New York 1979; and Michel Foucault, *The History of Sexuality*, vol. 1, New York 1980. In classical civilizations as well it was the middle classes rather than the aristocracy that most valued female chastity. See Arthur, 1977 and Pomeroy, 1974.

116. Reiter, 1977, p. 10.

hierarchization, some elite women may actually have gained privileges and influence. Precisely because women as a sex were already excluded from independent access to and control over the means of production within patrilineal kin corporations, some elite women could gain derived power as heiresses or trustworthy agents of men. Thus noble women of the ruling class could, and did, exercise unprecedented power over both men and women below them even though — and indeed because — they were subordinate to their fathers or husbands. The marriage ceremony of the Incas is revealing here: the Inca king took a valuable cloth, woven for him by the state service, and gave it to his wife, declaring that 'in the same way as she would be mistress of that cloth, so she would lord over all things, just as he did.' In return she gave him a garment woven by her own hands.[117] The symbolism is exact: she gets a share in the public tribute he commands in return for her personal service to him. She will share in the authority of his rule so long as the fruits of her own activities go to him.

Minoan Crete was exceptional in the freedom exercised by upper-class women, who seem to have mingled on equal terms with men, entered the professions, and played a pre-eminent part in religion.[118] But in many other kinship-based kingdoms or states upper-class women also had important roles, despite a theoretical framework of male dominance. In the archaic state of Dahomey, princesses exercised total authority over their husbands as loyal daughters of the king. They were granted exemptions from the rules of behaviour applicable to other Dahomean women.[119] In ancient Sumer aristocratic women were designated by their fathers for service to the gods, a position that gave them both respect and authority.[120] Homer's work depicts a few women as particularly powerful and influential in the ancient Hellenic world. In early medieval Europe, in the 'barbarian' kingdoms that grew out of the collapse of the Roman Empire, wives and daughters of kings and barons supervised monasteries, handled the treasuries, and wielded considerable

117. J. Murra, 'Cloth and its Functions in the Inca State', *American Anthropologist*, 64, 1962.

118. Glotz, 1968; Rohrlich-Leavitt, 1977.

119. Polanyi, 1966, p. 55; Sacks, 1979, p. 237.

120. W. Hallo, 'Women of Sumer', in D. Schmandt-Besserat, ed., *The Legacy of Sumer*, Invited Lectures on the Middle East at the University of Texas at Austin, Malibu 1976; S. Kramer, 'Poets and Psalmists: Goddesses and Theologians', in Schmandt-Besserat.

political and legal power.[121] In many African kingdoms, the king's mother or sister was accorded a special sphere of power and influence.[122]

Part of the reason for the elevation of authority of upper-class women in such kin-based kingdoms was the continued reliance on kinship and marriage as means of political control and alliance. In the absence of a strongly developed state apparatus or bureaucracy, the ruling class must use for new purposes traditional forms inherited from kinship society.[123] This can temporarily elevate the role of women in dynastic alliances. In Mari on the Upper Euphrates as late as the Old Babylonian period (c. 1750 BC) King Zimri-Lin married five of his daughters to vassals, and one was even made mayor of the city in which she lived. These women played vital roles in alerting the king to impending problems in the outlying areas of his kingdom.[124]

Another reason may lie in the fact that much subsistence labour continued to be done by local villagers rather than by slaves, along the lines of the traditional division of labour by sex and age. This may have involved a dual power structure, where upper-class women had authority over lower-class women's work groups, while upper-class men supervised lower-class men. Among the Bamilke of South Cameroon, for example, the mother of the chief 'directs all feminine activities, thereby controlling the agriculture work of the whole community'. She has her own residence, her own estates, and her own jurisdictional rights.[125] In ancient Crete, the queen's room, like the king's, originally had direct access to the public rooms where state business was conducted.

The presence of such powerful women in ancient kinship-based aristocratic kingdoms or states should not be taken as evidence for an earlier matriarchal stage, however. It is perfectly compatible with a general devaluation of womanhood and may even, as we have argued, depend upon this. Thus letters from King Zimri-Lin's daughters reveal that in at least some cases the marriages were made against the daughters' will, and they contain pleas to be allowed to return home. The chief's mother in South Cameroon has the exceptional nature of her power con-

121. McNamara and Wemple, 1977.
122. Lebeuf, 1971.
123. S. Diamond, *In Search of the Primitive: A Critique of Civilization*, New Brunswick, New Jersey 1974, pp. 260-74.
124. Hallo, 1976.

148

firmed by the fact that she dresses in masculine clothing and passes on her name to her children, despite the general rule of patrilineality. Thus elite women are pawns as well as important links in male alliances. The power and privileges of individual aristocratic women are exceptional, while the labour of the majority of commoner women is increasingly privatized and stripped of its social content.[126] Nevertheless, the fact remains that aristocratic kin-based kingdoms, even though they subject the majority of women to increased exploitation, allow special opportunities for elite women that disappear with the rise of a civil state.

Gender and Class in the Civil State

The chiefdoms and kingdoms which arose out of and began to transform the kin corporate mode of production were capable of only limited development of the relations and forces of production. The ambitions of the aristocratic clans were often thwarted by their own organization. Personal ties were transitory and could be undermined by distance, time, or the frequent feuds that stemmed from the personal nature of political and judicial relations. Such feuds made individual positions of power unstable and weakened the ability of the entire ruling class to extract labour and tribute from the subject classes. Thus those elements of the ruling class that required a more permanent, stable power base from which to organize production and extend their rule in both time and space, often supported by dispossessed or debt-ridden members of the lower classes, sought to replace the essentially private nature of aristocratic rule with a more objective, rational form of class rule. In Mesopotamia, around 2500 BC, the parochialism and excesses of the community aristocracy and the priestly elite, to which it was closely tied, interfered with the coordination of long-distance trade, craft development, and centralization of water resources. A secular power with military force at its disposal began to challenge the hegemony of the priesthood and the aristocratic clans, eventually creating a much more highly centralized state. In the

125. Lebeuf, 1971, p. 100.
126. Unfortunately the historical sources are always more explicit on upper-class women than on the peasantry or slave class. See the discussion by Sacks, 1979, pp. 208–9, on the fate of peasant women in Buganda.

Aegean world the disruptive feuds of leading clans and their ruthless dispossession of the small farmer created contradictions that were only resolved when a tyrant, usually from the aristocracy but appealing to other elements in the population desiring more order and stability, was able to curb aristocratic power.[127]

In place of a judicial mechanism involving blood vengeance by kin, a political system sustained by marriages, sworn friendships, and personal military loyalties, and a method of labour mobilization based on kin affiliation and personal power, a more objective, regularized system of class rule began to emerge: the civil state, resting on absolute private property in land and slaves, a professional administration and army, and a legal structure immune to shifting personal and kin ties. It is no accident that the centralization and professionalization of class rule in the ancient world was often accompanied by a qualitative increase in slavery. The development of a highly centralized bureaucratic state in ancient Sumer, the Ur III Empire, coincided with a vast increase in public and private estate-based slavery.[128] Classical Athens, the culmination of these rationalizing processes in the ancient world, witnessed the greatest development of slavery as both the central productive institution of society and as an absolute form of property freed from customary restraints and personal ties. As labour could now be mobilized independently of personal force or power, so society could now be ruled by law instead of private agreements. This was the objective base for the defeat of the personal character of aristocratic rule.

In most ancient societies, the establishment of the civil state required the subduing of the aristocratic clans, which had parlayed the use of affinal labour, bridewealth, kin ties, clientage, military booty and marriage alliances into a series of localized political and economic power bases. Often this curb on aristocratic power was accomplished by an individual acting as dictator or tyrant. The fact that many early tyrants and dictators

127. On the rise of 'despots' in ancient Mesopotamia see N. Bailkey, 'Early Mesopotamia and Constitutional Development', *American Historical Review* 72, 1967; I. Diakonoff, 'The Rise of the Despotic State in Ancient Mesopotamia', in *Ancient Mesopotamia: A Socio-Economic History, A Collection of Studies by Soviet Scholars*, Moscow 1969; among the many sources on Greek tyrants, see M. Arnheim, *Aristocracy in Greek Society*, London 1977; C. Starr, *The Economic and Social Growth of Early Greece 800–500 BC*, Oxford (New York) 1977.

128. A. Tyumenev, 'The State Economy of Ancient Sumer', in *Ancient Mesopotamia: A Socio-Economic History*, Moscow 1969, pp. 82–4.

came from the aristocratic class should not blind us to the anti-aristocratic nature of their rule. As the aristocracy was tamed, such individual rule was replaced by a structured, permanent state apparatus.

A vital part of the process of establishing the primacy of the civil state was the subversion of traditional, kinship-based forms of social control, through a process which Diamond[129] calls 'double institutionalization'. Adams[130] describes how kinship changed in the early Mesopotamian state, taking on new public functions as the basis of recruitment to the state-controlled army, labour brigades, and craft guilds. In Greece the civil state used old kinship terms to impose an entirely new principle of association — territoriality — on its citizens, and actually split up traditional kinship groupings among newly-created tribes.[131] In other cases, the centralizing state usurped the customary functions of the kin group outright, as in making homicide and adultery civil crimes. In a later centralizing period, Anglo-Saxon kings passed laws providing for the physical removal to another area of individuals whose kin groups stood between them and the operation of the royal law.

The state increasingly tried to relegate kinship to a private sphere of life which was separate from but subject to the public sphere organized by the state. In *The Oresteian Trilogy*, Aeschlyus symbolically demonstrates the victory of civil rule and public order over the aristocratic family system when the Furies, who once punished wrongs 'To parent, god, or guest', are made to abide by the decision of a mortal jury and then taken, with rather patronizing ceremony, to a special sanctuary within and under the protection of the city.[132]

As part of this institutionalization of civil power at the expense of aristocratic kin groups, there grew up a new emphasis on the conjugal bond and the civil legitimacy of marriage. Where marriage once united corporate kin groups, it now broke them up, as husband and wife were urged — and often legally obliged — to identify with each other rather than with their kin. The state wished to deal with separate households, which it could control more easily than extended kin corporations. Thus ancient states regularly restricted inheritance rights of distant

129. See Diamond, 1974, p. 256, citing Bohannon.
130. R. Adams, 1966.
131. V. Ehrenberg, *The Greek State*, New York 1964; Lacey, 1968.
132. Aeschylus, *The Oresteian Trilogy*, New York 1959, pp. 147–82.

kin and attempted to deal directly with individual household heads in matters of taxation, labour mobilization, military service, politics, and law. In Greece, for example, the household (*oikos*) supplanted the clan (*genos*) 'as the integral, organic unity of the *polis*. To the *polis* instead of the *genos* the family *oikos* began to look for protection . . . and to the *polis* in return the family *oikos* owed a variety of obligations.'[133]

While the state did not initiate the oppression of women or their . ideological devaluation, its development worsened women's position in a number of ways. First, to the extent that the state succeeded in monopolizing and centralizing the enforcement of justice, political power, and labour obligations, it coopted the older lines of authority that had often included women, even if only as adjuncts to male heads of clans. The new public, hierarchical nature of authority put an end to the informal and delegated powers that aristocratic women had exercised by virtue of their family position. Whereas in early Sumer both girls and boys of the aristocracy were educated in the temple schools, by the time of the Ur III dynasty, the scribes were mainly professional men.[134] Similarly, as Greek city states centralized and developed professional bureaucracies, the influence of women in ruling aristocratic families gave way to their total exclusion from the political realm. Again, in Carolingian Europe and in the twelfth century, both periods of state centralization, the noble ladies and queens who used to act as treasurers and judges in the family-based political systems of the previous two centuries were replaced by professional male administrators, and women's activities were restricted to the home and the cloister.[135]

Religiously, too, the centralization of lines of authority worked against women. The ritual power often exercised by women within kin corporate groups was undermined as the state appropriated and transformed religion for its own purposes. Thus in Mesopotamia during the third millennium the religious ideology began to reflect the centralizing and hierarchical trends of society at large.[136] In the process the powers of the goddess and her earthly servants, the priestesses, as well as

133. Lacey, 1968, p. 73.
134. Rohrlich, 1980, p. 89.
135. McNamara and Wemple, 1977; A. Lewis, *The Development of Southern French and Catalan Society*, Austin 1965; S. Wemple, *Women in Frankish Society: Marriage and the Cloister, 500 to 900*, Philadelphia 1981.

152

the symbolic importance of the female principle in general, were supplanted by male gods, priests, and masculine symbols and values.[137]

Second, because kin ties through females were an important part of the old kin-based aristocratic political and social system, women were sometimes singled out for special attack as symbols of aristocratic misrule. In Greece part of the attack on the aristocracy took the form of legislation against ostentatious wealth displays by women or their participation in elaborate funeral processions. In ancient literature, the association of women with chaos, civil disorder, and primeval forces, and men with law, patriotism, and rationality[138] was often a metaphor for the two different systems of class rule.

Third, state conscription of lower-class men for warfare, public works projects, or as labourers on state land increased female responsibility for the domestic sphere. Upper-class women may occasionally have benefited from such increased responsibility, as when aristocratic men delegated supervisory functions to their wives while they were away at war, but as state institutions and professional administrators developed, these women lost such power. Lower-class women generally found their workload increased, and often the state legally restricted them to the domestic sphere to ensure the reproduction and maintenance of the labour force.[139] Women's access to public positions and even their exposure to public affairs were sharply curtailed; they were more and more confined to the household.

Fourth, the establishment of the individual household as the basic social unit of state society increased the power of the husband as the family's public representative and deprived women of a second place of reference and refuge in their natal kin group. The diffused authority that had allowed women in even patrilineal kinship societies to sometimes gain manoeuvering room between the spheres of the husband's and the father's authority was gone. Especially as the household began to be seen as a microcosm of the social order, male authority within the household was reinforced ideologically and even legally.

Finally, women's social status was undermined by the separation of public and private spheres and the association of women

136. T. Jacobsen, *The Treasures of Darkness*, New Haven 1976.
137. Kramer, 1976.
138. Arthur, 1977; Rohrlich, 1980; Aeschylus, 1959.
139. Sacks, 1975; Reiter, 1977.

with the newly isolated and powerless domestic arena, less prestigious than the public sphere because so thoroughly subordinant to state control. Within that domestic realm upper-class women tended to be restricted to the role of producing legitimate heirs, while the work of lower-class women was often disguised in their husbands'.[140] Women's productive and reproductive roles came to form 'the invisible background'[141] to the perpetuation of class relationships, and womanhood as a social category was even more closely identified with powerlessness, dependence, and non-productivity.

It is important to note, though, that the extension of state authority into the familial sphere had more complex and contradictory consequences for relations between the sexes than is sometimes realized. Thus the legislation of the household as the basic social, political, and economic unit involved a simultaneous subversion as well as reinforcement of male authority. As Ortner[142] has pointed out, the control of women in state societies was at least partly connected to 'the domestication of men'. As women were made into legal juniors in relation to men, men were made into legal juniors in relation to the state. The increase in the male's authority over the nuclear household disguised his loss of authority over the extended family of labourers and reproducers. Moreover: 'The husband/father was no longer simply responsible to his family, but also *for* his family vis à vis the larger system.'[143] Seen in this light, even the well-known tendency of the state to make female adultery a serious civil crime might be seen as a restriction on male as well as female prerogatives. While adultery laws gave legal status to the double standard, they also typically involved some reforms, defining the limits of individual male authority and providing some protections against abuse. The Code of Hammurabi, for example, while making female adultery a crime punishable by death, also stipulated that the sale of wives or children as debt pawns should be limited to three years, and it forbade the beating of pawns.[144] Early periods of state formation, from ancient Mesopotamia through the consolidation of the Roman Empire, even up to the

140. Sacks, 1975.
141. Reiter, 1975, p. 280.
142. S. Ortner, 'The Virgin and the State', *Michigan Discussions in Anthropology*, 2, 1976, p. 29.
143. Ortner, 1976, p. 29.
144. I. Seibert, *Women in the Ancient Near East*, New York 1974, p. 14.

154

Carolingian age in Europe, have been characterized by state-mandated protections of women's rights in marriage.

Recognition of these complexities should not blind us to the essential connection between patriarchy and the civil state, however. The protections mentioned above arose only in the context of a newly institutionalized subordination, which codified the second-class status occupied by most women already and reduced the freedoms enjoyed by aristocratic women in periods of decentralized rule. The destruction of the kin group entailed the elimination of the real protections that it offered its members, making them more directly exploitable by the political and economic powers of the ruling class. In the Old Babylonian period, for instance, debt slavery increased as both men and women found themselves confronted directly by an economic and political system which had stripped away the former buffers of clan, lineage, and community. In Greece, the centrality of the nuclear household to the operation of the state led to a whole series of laws designed to preserve the *oikos* by reducing any options for women outside of it and enforcing their subordination to the interests of the household head. Historically, only women of the industrial or commercial classes have really benefited from the increased nuclearization of family life and the unmediated relation between the household and the larger economy characteristic of state societies, and they for only so long as production and trade were organized from inside the home.[145] In most other classes, the 'freeing' of women from kin and community ties in state societies has resulted either in more severe forms of work exploitation or in their confinement to private household service.

Conclusion

The origins of female subordination are inextricably inter-woven with the origins of social and economic differentiation among subgroups or separate families within any society. If early forms of social and political inequality were based on the appropriation of women's products, the converse is also true: the elaboration of socio-economic and political differentiation was also the primary stimulus to the subordination of women's pro-

145. Eli Zaretsky, 1976.

ductive and reproductive powers. The rise of the civil state institutionalized both patriarchy and class rule, thus removing some of the excess inherent in the personal exercise of power over the lower class and over women, but ultimately securing that power all the more firmly. Anthropology and history offer no justification for the opposition some political activists make between the struggle against class rule and the struggle against patriarchy. Sexual inequality has been such a mainstay of socio-economic stratification that class rule cannot be attacked without confronting the patriarchy that props it up. At the same time, as shown by capitalism's inability to meet its promises of political and legal sex equality, it is impossible to eradicate patriarchy without attacking the economic inequality and the political structures of class society. The fact that the subordination of women has also been used to control and manipulate lower-class men provides an objective community of interest from which an intertwined struggle against economic and sexual inequality can be launched.

Slavery and Women

Nicole Chevillard and Sébastien Leconte

Slavery has existed both in the recent and in the remote history of many countries and most peoples. It has left its often brutal stamp on Africa, the Caribbean, Europe and Asia. As an integral part of human history, slavery cannot be ignored in discussions of the origins of women's oppression. However, one important question arises: Surely the appearance of slavery represented such a radical upheaval, such a deep rupture in the history of human society that, by comparison, previous forms of women's subordination do not ultimately amount to much? The present essay is intended as a response to this objection. It can indeed be demonstrated that the role and place of women is in every respect fundamental in the historical process leading to the appearance of slavery.

The slave system was not instituted overnight, and was not inscribed in human nature. It is therefore legitimate to consider the possible paths that may have led from lineage social structures (discussed in chapter 2) to slavery. Two major alternatives present themselves. Did the changes which led to the formation of an exploited class composed of men and women — the slaves — lead at the same time to the formation of an exploiting class also composed of men and women? Or did women, the wives and daughters of ruling men included, find themselves subjected to the same relation of alienation?

To tackle these questions and unravel the threads of change that led from lineage societies to slave societies, we have chosen to look exclusively at African societies. Africa has known not only lineage societies, but also kingdoms, empires, chiefdoms or great cities (the terms vary according to the imagination of the Westerners who encountered or studied them). These societies engaged in slavery under various forms, much in the same way as Athens or Rome, before the arrival of the colonizers. Domestic slavery still exists, in fact if not under law, in countries such as Mauritania.

From Captivity to Slavery

The first thing one can say about a slave is that he/she is an available person, someone taken away from his/her family, his/her close relations, detached from the status he/she has acquired; he/she is a captive with whom one may do as one pleases: he/she can be destroyed, exchanged for a ransom, made to fight, to perform specific work, assigned a new status, or integrated.

Certain lineage societies that take male and female captives in war, do not then treat them in a way that leads to slavery in the classical sense; rather they tend to reinsert the captive into the victors' social structures. If a woman has been taken captive, the process is quite simple: she becomes a woman of the lineage, she is to be a wife or mother and work like the other women. She is integrated into the dominant relation of exploitation of the female work force. On the other hand, for a man, the matter can be more delicate: how can he be kept in a subordinate status when the principles of lineage structure make such a position incompatible with his sex? Will he eventually be entitled to a wife, to progeny? To resolve this contradiction, the male captive will, except in particular circumstances, acquire female status: he will not be entitled to a wife, will not have progeny, and in practice, will be required to perform 'women's work'. If he is given a wife after some time, he will then lose his captive status.

Nonetheless, this does not make male and female captives slaves in the full sense of the word. They have not yet become the individual property of this or that chief or warrior; they are the property of the lineage. Moreover, their progeny will not be captive. In fact, the male captive has no progeny while he is not integrated. He may have sexual relations, but he does not transmit his captive status to anyone. Socially speaking he is merely a 'sterile woman'.

The female captive, on the other hand, has children, and these are socially reinserted through their father, the mother's master-husband. The child does not inherit a captive status; if it is a girl, she will be exchanged, like other girls, by her lineage. If it is a boy he will in effect be considered a man of the lineage and will be entitled to a wife. At the most he may sometimes encounter some difficulty in gaining access to certain high positions.

Hence, in lineage society, captivity may be resolved through integration based upon assimilation to female status; it then withers away on its own from one generation to the next. Within a context of this kind, slavery cannot emerge of its own accord, although the ground is prepared for it. For such a transition to occur, the captive, instead of being collectively appropriated within the lineage, must be individually appropriated by a chief or warrior. He has to acquire the status of a particular good, which can be exchanged, and his progeny must be defined as captive also.

Thus it seems clear that slavery could not have become a stable and lasting system (that is, one able to reproduce itself) out of the blue, so it is important to locate its origins in lineage society. Taking the model of women's alienation in lineage society as the point of departure, it would seem that, for slavery fully to develop its potentialities, the very structure of the lineage system had to be challenged. Slavery developed as a coherent system only when the ancient structures disappeared, when there was individual appropriation of goods and of the human beings who produced them, when individual rights of domination replaced collective ones.

Since there is nothing automatic or mechanical about such a process, it is obvious that we cannot accept a historical determinism that would stipulate that all lineage societies must evolve into slave societies through the same process, with the same consequences, and at the same pace. We can see the way in which social structures in certain societies evolved in effect by trial and error, toward a slave mode of production.

African Pre-Slave 'Kingdoms'

There are a certain number of precolonial African kingdoms which cannot, strictly speaking, be defined as slave formations. Many factors lead us to believe that such States[1] are at a point of transition. Where it survives, lineage organization exists only at the system's periphery. In the centre, the seat of political authority, lineages as such have disappeared. Kinship now only involves a small number of persons, closely related by blood, and relations between individuals develop mainly in reference to centralized authority, which is held by the king or the royal family.

In the course of periodic raids, these warrior kingdoms take numerous captives from neighbouring populations. But inside these societies, slavery is not reproduced: a captive's son is free, and slave status is not inherited. Yet these kingdoms were subject to slavery: Moslem merchants from the empires of the North carried on the slave trade and until 1880, for instance, purchased male captives from the Bandia kings who had made the trade a royal monopoly, as with ivory.

These kingdoms' systems of production were based upon women's work, and the massive influx of captive women. The key to the operation of political institutions lay in the organization of the circulation of women. Women were the main wealth in this type of society. Royal and princely courts were directly supplied by harems, hence by the wives of kings and princes. Each woman had her own cabin and her own garden; land for cultivation was also located in the vicinity. Women had to grow what they and their children needed, and then prepare their food as well as that of the subjects of the royal courts. Beyond these private gardens were the royal plantations, tended by the warriors (in time of peace) and their wives. A further source of food was the tribute levied by the king on his 'subjects', whose resources also derived mainly from their wives' work.

In such societies, the most important members of the society (the king, princes, noblemen) characteristically did no manual work and had a large number of wives. The more wives a man had, the more he could offer hospitality, and the better he could retain servants, clients and warriors.

Women were no longer exchanged between lineages, since these had disappeared. One man, and one man alone, received a wife, primarily for himself, in exchange for compensation, as a result of capture or as a gift from the king. Kings and princes with political power thereby instituted new mechanisms for the cir-

1. Such as the Bandia kingdom, studied by E. de Dampierre, in *Un Ancien Royaume du Haut-Oubangui*, Paris 1967, and the Zande kingdom, studied by E.E.Evans-Pritchard, in *The Azande: History and Political Institutions*, Oxford 1971.

culation of women, and built up a network of clients and allies: they gave a woman, often (though not always) a captive or captive's daughter, to a man without immediate compensation (there is no dowry in lineage systems). The beneficiary, however, had to give the first girl born of that union to the donor, or to his heir, and in relation to the donor, he acquired the same obligations as a client.

In the Mossi empires of Yatenga, an analogous system can be observed: the *napogoyure*. Every three years, a census is taken of all the women the king has rights over, an announcement is made to the families who will benefit in the future, and women are handed over at a ceremony. As compensation, the beneficiaries owe services and a reciprocal gift, the first-born girl of the union.

A similar institution can be observed in the Bamileke chiefdoms of Cameroon, the *ngkap*. Here too, a woman is given without immediate compensation: the master of a man gives one of his daughters, or any other woman over whom he has rights, in marriage through a *ta ngkap* union and he is then entitled to receive as *ngkap*, all the daughters born of that union. It is easy to see that such institutions are not egalitarian in their operation but tend to strengthen established hierarchies. They enable members of the ruling classes to own a great number of women, to ensure the reproduction of this female 'capital', to increase it and to surround themselves with clients or debtors. Of course the slave system is not yet established, but we can sense that it is emerging. The exploitation and alienation of women remain the basis of the relations of production and mechanisms of power: there is as yet no structure for the exploitation of male captives. Nevertheless we may note that new structures of power and appropriation of the work force have been set up. Wealth is no longer managed and accumulated within lineages, but by a few ruling men who transmit it to their direct heirs (priority being given to their sons, if they have any, not to their brothers). Women are no longer circulated according to the rules of exchange developed in lineage systems; women are exchanged and made to work on an individual basis, within the framework of hierarchical and personalized relations between men; they are no longer a collective possession but almost entirely an individual, negotiable, exchangeable good. Their condition prefigures that of the slave.

Slave States

Some 'genuine' slave societies also existed in Black Africa. The Nupe kingdom of Nigeria, for instance, studied by S.F. Nadel,[2] features an elaborate form of slavery. 'Before the arrival of the British, the Nupe had thousands of slaves: a prominent man frequently owned twenty or thirty; well-to-do craftsmen of Bida, blacksmiths and weavers, employed several; even in the villages certain families owned one or two.' Nadel explains how the Nupe had two ways of obtaining their slaves: through war and through purchase; they were the property of their masters in the full sense of the word. The ruling class of noble and royal families owned the most slaves. They served in the household and in the fields. Some court slaves were promoted to high-ranking positions. Among these were a large number of eunuchs.

Here then, slave status applies to both men and women, and is transmitted to their offspring. The male slave, like the captive in lineage societies, is not entitled to progeny. The children of a slave couple belong to the owner of their mothers. However they enjoy a slightly better condition than their parents: they are slaves but cannot in theory be sold or slain.

The Kotoko principalities, studied by A.M.D. Leboeuf, are based on a similar system.[3] The Kotoko carry out raids, capture large numbers of slaves and supply neighbouring kingdoms with them. Kotoko princes own vast stretches of cultivated land around the capital which are tended by their slaves.

Slavery is not uniformly imposed throughout society. It is the ruling classes, in the cities, that are mainly involved. At the periphery, in the rural and peasant communities, 'les captifs de core'are reintegrated into society after two or three generations. They are children of captives but not war captives. By the same token, marriages between free men and female slaves are allowed without any restrictions and the children of such unions are free as a result of their father's status. In the centre, in the cities however, such unions, though still possible, are not recommended.

Slavery here has assumed forms which do not radically differ from forms it has taken elsewhere, for example, in the Mediter-

---

2. S.F.Nadel, *A Black Byzantium*,London 1942.
3. A.Leboeuf, *Les Principautés Kotoko: Essai sur le caractère sacré de l'Autorité*, Paris 1969.

ranean basin.

It could be argued that slavery emerged from lineage structures, taking as its model the ancient forms of exploitation and
subordination of women. It could be said that these latter served
as a ground for the first testing and accumulation. At the same
time the entire social structure was profoundly changed by the
emergence of relations of authority and of dependence which
were radically different from those appropriate to lineage structures.

Slavery was not superimposed artificially and externally on
previous forms of women's oppression. But surely slavery radically changed one of the main features of lineage systems,
namely, that all women were subjected to the same relation of
alienation? In slave systems, the 'free women'/'slave women'
distinction seems to suggest a radical and fundamental division
of women into two classes.

'Free Women'/'Slave Women'

At first sight, it does look as though there is a world of difference — a class barrier — between slave and free women (that
is, the wives and daughters of ruling men). Free women must
surely enjoy better material conditions, have higher social
status, wield power over male and female slaves, give birth to
children who are also free, inherit certain goods, and hold important offices in the political sphere. A number of examples,
again from Africa, can be quoted in support of this claim. Thus,
among the Kotoko, three women hold senior positions. They are
the *Gumsu*, the first wife; the *Magira*, the mother; and the
Rolanduma, the king's eldest sister or the sister of his father.
These women exercise undeniable influence over the female
population, both inside and outside the palace. In the Waalo
kingdom,[4] women held two important positions: the *Linger* was
the first lady of the kingdom and had, more often than not, to be
the mother or mother's sister of the king who chose her. The *Awo*
was the king's first wife and was thereby second in rank in the
hierarchy of women. The *Linger* and *Awo* ruled over districts
linked, in a hereditary sense, to their titles and administered by a
captive of the crown nominated and supervised by them.

From such examples, it would seem that in slave societies, or at

4. Boubacae Carry, *Le Royaume du Waalo*,Paris 1972.

least at their core, among the ruling classes, certain women
a 'dominant' status. During this historical period the valu
power of certain women seems to have been socially recogn. ed
and accepted.

We accept that, with the institution of the slave system, the
withering away of lineage structures and the institution of centralized kingdoms, the condition of women changed significantly. On the other hand, we are not convinced that so-called
'free' women can be classified with the ruling classes, and
opposed to female and male slaves. A number of paradoxes have
to be resolved, if our analysis is to be advanced any further.

First, what is the status of 'free women'? The biography of a
Hausa 'free woman', Baba of Karo, born around 1890, before the
British occupation of Nigeria and in the midst of the slave
period, scrupulously transcribed by Mary Smith, is an invalu-
able account of the day-to-day life and status of women in an
African slave society.[5] A woman's first marriage was always
arranged by her family (around the age of fourteen) and possible
subsequent marriages required at least the consent of one of 'her
fathers' (her biological father and her father's brothers). The
ideal first marriage was with a cousin on the father's side. Baba
of Karo relates, 'When I got to be fourteen, the moment came to
marry me off. I grew with our six fathers, the sons of Ibrahim
Dara and his younger brother Maidamishi; when the moment
came, they arranged the marriage with someone of the family.
They married me to Duma, son of Sidi: Sidi was the son of my
grandfather Mai Yana, Mai Yana and Ibrahim Dara being the
sons of two brothers.'

When a woman marries, she brings a dowry, offered by her
own family: The parents of the bride brought mats, bowls,
millstones, a mortar and pestle, jugs, a curtain and mat for the
door of her cabin, a pot to cook porridge and stew, and a small
bowl. Such is the bride's dowry. The dowry is not unilateral as is
bridewealth in lineage societies. At weddings there was an
exchange of goods, services and gifts between the wife's and
husband's families.

During her first wedding, Baba of Karo was sad. She cried. She
didn't really like this husband she had not chosen. She was to
become a woman; that is, she would never again go into the
marketplace, nor dance with the other girls. From now on she

5. *Baba of Karo, A Woman of the Muslim Hausa*, recorded by Mary F. Smith, Yale
1981.

was to live secluded inside her husband's compound. For all Hausa girls, the first marriage was a rite of passage which subsequent divorces and marriages would not undo.

Thus, the various elements that determine the life of a 'free' woman in an African slave society bear an odd resemblance to those described in Athens or Rome at the height of the classical period. They are indeed directly linked to slavery.

First of all, the Hausa women's seclusion is only possible because there are female slaves in the household. Baba of Karo provides firm evidence for this: 'After they finished preparing the porridge with us, the wives of slaves washed, then, with a hoe over their shoulder, went off to the fields to bring food to the men; once the men had eaten, they began work too.They worked until the afternoon prayer, Azahar. Then they stopped; female slaves went to get wood for the fire. Meanwhile, we would stay inside the compound. In the evenings, they would bring back the wood and we would cook together, then they washed and took their food to their corner of the compound.'

However, the Hausa *'free'* women do not remain idle inside their 'compound'. They are involved in handicraft production. Slave and free women share tasks. But this sharing benefits only the free men of the household. In truth, the term 'free woman' seems quite ill-suited to describe conditions where women live in seclusion in this way. The Greek *gynaecea* played the same role.

It is paradoxical to consider a woman subjected to such constraints as a full member of the ruling class. Her situation is reminiscent of the fate of Chinese women whose feet were bound so that they were unable to walk far, confined by an infirmity which was only imposed on those women destined to be the wives of rich owners, traders, civil servants or mandarins rather than servants or peasants. It is also reminiscent of the obligation imposed to this day on women in Saudi Arabia, who may only travel entirely veiled and accompanied by a man from their family; as though they had to be prevented from escaping.

A second paradox is the fact that not only certain high-ranking women but also certain slaves had very high positions. In the Waalo kingdom, for instance, the roles played by the *linger* and *awo* are no different to those of officials of servant origin. One of these, the 'chief of the crown's captives' plays a role equivalent to that of prime minister. Another occupies the post of minister of foreign affairs. The authority of both the great women and the high-ranking slave officials derives from the king and is not autonomous. All developed slave societies functioned through delegating power to slaves and women giving them the right to manage and supervise others, and granting them living conditions that were frequently better than those of many a free man. This was really a question of the mechanisms of power, rather than emancipation or power-sharing measures. To be effective, all coercive systems have to entrust some repressive functions to members of the dominated group. One thus kills two birds with one stone: one divides the oppressed by allowing them the illusion that there is a 'way out' other than revolt, and one secures the loyalty and services of persons well-acquainted with the concrete conditions of exploitation. Should these 'mandate-holders' not give satisfaction, they can easily be disciplined or replaced, for their inferior status deprives them of any guarantee of support. Such mechanisms operate at various levels in all class societies, sometimes reaching the most heinous extremes, as was the case in Nazi concentration camps, where most of the day-to-day repression and extermination work depended on a small number of the inmates themselves, the 'kapos' or 'block leaders', who were involved in the closest collaboration with the SS, sometimes acting even more inhumanly than some of the SS, if that was possible.

We are not attempting to conflate slave societies with concentration camps, rather to emphasize that in a slave system, which rests upon a form of coercion, mechanisms for the exercise of power existed involving the processes of 'delegation' and the apparent integration of certain subordinates into the ruling group. In this instance, women and slaves were incorporated into the political and administrative hierarchy of kingdoms and other kinds of slave states.

It is in this context that we can interpret the fact that monarchs of certain African kingdoms came to rely chiefly on slaves and women to exercise their authority, and avoided members of their own dynasty and of other noblemen. Thus, the king's closest kin (his brothers and adult sons) were frequently kept away from the royal residence. In the Kotoko principalities, the children of the *Miaire* (the king) born of the official marriage with one of the four wives, were automatically excluded from succession. Only concubines' sons were entitled to lay claim to the throne. Thus the king was protected from the influence of his maternal family and his family by marriage.

It would seem therefore that the line between the 'free' wife, the slave wife, and the plain female slave, is in fact quite thin. Under the law it hardly seems to exist. In Roman law (and also, apart from minor differences, in African customary law and Islamic law applied to African societies too) the term *alieni juris* means he who is subject to another's law, or to the right of the *pater*. It applied both to married women and slaves. The *alieni juris* has no patrimony, and no personal legal capacity to act on his/her own behalf; he/she may only borrow the capacity of the *pater* to engage in matters that concern the *pater* as a legal person. Under Roman law, the only lifelong *alieni juris* are women: first of all, as girls, they are subject to their father's *patria potestas*, then as wives they are subject to their husband's authority or that of their husband's father.

In the last analysis, the 'free' women enjoy neither property nor freedom. And if their children are 'free' too, it is not on their mother's account, it is the father (or the person socially recognized as such) who gives them this status. There is no better expression or symbol of this power than that given by Roman custom: the newborn child had to be presented to the head of the family, the *pater*, who then held power of life and death over the child, the power to recognize it as his, or to deny it life.

We would therefore argue that in a slave system the 'free' woman cannot be seen as the free man's equal or as part of the ruling class even though, to a limited extent, she shares its existence. Depending upon her personality, circumstances, the importance of the family she comes from or the family she marries into, she may sometimes lead a well-to-do, prestigious, or exceptional life. But certain male and female slaves also had brilliant social careers. More fundamentally, we would argue that 'free' women constitute an alienated group, its main function being to guarantee the biological and social reproduction of the group of free men.

Slave society needs slaves (that is, individuals who 'inherit' their parents' slave status), and free men (and among these, potential leaders and rulers) to be 'born'. Moreover, the right number of slaves must be born, otherwise the relations between classes would be unbalanced. Nor can too many free persons, nor too many or too few pretenders to positions of power, be born. Free men cannot therefore be given the freedom to designate who is to be a slave and who is to be free, nor are princes and noblemen free to choose their heirs as they please. If they could imbalances, tensions, conflicts and complaints would constantly arise.

Therefore, certain rules have to be established: only the children of certain women can be considered free, and such women may only have children, as far as possible, with free men. These free men obviously cannot be physically certain of their paternity and are not able to prove it publicly so free men secure paternal power for themselves (it is during such periods that theories stating that the mother only bears the child, whereas the man is the only true procreator emerge). They sometimes have children with a slave, but reserve the sovereign right to decide whether or not to emancipate them or their mother. The legitimate social reproduction of free men takes place, in fact, through marriage with these 'free' women. The latter therefore have to be kept under watch and secluded to ensure that they do not publicly flout the rules constituted outside their control but involving the use of their bodies. Such a marriage bears only a distant relation to previous forms of exchange of women.

In slave society, lineage structures have disappeared, especially at the centre of the system, although they sometimes survive at the periphery, among 'subject' peoples. Kinship is no longer organized within the framework of lineages but within the narrower and deeper framework of family 'lines'. In a 'line' the inheritance and devolution of power operates from father to son. At the death of the 'line's' founding father, it is not his younger brother who inherits and takes control of the wealth, but one of the sons, designated by the father. And when this son dies it is not his brother or cousin who takes over the 'line' but one of the son's sons, and so on. Such a kinship structure was indispensable for the proper organisation of power and property relations and it enabled small groups of ruling men to emerge and accumulate wealth and power. At the same time, such a structure is more fragile than the lineage because fewer men are involved, and because it is easily threatened with extinction through lack of descendants. The 'line' no longer bases its power on a 'women-capital' but on its goods, its wealth, its slaves, its alliances with other 'family lines' and on the number of its clients and debtors. Hence, marriage is no longer the only means of acquiring a female work force — it is better to buy captives and slaves — it is rather a means of bargaining from 'line' to 'line' to form and tighten alliances. Marriage has also been freed from the ancient rules of exogamy and, in a practically 'incestuous' manner, marriage increasingly takes place between cousins. Women are no longer acquired with bridewealth but through an exchange of goods between two 'lines' at marriage. It has been said that dowry and bridewealth are mutually contradictory. A father does not have to give goods to marry off his son, but by marrying off his daughter, he entrusts the management of some of his goods to a son-in-law (or rather to his 'line') to widen his own 'line's' social base and extend its influence and defence network.

In such a system, therefore, 'free' women are merely hostages, instruments for the reproduction of social relations. This is hardly surprising: the 'social revolution' that occurred with the institution of the slave system was never undertaken by women or for their benefit. It was 'men's business', bad business at that for some of them, since in this case a good many ended up as slaves themselves.

The upheaval of social relations that was involved in the transition from the old lineage base to slave societies, occurred at the expense of and by means of women. Precisely because this was the case it is not surprising that in class societies based on slavery, 'free' women do not stand in a genuinely antagonistic relation to slave women and slave men. Like both of the latter categories they find themselves in an alienated and oppressed position, due to, and in the interest of, the ruling class, the dominant men.

In slave society, then, male and female exploiters do not confront exploited men and women as two opposed groups. Nor, and this is what is new in comparison with lineage societies, does the opposition simply rest between men on the one side and women on the other. Women's oppressed and exploited status has changed, in the sense that some men have come to join them in the camp of the alienated. Sex war no longer has any reason to exist, but women's oppression is not lightened, nor does it vanish.

The Processes of Women's Subordination in Primitive and Archaic Greece

Monique Saliou

For a century, ancient Greece has been a favourite area of investigation for those constructing theories of the origins and forms of women's subordination. The wealth of archaeological and mythological material, the ideology that makes the Hellenic world the cradle of Western civilization, have led to numerous interpretations representing a wide range of methodologies and conceptual schemes.

The matriarchy debate was initiated in 1861 by the publication of Bachofen's *Das Mutterrecht (The Mother Right)*. From the existence of myths that illustrate the religious sovereignty of the female principle (great warrior goddesses), Bachofen argued that humankind had passed through a matriarchal stage, a sort of primaeval savagery which, fortunately (according to the author), had been superseded by patriarchal civilization. The discovery at the same period of primitive matrilineal societies, in America in particular, gave weight to this thesis.

It is worth reconsidering Bachofen's approach. In his view, myth reveals the true nature of archaic societies: 'Does mythical tradition give an accurate picture of those early times when the development of the ancient world took shape? Our answer is yes: it is indeed a most direct expression, therefore the most truthful and most certain. Thus we can say that myth is the history of primitive times.'[1] Hence, listing the myths that confirm maternal descent and then those that evoke a sovereign goddess proves the existence of a matriarchy. Bachofen's position is in part a

1. Jacob J. Bachofen, *Myth, Religion and Mother Right*, New York 1967.

reflection of the limited state of anthropological knowledge at that period, but it also emphasizes an idea dear to nineteenth-century sociologists, namely, that a society cannot contain intrinsically contradictory elements. In the totally patriarchal world of the last century, nothing seemed more contradictory, and therefore impossible, than matrilineal descent and a feminized religion coexisting with a masculine power structure. Engels, who attempted to provide a materialist base for Bachofen's assertions, remained a prisoner of this logic, and failed to see that contradictory social traits are the very mark of transitional, pre-slave formations, or the beginnings of the slave mode of production.

One of the starting points of this article is a consideration of the inadequacy of this thesis which confuses matrilineality with matriarchy and, incorrectly, sees women's oppression as a historical product that began only with class society. However, refuting the concept of primaeval matriarchy in Greece does not entail uncritical acceptance of the idea that 'the world has always belonged to men'.[2] This is a belief which in contemporary France is an aspect of the revealed truth.

The origins of this belief are found in Lévi-Strauss and *The Elementary Structures of Kinship*. As is well known, the author claims that all human societies are based on the laws of exchange, the fundamental exchange being that of women. The passage from nature to culture began with the prohibition of incest, that is, a rule that men set themselves to exchange women of their blood for foreign women, and this is the basis of social life. In short, men assert themselves as social beings through the mediation of women: 'The fundamental fact is that men exchange women and not the other way round.'[3] Authority is therefore always masculine: 'This masculine priority is a constant trait'.[4] Lévi-Strauss's goal is not to explain but to observe. He points out, correctly, the driving force of patrilocality in asserting male dominance, but remains silent on matrilocal societies, which certainly existed, however limited they may have been in number. When the founder of structural anthropology ventures to explain the origin of the inequality of the sexes, he resorts to 'the sexual passivity of women', as if

2. Simone de Beauvoir, *The Second Sex*, London 1972.
3. Claude Lévi-Strauss, *The Elementary Structure of Kinship*, London 1969, p. 147.
4. Lévi-Strauss, p. 150.

Freud had never existed.

It is in dealing with the woman question that structural anthropology can be most effectively criticized, since its method in effect justifies the reification of a human group. Indeed, to regard primitive societies as 'cold' (without history), to limit oneself to the study of kinship structures and to regard economic production, the division of labour and exogenous influences as secondary is tantamount to considering the constants of primitive society as facts of nature. Moreover, this method is ill-suited to archaic societies that have a known history, that can only be understood through a dynamic perspective. The interest of the Greek material is that it shows the evolution of women's oppression and the change in the balance of power between the sexes.

We are not, in this article, intending to find a hypothetical matriarchy, but we do refute the idea that the subordination of Greek women is self-evident. We propose to demonstrate that the mechanisms that lead to women's oppression are constructed through processes that involve all levels of the social formation and are not given as an immediate and necessary form of socialization.

Our study exclusively concerns the historical period, and all the social formations mentioned are class societies. Nevertheless, the forms and degrees of women's oppression over this period are very different and cannot be reduced to a single model structured around exchange. We have adopted a resolutely historical method and will attempt to underline the changing elements in the forms taken by women's oppression by analyzing its function and its role in the development of a given society.

The use of mythological material is inevitable but demands a justification of the hermeneutics adopted. It is obvious that myth is not the certified copy, the mere reflection of the social reality that produces it. All the accounts of Amazons by no means prove the existence of these female warriors. When Greeks say that 'myth is the word of truth', they place themselves in the realm of the Sacred, in the realm of the ultimate reasons that made the world as it is. But this aspect of myth also means that we are not dealing with stories invented by the fertile imagination of some bard; myth is political, it explains social and sexual hierarchies. Hence in our view the interpretation of psychoanalysts, in particular of the Jungian school, which claims that Greek mythology is the most developed expression of mankind's collective Unconscious, has to be rejected.[5]

For one thing, this approach chooses to ignore the historical foundations without which these myths would not have existed. Furthermore, it presents them as having unequivocal meanings and symbols, whereas these legends are nearly always a heterogeneous set of sequences that stem from various historical periods and traditions, and their meaning is often unknown to the ancient mythographer. Thus the symbolic polarity of Male and Female, which supposedly encompasses a set of archetypes (Women = Earth, Moon, Matter, Passivity; Man = Fire, Sun, Spirit, Activity), is a late construction by rationalist philosophers of the classical period and does not stand up to an examination of the earlier texts.

However, while we reject the idea that myth is a pure projection of social reality as simplistic, we no longer accept the explanation that some authors apply, oddly, only to matriarchal sequences, the explanation that: Myth is fear,[6] fear of a topsy-turvy world, of Chaos, of Non-Being, which could not be better concretized than through women's power. This explanation, which is favoured by contemporary Hellenists, readers of Claude Lévi-Strauss and of Simone de Beauvoir, explains nothing. Why are men so fearful of women if they have been subjugated since the stone age?[7] Why have women been chosen as a symbolic medium for all otherness, all negativity, why has so much creativity been exercised to invent conflict between sexes (that is, at least half of Greek mythological production) if the subordination of women has always been 'experienced' as immediate, natural, and undisputed?

Although mythological material is indispensable to any serious study, it can only be deciphered in the context of economic and political data, as well as that of a spiritual realm of which it is an active component and with which it clashes. It is by drawing on archaeological, mythological, and literary evidence, real and fantasy women, that we will explore the basis and evolution of their subordination. The themes of women and work, women and power, and women and the sacred will be examined.

5. Carl G. Jung, *Symbols of Transformation*, London 1956; *Modern Man in Search of a Soul*, London 1961.
6. For example, see Pembroke, 'Women in Charge', in *Journal of the Warburg and Courtauld Institute*, XXX, 1967, p. 137.
7. de Beauvoir; Lévi-Strauss asserts the universality of the exchange of women and argues for its ahistorical character, which he attributes to men's greater capacity for sexual initiative.

A brief chronology

	4000 BC:	beginnings of agriculture
	20th to 16th century:	Cycladic civilization in the Aegean Sea, probably centred around Crete. Minoan civilization at its peak around 1550/1500. From 2000, arrival of the first Indo-Europeans in continental Greece.
PRIMITIVE GREECE	16th to 12th century:	Mycenaean domination (Indo-Europeans: influenced by the civilization of Crete, which they rule from 1450.)
	12th to 10th century:	Arrival and settlement of the 'Dorians', the last wave of Indo-Europeans, who destroy Mycenae, close Greece to large-scale trade. Writing disappears.
	9th century:	Writing reappears. Homer writes around 850. The country is ruled by a warrior aristocracy that controls village communities.
ARCHAIC GREECE	8th to 6th century:	Demographic crisis → shortage of land → colonization in the Mediterranean → development of trade, urbanization → a class of tradesmen become rivals of the aristocrats and allied to the peasants → many cities evolve toward tyranny, a governmental form involving curbing of aristocratic power.
	The example of Athens:	750 BC end of the monarchy.
		625 birth of secular written law (Draco)
		594 founding of Athens's institutions; suffrage based on property quali-fication (Solon)
		560—528 tyranny of Pisistratus.
		507 Cleisthenes → beginning of 'democracy'.

Women and Work

One of the most destructive of all associations is that between Earth and Mother, an association which supposedly encom-passes all femininity, an inevitable fiction in all Hellenists' books about women, and the highpoint of psychoanalytic sym-bolism. Demeter and Jason, united in the furrow of a wheat field, are said to present the archetype of the 'natural and functional identity' between Mother and Earth. Some have inferred from the constellation of myths around Demeter, which are of very ancient (probably Cretan) origin, a privileged relation of women to agriculture. Reality is far more complex.

Women of the archaic period, a period known as the Greek Middle Ages, subsequent to the Indo-European invasions and prior to the domination of the City, are virtually excluded from agricultural work. Yet agriculture is the essential activity in a society that is, incorrectly, described as 'feudal', where social relations oppose noble families, owners of vast estates, to small landowners who pay them a tax, and slaves (probably still limited in number). Homer, who primarily describes his own period (though with reminiscences from the Mycenaean period, which he claims to recall), mentions only men plowing and harvesting (*Iliad* ch. XVIII); women are limited to preparing workmen's meals; girls (slaves?) appear only for grapepicking. In Ulysses's manor, female slaves, more numerous than their male counterparts, seem confined to domestic tasks. Penelope weaves and, though Nausicaa washes the laundry with her servants, neither drives the plow. In *Works and Days*, Hesiod does mention a little slave girl who helps him with agricultural work, but part of the poem is devoted to denouncing the idleness of wives, those 'famished stomachs', 'bumblebees of the hive', who were created for men's damnation. In Homer, fallow land, not civilized by grain culture, is considered feminine: the realm of Calypso, of Circe, of the Sirens. Yet in the archaic period, and in this respect the classical age retains these values, agricultural work is seen as the only kind that befits a free man and honours the gods. The ideological link between femininity and agriculture is nonetheless given as structural, but within a purely negative framework. In Hesiod, the gods create the Woman/ Wife Pandora to avenge the theft of fire by Prometheus, who introduces cooking and agriculture. Agriculture and the appearance of the female race mark the beginning of civilization. 'Before' was the golden age when men did not toil, while women either did not exist or were abandoned to natural savagery and procreated outside marriage. Just as he domesticates the earth through labour, man domesticates woman through marriage.

The Athenian Cecrops myth has the same thematic system as the Pandora myth in Hesiod: the civilizing hero is the inventor of both agriculture (for men) and of monogamous marriage (for women).[8] Hence femininity and agriculture are in a relation of

structural symmetry instead of a relation of sympathy, which
would fuse women's fecundity with the earth's fertility, as in the
Demeter myth. Both women and land are the objects of domination, exercised through masculine labour: the hard but honour-
able labour of the small landowner; the exhausting labour of a
husband endowed with a wife with an insatiable sexual appe-
tite, but who bears sons.

J.P.Vernant,[9] from whom we take the main part of our analysis
of Hesiodic myths, does not ask what is, in our view, one of the
major questions that arises from these texts. Where does
women's exclusion from agricultural work come from? This
exclusion undoubtedly affects wives rather than slaves, since
Hesiod's 'purchased but not married woman' (v. 405-406) takes
part in the plowing. Yet the exclusion is real, or else the poet
could not, in the most concrete and practical passages of *Works
and Days*, have denounced the 'female race' as basically idle. It
should be added that he calls anyone who lives without doing
anything a 'stingless bumblebee' (in the masculine).

This idleness of women is all the more remarkable since it
seems to cut any connection with primitive societies and represents a break with earlier periods, for women of the archaic
period undoubtedly work; free wives and slaves spin, weave
and perform various domestic tasks. This we know not only
through iconography, but from all texts, beginning with those of
Hesiod himself, who is unstinting in his advice. According to
the myth, Pandora had barely been kneaded by the gods before
they endowed her with a distaff and Athena taught her the art of
weaving.

In the classical period, all girls received a tuft of wool at birth,
the symbol of their women's status. The wife of the aristocratic
Xenophon is asked to spin and weave at the back of the gynaeceum while her husband, who speaks highly of agriculture ('it
makes man virile'), contents himself with being the owner of his
land. Another Xenophon text shows Socrates advising a ruined
disciple of his to put the women of his noble family to work to
make cloth that he himself could sell. In the popular districts,
again in the classical period, there are women artisans and shop-
keepers. Such activities are nonetheless deprecated: Aeschines,
the orator, Demosthenes's rival, is constantly reminded by his

8. Pierre Vidal-Naquet, *Le Chasseur Noir*, Paris 1981.
9. Jean-Pierre Vernant, *Myth and Society in Ancient Greece*, Brighton 1980.

opponents that his mother sold in the marketplace. Thus all women, slave and free, work — but unlike men it is not really work, it is 'women's work.' Women exercise no control over what they produce, free women being excluded not so much from the formal right to own but rather the right to manage. In addition, recent studies of the dowry system in Athens during the classical period show that the dowry was nearly always made up of money, and rarely of land, the most significant means of production, or of workshops with slaves. The money was used by the husband as capital to invest.

Around 1150 BC, the Mycenaean world presents a rather different picture. Texts in linear B provide precious information about economic reality, and reveal the major role played by female labour. As slaves on royal estates, or wives of small farmers of varied and complex statuses (from the free tenant farmer to the serf), they perform most agricultural tasks. When the tablets of royal palaces mention landless manual workers, employed at home or for olive picking, they are nearly always women or children. Relatively prosperous small landowners obtain women slaves, and the same is true, of course, of monarchs. The royal palace archives of Pylos and Knossos mention servant women with highly specialized tasks: there are 'those in charge of barley', 'of reaping', 'of wheat handling'. Threshing is nearly always a woman's task, and grain grinding always. These same women pick grapes and olives, and press them. Lastly they make up the contingent of textile workers (between 600 and 800 according to the tablets) free or slave, who weave wool and linen in the palaces. And it turns out that the monarch's wealth rests on cloth, oil, and the wine trade, in other words on the products of women's labour. It is also probable that in reputedly masculine (potters, blacksmiths, goldsmiths) artisans' corporations, the artisan's wife takes part in the work (statuary shows women potters, tablets speak of a 'dyer woman'). We can, with some confidence then, infer the universal character of female labour.

However, even when they do not belong to noble clans, men carry out less thankless tasks, and above all appear to enjoy a greater freedom of movement. In the countryside, they are horse breeders and herdsmen; and in a society where breeding for war or for wool plays a decisive role they enjoy a valued status. Myths show gods engaged in pastoral activities; the king is the 'pastor' of his people. These shepherds are independent, and readily become bandits who threaten the settled people assembled around fortresses. Where are their wives? Tablets show that these herdsmen may rent their land and their wives are likely to be the ones farming it, since transhumance rules out permanent residence. Likewise for sailors, as women go on board Mycenaean boats only as goods to be shipped. All royal functionaries appear to be men. With the exception of those that tablets call the poor (serfs-slaves), all men — but not women — are liable to become soldiers, in Mycenaean society the noble activity *par excellence* for which Homeric poems reflect a distant nostalgia. Nevertheless, and this is a fundamental difference from the archaic period, women hold certain privileged positions that give them some economic control. Priestesses own land as do Queens.

Cretan civilization around 1500 BC, which used to be presented as the homeland of matriarchy, is more difficult to grasp. Although there are no written texts, some evidence of female autonomy is provided by archaeology and iconography. Nevertheless, all ancient authors (Heordotus, Plato) stress the fact that one thousand years after the Minoan period, Cretans had maintained seemingly anomalous ancient customs. Thus the laws of Gortyn, whose rediscovered inscription dates from the fifth century BC, give valuable information on women's condition. Not that after one thousand years and the Achaean and Dorian invasions this code reflects the exact situation of the women of 1500 BC, but its strangeness in comparison with Athenian legislation, the fact that Aristotle mentions that these antique laws applied mostly to serfs, descendants of vanquished peoples, allow us to deduce the existence of a situation more favourable to women. Indeed the code displays a system of clan property within which women have significant rights. A girl keeps her share of inheritance in her tribe; her husband may neither sell nor mortgage her dowry. A wife keeps control of her own goods after marriage. In case of divorce, she takes back her dowry, half the couple's assets, and all the household clothing. If she dies without any children, the husband hands back to her tribe half her goods and half the latest crop. If she marries a serf, and stays on her land, her children are free; the opposite is not true. When a girl plans to marry, the men of the clan have precedence for thirty days; if none volunteers, she herself chooses outside the tribe. Texts (Homer, Plato, Strabo) appear to bear witness to the existence of collective marriages during the great agrarian festivals, with matrimonial unions following rites of passage from youth to adulthood. A widow or divorcee who does not wish to marry a man of the clan may avoid this by giving him financial compensation. Finally, before leaving to live with her husband, a bride waits until she is able to cope with domestic problems, an evident remnant from a matrilocal period. Children are named by their mother, and matrilineal descent is confirmed by Herodotus's descriptions of tribes in Asia Minor that claimed Cretan origins.

Thus, in the fifth century before our era, within a rigorously patriarchal Greece, we see a matrilineal, endogamous, island society with matrilocal survivals. What would the status of Cretan women a thousand years before the code have been? While it is clearly matrilineal, there is no formal proof that this society was predominantly matrilocal. Nevertheless, it seems likely, given the persistence of endogamous customs such as those cited above. The iconography depicts Cretan women farming the land with men, spinning and weaving, and engaged in artisan trades. On the other hand, women seem to practice neither fishing — at least not fishing from boats — nor seamanship. Priestesses appear much more numerous than priests. Women's freedom of movement must have been great: frescoes show them strolling and taking part in religious ceremonies. The famous rite of jumping over the bull reveals a certain amount of physical training. Before marriage, young people of both sexes belonged to phratries inside a tribe, and led a very free life.

Nonetheless, it would be futile to imagine a Cretan matriarchy. It is a slave society, and all authors are agreed that the majority of slaves acquired through war or piracy were women. Noblemen have to have concubines; female workers are needed in temples and to build them, servants to farm the land. This society is not egalitarian; today historians accept the idea that free individuals were divided into four castes: the priest-kings and the great sacerdotal families who control trade; warriors; farmers and breeders — the mass of the population; and artisans supported by the community.

The king is a man; certain myths evoke an enthronement ritual through sexual union with a priestess, but this does not detract from the dominant position of the male monarch. The originality of Cretan social structure lies in the fact that women are regarded as full members of the four castes; they are not 'outside' the people, as in classical Greece. The Minos legend reinforces this.

As we know, this is a generic name designating the 'king'. The myth that historicized him endows him with four sons and four daughters, each with characteristics that connect him/her to one of the castes. A purely patriarchal society would have contented itself with four sons, or would have had the two lower classes of society personified by girls.

Nevertheless, male/female relations are not rigorously symmetrical. Rules prescribing endogamy, in the Gortyn code, bring out the fact that the girl is 'offered' to the men of the clan and not the boy to the women of the tribe. Myths pertaining to Minos's family show the king punishing one of his daughters (Akkallis) for allowing herself to be seduced by Apollo, that is, a foreigner to the clan. The legend underlines both the hold of the tribal group over its women and the exercise of that authority by a man.

What can we deduce from an analysis of social relations during three periods of Greek history? How are we to explain an evolution that is consistently unfavourable to women?

An examination of the relationship of women to work illustrates how impossible it is to uphold the thesis of a natural division of labour. Agriculture, for example, is masculinized in the archaic period, whereas during the Mycenaean and Cretan periods it involves considerable female labour. Only one activity appears to be exclusively feminine throughout that millenium: spinning and weaving. This permanence cannot be taken for granted, bearing in mind that in some North African societies such work is reserved for men.

There are more female than male slaves, and slave labour plays a decisive role in the wealth accumulated by the ruling classes in all three societies. This emphasizes the importance of putting women to work, and they are invariably entrusted with the most tiresome and above all the most disvalued tasks.

Another constant is the real and also ideological feminization of activities which are seen as both necessary and dangerous for the dominant relations of production. The study of myths is enlightening on this point. In Crete, as in Mycenae, artisans, who stood outside the fundamental relationship to the earth and were frequently foreigners, were feminized: their productive divinities were female, or connected to feminine principles. Dactyls, Cabiri, Telchines — the sons of the Earth share the cunning and magic of women and the vocabulary that describes their abilities and production is the same as that applied to female weavers. Much later, the very patriarchal Indo-European pantheon allowed the Haphaestos figure to remain, as the god of blacksmiths, a god who was born from his mother without a father, Aphrodite's constantly deceived husband. This deprecation of artisanal and trading skills survived into the classical age. M. Finley,[10] whose theses are generally accepted, holds the view that Athenian citizens kept agrarian capital for themselves, leaving less noble activities to the Metics.

Having identified the elements which remain constant, we must now consider the nature of the evolution of the relations between the sexes from the Cretan period to Hesiodian Greece.

We start from the hypothesis, in our view the most plausible, that Minoan Crete has all the characteristics of a transitional society, not only in the classical Marxist sense of the term (the transition from one mode of production to another), but in the sense of the transition in the relations between the sexes. In terms of the relations of production as a whole, there appears to be an interpenetration of contradictory elements characteristic of a transitional stage. Thus clan property and forms of individual appropriation coexist; there are the beginnings of a differentiation of functions (artisans) and of a slave system, but the economic role of this slavery is indispensable only for the ruling clans and for ostentatious rather than productive activities. The particularity of Crete is that the form of relations between the sexes seems to lag behind the stage of development reached, compared with other societies of comparable evolution in the Near East which are already resolutely patriarchal. It is because of this backwardness, the causes of which are unclear (insularity, strength of religious tradition?) that we are able to reconstruct elements of the process that leads to women's subordination.

It seems that at the end of the Neolithic Age, Cretans lived on agriculture in a system of clan property (as is shown by collective tombs); clan ancestors were women, as is proved by the exclusive presence of female idols in the religious statuary. Matrilineality and matrilocality are established beyond doubt. The capacity to accumulate surpluses emerged, in the islands of the Aegean Sea, not only with the communal practice of agriculture and breeding, but with the spread of more specialized, and more individual artisanal techniques. It is unclear why women specialized in spinning and weaving wool, both relatively recent

10. Moses I. Finley, *The Ancient Economy*, London 1979.

activities (in 5000 BC humans still wore animal skins). Louis Gernet,[11] in his work on the economic function of gifts, stresses the importance of the giving of clothing by women in myths and in rituals. He infers from this that the most ancient exchange system is the exchange between the sexes, with women offering cloth. We do not know what they received in return. Perhaps men themselves, since according to Gernet it was particularly at marriages that this exchange took place and this is a matrilocal system.

What happened next? Did men, taking the opportunity of serious upheaval, for which there is archaeological evidence, and of clashes between clans, consider controlling the labour power represented by women — the first stage being patrilocality? Or did the arrival even before the Indo-European invasions of immigrants from different kinds of systems and contact with civilizations with female slavery lead to a grafting on of patriarchal elements?

All that we do know is that in terms of the relations between the sexes, Minoan society appears to be the product of contradictory tendencies, which unite around the necessity of using female labour. The endogamous clan did not want to let its daughters leave for a first marriage, taking their productive powers with them; while the predominance of female slavery demonstrates the trend toward a devaluation of the status of women as a whole, a situation paradoxically reinforced by matrilineality. A male slave's marriage to a free woman is enough for him to become free, whereas the slave woman remains in servitude and transmits it to her children. Another indication of this increasing deterioration of status lies in the ideological-religious ties between femininity and artisanal trades. These, as we have said, are represented as both necessary and marginal; they represent a division of labour which is emerging from the first social relations; they demand a technology and know-how that come close to the art of weaving and which the community sees as magic. It is noticeable that, among many primitive African tribes, blacksmiths (in Greece the artisans *par excellence*) are subject to the same taboos as women and are frequently denied the right to bear arms, the community having found no better way to control their work than to give them a woman's status. This can only occur because women provide the model of

11. Louis Gernet, *The Anthropology of Ancient Greece*, London 1981.

182

an already dominated category, holding exclusive mastery of a specialized activity (spinning and weaving).

In Crete, the processes of evolution from a matrilineal and partially matrilocal society to a patrilocal and patrilineal society were arrested, as the code of Gortyn proves. Why? In our view the most likely hypothesis is a paradox. Indo-European invasions brought victors with increasingly patriarchal systems. It is quite probable that the odd survivals found in Crete in the classical age were the result of the vanquished people's resistance (a number of free peasants became serfs), and a common identity was provided by the unchanging customs. It is a widespread phenomenon. In this case, the element of violence in the relations between the sexes in myth is explained.

The various strata of the Indo-European populations came up against the ancient Aegean core everywhere (on the continent, in the islands, in Asia Minor). They imposed their own three-tier model for society (those who pray and lead; those who fight; those who work) and the hierarchy of the sexes. But all invasions borrow from the conquered even while victors assert their refusal to be contaminated. In the syncretic combinations that result, the group that offers the most efficient system ends up imposing its order and values and does so by defining itself in opposition to the social and ideological models of the conquered, particularly when these seem to impede greater economic and political efficiency. Aegean civilization was undoubtedly superior in its refinement, in the quality of its art, but it contained too many contradictory elements for it to last. In reaction to the threat it represented to all patriarchal society, male superiority was constantly and vehemently asserted. 'That is why our duty is to defend order and never endure that a woman has the upper hand.'[12] Thus speaks Creon on a stage where all actors are male, before an audience that is probably exclusively male, in a century (fifth century BC) when the seclusion of women is the rule.

Male domination began to be imposed as early as the Mycenaean period, through the clear predominance of female slavery, the sexual division of labour that gave the least valued tasks to women and through patrilocality. Nevertheless, certain Mycenaean royal women maintained high status. Priestesses, more numerous than priests, owing to the greater number of

12. Sophocles, *Antigone*, London 1951.

female divinities inherited from Crete, clearly held some economic and political power. According to the accounts given by
the tablets, the clergy held huge estates, and wielded control
over considerable donations. In Pylos the priestess of the great
Goddess opposed the Communal Council and claimed for the
Goddess (for herself) total ownership of its land. The political
influence of this female clergy, with its numerous female
prophets (Cassandra amongst others) and magicians (Medea,
Circe) is evident. The Queens, or even the wives of warlords,
played an important role. In their warrior husbands' frequent
absence, they defended the family property against the ambitions of overly greedy neighbours. Homer is informative in this
context. Clytemnestra, or the Queen of Pheatians, whom Ulysses
is asked to greet before her spouse, or even Penelope, were not
contemporaries of the poet of archaic Greece. They were the
equivalents of the 'Great Wives' of ancient oriental monarchies,
or of African kingdoms. Their pride, their inflexibility, their
crimes sustain classical epic, and also classical tragedy. It is as
though the Greeks as late as the Democratic period were continuously having to protect themselves against any claim to
power by women. The status of the Great Women does not
however undermine the patriarchal nature of Mycenae, those
kingdoms based on 'the frenzied exploitation of women and
children from morning to dusk in workshops for a liter of barley
and a handful of figs.'[13] Clytemnestra and Penelope are only
acting on someone else's authority, a power that is granted to
them all the more easily in that they are less dangerous to the
holder of sovereignty than some male cousin or vassal, who can
so easily become a usurper. We will return to this particular
relationship of certain women to power in monarchic systems.

We still need to explain the transition from economies where
women are actively engaged in agriculture to the situation in
archaic Greece, where free women are totally excluded from it.
What we know of the Greek Middle Ages can perhaps provide a
hypothesis. We know that the Mycenaean world was destroyed
'wholly and brutally',[14] leading to a period of migration, the
decline of economic activity through the disruption of Mediterranean trade, and the disappearance of writing. The world that

13. Paul Faure, *La Vie Quotidienne en Grèce au Temps de la Guerre 1250 ans avant
J.-C.*, Paris 1975.
14. Moses I. Finley, *The World of Odysseus*, London 1977, p. 210.

184

re-emerged between the eighth and sixth centuries BC, that of
Homer and Hesiod, was almost exclusively dependent on the
land. There was simultaneously an acute agrarian crisis, caused
by the lack of land and its unequal distribution, from which the
aristocratic classes benefited. Crafts were performed only by rare
specialists; the great textile workshops disappeared. Spinning
and weaving were reserved for mere private consumption; the
sexual division of labour had never been so clear-cut, nor had
women's confinement to domestic tasks. This development
seems to us to stem from a combination of factors. As a result of
migration, tribes arrived on the island with established patrilineal systems. In an economy with *individual* property and a
mass of small landowners, where agriculture is the only possible
resource, male labour becomes essential: Hesiod's peasant
cannot content himself with having his wife work, unlike
societies where all women are put to work on the clan's collective
property. As in the farms of traditional European agriculture,
there is work for everyone: for the landowning couple and even
for male or female servants. At this point the division of labour
intervenes and hardens the relations of domination between the
sexes. Land, the essential source of wealth, is increasingly the
property of the nobles; owning it is men's business, as is
farming, even though such work does degrade the person com-
pelled to perform it. Therefore, the man may thus present
himself as the only producer of goods, while the woman, who is
spinning, weaving, grinding the grain, preparing the oil, and
cooking is described as idle ('the bumblebee of the hive'). The
sharing of work is perfectly consistent with a system of inheritance which excludes women through the institution of the
dowry, which implies that the married woman renounces her
family's goods. The dowry seems to appear very early in archaic
Greece. Homer mentions the existence of Penelope's dowry
(*Odyssey* II, 132–3), which Telemachus is said to be forced to
hand back if he drives his mother out of the palace. Significantly,
the Homeric text shows the coexistence of the dowry with bride
price, since the suitors multiply gifts to the father, to the brother
of Ulysses's wife as well as to herself. This coexistence, which is
perhaps an expression of Homer's *parti pris* of archaism, is
quickly resolved in favour of the dowry which, as we have
already seen, was always money and never land in the classical
period.

It is thus clear why access to landed property in the case of noble families, other property and even agricultural work are denied to women (or at least to free women), since the system is much more flexible with regard to slaves, who do not represent the same threat. One final advantage completes the coherence of the system: the obligation to perform domestic tasks is synonymous with confinement, with exclusion from social life. The phenomenon is reinforced with the emergence of the Greece of the city states, as though political equality between slave-owning citizens, whatever their wealth, can only occur in the certitude that women remain subservient. It was as if the logic of the extension of democracy to free men's wives had been stifled, so strongly did Greek society feel the structural nature of the link between women's status and slavery. This link is remarkably outlined by myths, as Pierre Vidal-Naquet demonstrates.[15] When the Greeks have fantasies of the world upside down, what they see is rule by women and by slaves: male slaves marrying free women and governing in the place of the masters.

Women, Power, Conflict of Sexes

From Matrilineality to Women Aides of the Royal Office

Residual elements of matrilineal descent, which was well established in the Cretan period, remained in the Mycenaean period and after, and conflicted with the development of patrilineal lineages. With the exception of the Gortyn code there are no detailed legal documents, but mythology provides supporting evidence of this point.

Two sequences frequently occur: First is the theme of the special ties between the son and the mother's family. A number of male mythical heroes spend their childhood with their maternal families: Theseus, Perseus, Achilles. On the other hand, girls appear to stay with their father, a possible sign that they represent a valuable possession in view of future alliances. A variant of the myth lies in the hero being taken in by a foreign family (fostering?). In Cretan tradition, the child takes the mother's name; in myths it is the maternal elder who names the hero: this is the case with Ulysses, Achilles, or Theseus. Authors

15. Vidal-Naquet.

such as Marie Delcourt (*Oedipe ou la légende du conquérant*) interpret this stay at the maternal elder's, not as a matrilineal survival,
but as a rite of passage from childhood to manhood. The young
man certainly undergoes a rite of passage and initiation, but why
does it take place in the maternal family? In the classical age, the
young boy is sponsored by his father when he attains citizenship
and soldiership.

Louis Gernet, in an article titled 'Mariage des Tyrans',[16]
describes the continuing importance of maternal descent among
noble families of the sixth and fifth centuries, and challenges the
idea that it amounted to a vestige of uterine descent. He argues
that 'they are males maintaining their ancestor'. This is in fact
exactly the situation which exists in most matrilineal, virilocal
societies, where relations of kinship imply privileged relations
between the son and the mother's father, or her brother. The
woman is only a powerless go-between under obligation to the
men who are related through her.

The historical examples quoted by Louis Gernet are revealing.
He studies the matrimonial behaviour of various tyrants (in
Greece, tyranny is a regime of transition and arbitration between
the power of the aristocratic classes and the installation of democratic institutions). Tyrants come, more often than not, from big
noble families, and assert their legitimacy both through the age
of their lineage and popular support. Using archaic attitudes to
legitimise their overthrow of other clans they adopt marriage
patterns for themselves and their children which are quite different from those prevailing in the cities. Denys of Syracuse
marries two different women on the same day. One is Syracusan,
the other from Locres. Such bigamy can only be explained in
terms of a desire to intervene in the affairs of both cities. The
woman from Locres bears him a son who is destined to succeed
him in Syracuse. But, since he also has two daughters with the
Syracusan, he must neutralize them and he therefore marries
them off, one to his son, the other to his own brother, a good
example of endogamy which demonstrates that women 'transmit' power. Pisistratus, tyrant of Athens, is also bigamous; he is
married to an Argian whose sons stay in Argos where they
occupy powerful positions. He is also married to an Athenian
woman, from the illustrious Alcmaeonidae family, which
enables him to reconquer Athens after his first exile.

16. Gernet.

One could cite many examples that show the rights of a grand-son to the goods and particularly the sovereignty of his maternal ancestor, but we repeat that this does not amount to an example of matriarchy. The Greek language is in fact very precise: the word *metroios* (maternal) does not derive from *meter* (the mother) but from *metros* (the mother's father).[17] There are, however, undeniable reminders of a matrilineal system, particularly in view of the fact that classical Athenian law explicitly denies equality between the maternal and the paternal line. The dowry is the mark of the woman's (and her children's) renunciation of her family's possessions; in the case of the only daughter and heir (*epiclere*) the paternal uncle has the right to marry her. Therefore the tyrants who favour maternal descent are behaving in a totally anachronistic way which can only be explained as a conspicuous valuation of outdated customs.

The 'marriage with the princess' theme, to use Marie Del-court's phrase,[18] is a complementary sequence to the theme of the privileged relation between maternal ancestor and grandson. Myths and history provide three types:

1) The hero, seeking fortune and adventure, arrives in a foreign land where he marries the king's daughter, usually after having proved his valour. The marriage confers power on him. In the preliminary trial, the hero frequently risks his life (often the old king is put to death by the young king). Thus Alcmene marries Amphytrion who killed her father. Even Homer's kings are frequently seen to reign in their wife's country: Menelaus in Sparta, Achilles in Scyros, Peleus in Phtiotis, Telamon in Salamis. During the historical period, tyrants particularly adapted this model. Herodotus relates how Pisistratus married the daughter of Megacles the Alcmaeonide in 'the interests of the tyranny'. No doubt the case is somewhat different since the marriage does not naturalize Pisistratus, who is himself an Athenian, but it does confer the ability to rule through an alliance with an illustrious family.

2) The hero marries the dead king's wife. The most significant myth, is, of course, the legend of Oedipus. But there is also Gyges (Herodotus I, 10, 11) who kills the king of Lydia on the queen's order, marries his queen and becomes king; and there is Penelope who appears, despite the ambiguities of the text, to give access to the throne of Ithaca.

17. Emile Benveniste, *Indo-European Language and Society*, London 1973.
18. Marie Delcourt, *Oedipe ou la légende du conquérant*, Paris 1944.

3. The princess's son attains power, on condition he has no father. The lack of father is expressed by the myth in a manner compatible with the ability to reign: the father is a god and the child is therefore legitimate with respect to the sacred, but the father does not partake in kinship relations and in claims to the throne. In that case, the trial usually takes place after the child's birth, 'exposure', attempted drowning and so on, along with the mother who is subjected to the chastity ordeal. The most common sequence shows the child taking power in his mother's country, possibly after having assassinated the ancestor or the maternal uncle.

These myths pose an interpretative problem with regard to women's status: the fact that women do not exercise power but transmit it is an only too familiar situation; what is more unusual is the way in which men attain power through women. Myths display the most diverse and contradictory situations. Sometimes the king reigns in his wife's country (uxorilocality) and a son succeeds him, or, on the contrary, leaves and reigns elsewhere. Sometimes he reigns in the country of his mother (or of the father of his mother), who resides with her spouse. Matrimonial unions sometimes reflect strict endogamy, sometimes the most pronounced exogamy, as in the case of the 'adventurer' who marries the king's daughter. One hero is credited with different kingdoms by different sequences. Thus Neoptolemus (Pyrrhus), Achille's son, is described by Euripides in *Andromache* as king of Scyros (his mother's country) and of Phtiotis (country of the first wife of his paternal grandfather, Peleus). Another mythical sequence makes him the king of Epirus, where he settles upon his return from the Trojan war, following the advice of the goddess Thetis, his paternal grandmother. Although king of Athens like his father Aegeus, Theseus nonetheless appears to hold rights over Troezen, of which his mother is a native and where he has left his illegitimate son Hippolytus. These complex and contradictory systems stand in contrast to Pericles's definition of a citizen of Athens in the fifth century: the son of an Athenian father and mother (having a non-Athenian mother is a cause of illegitimacy) who inherits his father's possessions.

Each myth, with its variants, would require a detailed analysis. In the framework of this article we can only consider the meaning of the 'incoherence' and ambiguity of myth, in comparison with the logic of the rules of force in the classical period.

One internal explanation is that myths point to realities that existed prior to their transcription, reinforced by the fact that they concern royalty, the supreme custodian of ancient customs. The second explanation is that primitive and archaic Greece seem to have remained uncertain (probably for centuries) about the nature of the links between a male individual and the paternal and maternal clans.

The combinations myths present are sufficiently diverse for us to deduce considerable flexibility and a capacity to adapt according to the needs of the clans or of a dominant clan, or even individuals, in their search for power. It is quite logical to assume that aristocratic behaviour had its equivalent among the populas. In any case, the image (given by certain anthropological schools) of primitive societies which exist only through rigid and immutable kinship rules does not seem to apply to primitive, nor even to archaic Greece. Herodotus (III, 50, 53) puts these words in the mouth of the daughter of a Corinthian tyrant, Periander, when she is addressing her brother: 'Many others, already, by claiming their mother's rights, have been denied their father's inheritance.' The anecdote is all the more meaningful in that the young man is faced with the question of reigning in his father's country, which he refuses to do because the latter killed his mother. Yet he cannot hope to rule in his maternal grandfather's country since his father has taken all his possessions: he simply takes his mother's clan's side. The hero's behaviour and the sister's remark demonstrate that belonging to two lineages is experienced as a conflict, but that the individual has the freedom to choose the maternal side.

There is the same ambivalence with regard to the advantages gained by keeping daughters and those gained by exchanging them. By keeping them the men of the lineage preserve the ability to reign, which may be passed on through the daughters. To exchange them is to ensure beneficial alliances and a right to watch other clans. In all instances, the paternal family keeps the daughters close at home before their marriage, very different to the attitude to boys. Fostering (education in another family or in the mother's family) is extremely rare among girls, as is the theme of the exposed child, particularly since it concerns a test of capacity to rule. Nevertheless (quite logically), the myth surrounding Semiramis contains an exposure sequence.

Mythology gives more importance to the father-daughter relationship than to mother-daughter relations. The most extreme example is of course Electra, who has her mother killed to avenge her father, or the goddess Athena who comes forth fully armed, from Zeus's skull, without having been born by a mother. But there are also Oedipus's daughters, who accompany their father to exile while his sons abandon him. The nymph Erigone, Dionysus's lover, hangs herself upon hearing of her father's death. The wide number of daughters who kill their fathers (whereas sons have a tendency to kill mothers) is the other facet of this privileged relationship. This contrasts with the Cretan couple Demeter/Persephone, organized around the mother-daughter relationship. We are therefore looking at sequences of different dates. Demeter and Persephone belong to the ancient Aegean heritage and evoke a strictly matrilineal kinship system. On the other hand, the appropriation of daughters by their fathers suggests transitional forms.

The period where possessions and power are transmitted solely through women gives way to a period where men, of the paternal clan where the daughters reside, are capable of controlling women's ability to transmit power for their own benefit. It is all the more necessary at this stage for daughters to remain at home, since matrilineal forms of inheritance of sovereignty are maintained. On the other hand, the ties between the son and the maternal family have little relevance since the boy can inherit only from his mother and cannot bring his father's possessions to the maternal clan. It is women's inferior status, their incapacity to exercise power directly, combined with their role of carriers of that power, which makes them valuable and dangerous for the paternal lineage. Hence, daughters inherit from their fathers, but rarely from their mothers, since that would reintroduce a coherent matrilineal system and give the maternal lineage a right of control over them. Where elements of matrilineal inheritance continue, it benefits the sons. Meanwhile, the need to control daughters is resolved in primitive Greece in a range of ways: one may either keep the daughter, who transmits power to a cousin or a complete outsider (the result is the same); or she is married into another lineage but keeps close ties, which may very well cause problems with the husband's family.

Thus, Euripides's tragedy *Andromache*, although it dates from much later than the period of mythical elaboration, shows Menelaus about to slay the concubine and the bastard son of his son-in-law (while the latter is absent) at his daughter's request. 'That which is mine is his, that which is his is mine', says

Menelaus of his son-in-law (verse 585). In this much later case of exogamic union, which is less favourable to the woman who will reside at her husband's house in a foreign land, the honour she brings through the nobility of her blood still entitles her to some rights.

In the same tragedy, Euripides has Hermione say (verse 146–152): 'This golden ornament glittering on my head, my clothes embroidered with all colours, were not given to me by the house of Achilles or of Pele [the husband's lineage] . . . They come from Laconia, *from my country* of Sparta. 'Tis Menelaus my father who gave them to me in my splendid dowry. *I have a right to speak up.*'

As for the princess who stays in her country, or the widowed queen who keeps the kingdom, her prerogatives are even clearer. She transmits legitimacy, a virtue embodied in the possession of the royal attributes: treasures, jewels, precious cloth, conferring sovereignty on the person who holds them. But in Greek, treasure room and nuptial room, which remains the Queen's room, are described by the same word: *thalamos*. The chest where the treasures are locked away (*larnax*) is also the chest where the exposed royal children and their mother are locked up in mythical ordeals. Sequences abound around the theme of the inheritance of royal talismans and the role of women. Medea enables Jason to conquer the golden fleece, property of her father. Atreus's wife gives her brother-in-law, Thyestes, the golden lamb, symbol of power, and this is the starting point for the series of murders in the lineage of the Atrides. Amphytrion manages to kill one of his enemies, Pterelaus, by seducing the daughter, who cuts the golden hair that made her father invulnerable.

What do all these myths reveal about the real status of women living in the Mycenaean, then the archaic period? Not much with regard to the concrete living conditions of female slaves, female serfs, or wives of small landowners. On the other hand, the legends confirm what the Mycenaean tablets suggested about the role of women of high lineage, a role which seems to have been maintained several centuries later. Their status seems to us very close to that of the princesses and queens of medieval and modern Europe, although the latter were subject to more rigid succession rules. They were subordinate to their fathers, objects for transactions which secured alliances, and therefore without any freedom of matrimonial choice, but they were also associated with power and possibly able to exercise it directly. Homer's queens rule when their husbands are fighting the Trojan war. The reproach made to Clytemnestra is not to have ruled over Argos while Agamemnon was away, but to have taken a lover on her own and not on her father's order, and of course having tried to retain power on the return of her husband by killing him.

The Downward Levelling of Greek Democracy

'Democracy' could not accept the status of women who had 'a right to speak up' because it would have had to extend it to all citizens' wives. It is significant that women's status in Sparta during the classical period was far higher than in Athens: Sparta had kept an aristocratic government. Similarly, the French Revolution of 1789 deprived all women of political rights, whereas the old régime accepted women holding fiefs and the rights that derived from it. But for the Greeks the situation was not so simple: centuries of patriarchy and of patrilineal descent were not behind them. On the contrary, they inherited a complex and contradictory web of systems for the inheritance of possessions and power. This web is acceptable when the unwritten laws of lineages are the rule, with the relationship of forces between clans who adopt this or that solution depending on the interest of the most powerful clan. But when it becomes a matter of writing laws, of making them applicable to all, it is evident that an exclusively patrilineal kinship system, compulsory exogamy, and the rupture between the woman and her family expressed by the dowry appear much simpler and above all much more beneficial to the male community. Henceforth, there is a correspondence between those who exercise power (in this case a right: citizenship) and those who transmit it. This is well expressed in this strophe, attributed to women, from Euripides' *Ion*:

> Men's greatest happiness
> is firmly established
> when in paternal rooms
> bloom young lives that promise to bear fruits.
> The sons will receive from their fathers
> the rich heritage which they will pass on
> one day to their own sons . . .[19]

19. Euripides, *Orestes*, Paris 1962, verse 560–62.
20. Aeschylus, *The Eumenides*, Paris, verse 658–61.

Contrary to the belief of Bachofen and Engels, the advent of the city-state did not mark 'the historical defeat of the female sex', which had occurred a long time before. But it marked a pronounced deterioration in the status of noble women, and hence of all women as a result of the ideology that accompanied it. In order to attack the last remnants of maternal descent, the Greeks denied that women played any part in the reproduction of the species. As Apollo declares in Aeschylus's *Eumenides*, 'It is not the woman who begets the one who is called the child: she is merely the nurse of the germ she has conceived. The one who begets is the male; *like a foreigner* she preserves the young shoot.'[20]

This famous declaration is no doubt extremist in comparison with the true practice of the Athenians. If the mother is a foreigner, then why does marriage between children of the same mother and of different fathers have to be proscribed? Why does Pericles require that a citizen be born of both an Athenian father and mother? This tragic extremism, taken up by the scientists (Anaxogaras, Aristotle), accurately reflects the fantasies of a male community which knows it needs women for reproduction, but dreams of doing without them. A dream which explains the importance of matricide in mythology.

Matricide appears as a defence/vengeance for the father by the son. The mother is punished for having been a bad wife, either because she asserted her independence or took sides with her clan against the interests of her husband. Orestes kills Clytemnestra; Alcmeon kills his mother, Eriphyle, who had sent her husband to fight and die along with her brother. Masculine solidarity is formed in the blood of the mother. While Orestes's crime is merely one mythical element among many others at the disposal of the imagination of Athenian poets, it is the one they have most widely used. The Orestes character appears in nearly half the Tragedians' works that have been passed on to us.

Nicole Loraux in *Les Enfants d'Athéna*[21] argues very convincingly that, in order to justify women's subordination, 'the Greeks set forth a sea of speeches'. First they deprived women of any civic identity through language itself. There is no feminine Greek word for Athenian; there are only women of Athens or wives of Athenians. On the other hand there is a feminine word for Spartan. The fatherland is, of course, the land of the fathers. From Hesiod on, most authors used the expression 'the female

21. Nicole Loraux, *Les Enfants d'Athéna*, Paris 1981.

race' (*genos gunaikon*) to speak of women; on one side the Athenian people (*demos*) made up of the men of its tribes; on the other, a race from nowhere, which is solely a sex. And since in Athens citizenship derives from being a native, the equation between femininity and uprooting had to be proposed. Women do not and cannot have a fatherland; and so that everyone will know it myths of origin are there to justify it irrefutably. Nicole Loraux shows there indeed exists a first Athenian man, Erichtonius, but no first Athenian woman: only Pandora, the first woman whom the gods made be born in Athens. Another myth: after the city of Athens was founded, Athena and Poseidon quarreled over who would rule over it. In that non-civilized period, women as well as men voted, and there were more of them. They tilted the vote in favour of Athena. Poseidon was furious; men comforted him by depriving women forever of the right to vote and the right to bear a name and pass it on.

Finally, since the protection of the City by a female deity was suspect (Athenian democrats had inherited Athena from a remote past), she was featured as a warrior virgin, born without a mother, out of Zeus's skull, and resolutely on the side of men. What Athenian citizens retained from the eponymous goddess is that she was a negation of femininity: she had no mother, was not a mother; she waged war; and she embodied creative intelligence at the service of Power.

The Expression of Sexual Conflicts in Tragedy

With the exception of a few fragments from Sappho's work, which demonstrate the high culture and relative autonomy of aristocratic women in the islands of the Aegean Sea in the seventh century, Greece has left no female writings. On the other hand, Greek tragedy and comedy dramatize the struggle of the sexes, and it is a sex struggle that has the force of class struggle, not a codified joust of the kind featured in Western traditions of the theatre or the novel (from Shakespeare to Racine and from Madame de la Fayette to Balzac), where the confrontation takes place in the context of a status accepted by all.

Greek tragedy lasted only one century, the sixth century in Athens. Organized by the City's magistrates, it was more a political act than a literary genre, with the City representing itself through the legitimizing of its values. It illustrates a transitional moment, not in the economic and political sense (such that 'democracy' triumphs as the aristocratic clans are weakened) but in a moral sense: it is the product of what could be described as the lagging behind of collective psychology. As Jean-Pierre Vernant puts it: 'The tragic turning point thus occurs when a gap develops at the heart of social experience. It is wide enough for the oppositions between legal and political thought on the one hand and the mythical and heroic traditions, on the other, to stand out quite clearly. Yet it is narrow enough for the conflict in values still to be a painful one and for the clash to continue to take place.'[22] The clash between sexes obsessively punctuates that confrontation.

The very nature of theatre means that value conflicts are embodied in characters, and thus in female as well as male characters. Railing against the 'race of women' as Hesiod had done and as Aristotle will do is no longer adequate. Women have to be made to speak on stage, rather than be advised to remain silent (Pericles). Despite the fact that actors and audiences are all men, the tragic authors did not manage to dramatise the woman-less world the City wanted to be. Even though they are acted by men, the female characters embody women and embody them with rare vigour. Whether this is achieved through a miracle of genius transcending the ideas of the period and of the author or through the logic internal to the work itself, which feeds on the conflict and dies in its resolution, is unimportant. None of the female stooges of whom contemporary literary hacks and film-makers are so fond are found in Greek tragedy. Better: the only voice to come from Greek women, however deformed and mediated by the rules of the theatre, is that of tragic heroines, a voice of revolt and hatred.

Several themes are worth underlining because they are common to the entire tragic theatre: 1) Women personify and claim the past. There is an obvious symmetry between the rejection of ancient, aristocratic society and that of feminine influence in all domains. Women are the ones who defend the ancient values: those of clan kinship, those prior to the emergence of law, those of the old religion. First kinship: there is a confrontation between the solidarity of blood ties, the preeminent role of maternal descent on one side, and on the other, the superiority of paternal descent and of marriage over kinship (cf. Clytemnestra's murder by Orestes). Next, the values which existed

22. Vernant, p. 4.

prior to the emergence of law; we know to what extent they were linked to the structures of kinship: Antigone buries her brother to obey the unwritten laws of family piety against the written laws of Creon, those of the City. Finally, the values of the old religion: women deities are the ancient gods like the Erinyes, bound to the clan, or those ancient statues one embraces at a time of peril with a great deal of emotional fervour (Aeschylus, *The Seven against Thebes*). Opposite these stand the young gods of Olympus who are revered with measure and distance as befits the citizen.

Why was the past thus equated with women and why was victory over the past described as a victory (sometimes dubious) over women? This could only be because Athenian democracy represented the outcome of a process begun several millenia earlier, and the Greeks sensed — confusedly — that the past had been more favourable to women. Moreover, since the mythical or historical past was experienced as the reverse of the present, it was logical to personify it as what in the city represented its opposite, women. But this symmetry could not be only symbolic; it now rested (and this was the key to its efficiency), on tangible realities: memories passed on from generation to generation of a more balanced relationship between the sexes, and above all of the power of certain queens or priestesses; anxiety at the thought of a regeneration of any share of feminine influence as was suggested by the mere physical presence of women in the City. It should also be acknowledged that tragedy reflects the real feelings of women of the classical age, taking refuge in the only values they were left with: a fierce defence of a family unit which is made up of their children, themselves, possibly their own clan, and a proclaimed alienation from the *genos* of the husband they were supposed to be part of; indifference to the laws of the City and preservation of the cults rejected by the civic ideal. The last feature is in fact common to all antiquity: women adopt unofficial gods in greater numbers than men. Again, Antigone's tirade best delineates the conflict of values: 'I did not think that your edicts held so much force that they permitted a mortal to violate divine laws: unwritten laws, these, but intangible. They have been in force, not since yesterday or today, but since the beginning, and no one saw their birth . . . Had I been forced to leave a body that my mother bore without sepulchre, I would never have been consoled.'[23]

2) Women are not deceived by masculine values. Tragic

dialogue suggests this capacity for derision with regard to the dominant sex, which seems to have been a defence of the oppressed for millennia. In the classical theatre, with rare exceptions, when a woman adopts the accusations of men against the 'female race', it is in order to deceive the man concerned. Euripides' *Medea* is a good example of this two-fold language. 'A woman is weak and inclined to weep', says Medea to Jason when she pretends to obey him. Before this point, in front of the women of Corinth who support her, the foreigner, in the name of feminine solidarity, she had drawn this picture of the status of women:

Of all that breathes and is conscious
None is more to pity than us women.
First, we have to auction
And buy a husband who will be the master of our body,
A misfortune more costly than the price paid for it.
And yet, our greatest risk lies there: is the status quo good or bad?
To part from one's husband is to dishonour oneself,
And to deny him is forbidden to women.
Entering an unknown world, new laws
of which the native home taught nothing,
A girl has to guess the art of using them with her bed companion . . .

There is, furthermore, this rejection of male superiority based on valour as a warrior:

We are told that in our houses we lead
a life free of danger while they go to war!
A bad reason: I would rather go three times to combat
than give birth once to a child!

A series of very mundane remarks that Euripides probably heard from all the 'ill-bred' women of Athens — except for this: that he puts these words in the mouth of a mythical princess plotting to kill the sovereigns of the City and her own children in order to destroy the husband who abandoned her. The fact is, however, that the women of Corinth whose king is being slain, remain complicitly silent. The contrast shows the extent to which Euripides was aware of the potential for violence contained in women's subordination. The *Bacchae* — by the same author — illustrates this on another level: a new cult is enough impetus for women's civilized nature (that is, their domestication by men) to

23. Sophocles, *Antigone*, verse 445–60.

give way to their savage nature.

The entire tragic theatre seems to prove that women's internalization of their inferiority was far from established. Another example, among so many others, is the dialogue from Aeschylus's *Seven against Thebes* between Eteocles, the ruling king, and the women of the city. The city is under siege and women have flung themselves at the feet of the statues of the ancient deities to implore salvation; the king threatens them (to no avail) with stoning if they do not go home and let men take care of praying to the gods, in a decent manner. Exasperated, Eteocles exclaims: 'O Zeus, what gift hast thou made unto us with the female sex!' The Chorypheum's (women) answer: 'Pitiful sex . . . like that of men when their city is taken.' The remarkable insolence of this statement provides, at the least, evidence of some resistance to male domination.

3) Women are rarely described as weak, as unable to fight. Rather the opposite — as is demonstrated by readings from Hesiod, Semonides and Herodotus, who compile with relish all the tales (real or invented) of women warriors around the Mediterranean. The civilizing role of the male community consists of harnessing female savagery, which expresses itself in two directions: thirst for power leading to attempted murder, and sexual energy. The only remedy is marriage, on condition that the husband is capable of dominating his wife. Tragedy, through its very nature, dramatizes the failure of this civilizing endeavour. Clytemnestra, Hecuba and the Danaids are not virile women, as all explanations continuously reiterate: they are archetypes of Femininity left to itself. Tragic heroines behave like men. They give orders, dominate, defy their enemies, and even kill them as did Clytemnestra who, as J. P. Vernant has shown,[24] executed Agamemnon by following a sacrifice-hunting ritual, two male prerogatives *par excellence*. In tragedy the misdeed lies in a woman doing what a man does and inverting the social relations which guarantee the order of the City and are guaranteed by the gods. The misdeed does not stem from not conforming to a pseudo-feminine nature (gentleness, fragility, congenital masochism) that the Greeks had not yet invented. The citizen of Athens thinks in political categories: those who vote in the City versus those who are kept out of the civic body (women,

24. Vernant and Vidal-Naquet, *Tragedy and Myth in Ancient Greece*, Brighton 1981.

slaves, aliens) and must behave in accordance with the inferior status assigned to them. A woman, or a slave, is like a man, but a defeated man (thus they are always potentially in revolt and have to be crushed). Only with later philosophical thought was the idea developed that slaves or women were inferior not only because of what they did, but because of what they were.

From Old Goddesses to Young Gods

The relationship between women and the Sacred, or more accurately between femininity and the Sacred, has been much more widely studied by Hellenists than the aspects we have focused upon so far.

The dominant thesis is briefly as follows: from the Upper Palaeolithic on, pre-Hellenic civilizations were involved in the cult of one or several Great Goddesses, designated by the term Mother Earth, or Great Mother. Around her was a symbolic constellation connecting her to certain elements of the cosmos (moon — night) and of nature (water — plants — wild beasts). The Goddess personified Woman Mother whose fertile power demanded veneration, and was identified with the Earth's fertility. With the arrival of the first Indo-Europeans, the Goddess was assigned a *paredre* (child or young lover) who was at first her subordinate; then, with the passing centuries and invasions, the *paredre* took on a dominant position, until the formation of the very patriarchal Indo-European pantheon. Except for the interpretation of the attributes of the goddess, to which we shall return later, this thesis is confirmed by arch-aeology, by mythology, and by the persistence of archaic rituals in classical Greece.

The problem lies in what this periodization tells us about the real condition of women. Does the existence of one or several female goddesses imply a situation of dominance by women? Does their existence indicate that women are at the root of religious phenomena and thus that women make the goddesses? Or is it men 'who partially alienated their existence in Nature and in Woman and later reconquered it'?[25] This last thesis, popular among contemporary anthropologists, rests on the old idea that the femininity of the Sacred is attributable to the terror

25. de Beauvoir, p. 100.

that men experience before the mystery of feminine fertility; as the development of rational thought progressed with the evolution of technology, men freed themselves from their fears and invented male gods corresponding to their domination in the material world.

We believe these allegations to be grossly simplistic. First of all, the religious periodization mentioned above corresponds precisely to a social and political periodization marked by a deterioration, sometimes gradual, sometimes brutal, in the status of women: there is indeed, then, a relation between the femininity of the divine and real women. Anyone who doubts this only has to consider the impression made by a contemporary remark: 'I encountered God; He is a woman and is black.'

Secondly, the concept of fear inspired by maternity explains nothing. Pre-scientific people are 'fearful', or better, respectful of everything, water and fire, the sun and night, wild beasts, the neighbouring tribe, and, no doubt, the magic contained in women's fertility. Even then, this last point may be qualified: men appear to have known about their responsibility in the reproduction of the species for a very long time; the countless Palaeolithic Venuses do not seem to convey terror. Actually, the Sacred is never the pure projection of human fear but much more an attempt to explain the world as it is, from cosmic phenomena to political realities.

Supposing that we accept the explanation of fear for very primitive societies, how can it be applied to Crete and its civilization? If technical progress, the artisan's skill at shaping matter as opposed to the routine of the agriculturalist, is the means by which men free themselves from deifying femininity, Crete should have a pantheon dominated by gods, and archaic Greece Great Goddesses; but it is in fact the other way around. If technology were an exclusive prerogative of men, and the earth experienced as essentially female, artisanal professions and their protective deities would not have feminine attributes in periods of patriarchal triumph.

We believe that the fundamental mistake lies in the incorrect idea that goddesses are exclusively fertility deities. Archaeology and mythology actually prove quite the opposite. Most specialists on Crete (Charles Picard, Paul Faure) reject the idea of Cretan monotheism; there were several goddesses, protectresses of specific geographical locations and endowed with diverse functions. The deities were goddesses of the Earth, but also of heaven, of water, of mountains; they protected the fertility of fields but also wild plants; they stimulated the fertility of herds but they were also mistresses of wild animals. Fishermen and navigators invoked them as frequently as agriculturalists. Agrarian cults were undoubtedly predominant but they were also predominant at the time of the masculinized pantheon of archaic and even classical Greece, when the majority of the population lived from the land. To sum up, these deities were sovereigns of the entire society (Paul Faure). They were *potniai*, in archaistic Greek, which translates as mistresses or sovereigns, and from which the Latin *potens* derives. In fact maternity was not a mandatory attribute: Diktynna and Britormartis, two Cretan *potniai*, were virgins. Neither the excavations in the island's caves that harboured cults in the Minoan period, nor the iconography, point to a male god; the thesis that makes the bull a deity is much debated today. Even if we accept the divinity of the bull, it could only be subordinate to the goddess, as the animal to the human. Deities seem to be venerated by colleges of priestesses who are pictorially depicted performing sacrifices; male officiants are rare. In the caves groups of young men and young women probably went through rites of passage under the goddess's protection.

There can be little doubt, then, that the Sacred, all the Sacred, was feminine in Crete, as it is masculine in our age. When Cretans think of the Divine, that is to say, Power, they see a woman or, if we prefer, a feminine principle. To conclude that they had a matriarchy would be extrapolation with no basis and would contradict what knowledge we do have of the social reality of Crete. Nevertheless, the existence of Great Goddesses tends to be incompatible with a patriarchal system. No doubt, Asiatic patrilineal and patriarchal monarchies did have a Great Goddess (examples abound); but all such societies evolved inexorably and quickly toward polytheism with a dominant male god, at least in official religion.

We would propose the following as the most likely explanation: Goddesses were a survival which was particularly vigorous in Crete as a result of the gap we have observed between its civilization and its environment. This survival may be explained by the extreme conservatism inherent in religious phenomena; a survival from an epoch in which the tribal ancestor must have been a woman. We know how important founding myths are in most primitive periods and the way in which the time of the ancestors is assimilated to the time of the Sacred. Though the continuing feminization of the divine can temporarily coexist with male political power (the king is the Goddess's lover), it nonetheless generates a specific relation to the Sacred on the part of real women. It would be useful if psychoanalysis (particularly Lacanian) would let us know around what 'primacy of the phallus' individual personality was constructed in Crete. But this is not the purpose of this study. On the other hand, it is clear that women found a support, a source of social and individual dignity, in their potential identification with goddesses.

The Sacred was their domain, not as objects incarnating the divine, but indeed as subjects. Apart from the King, there seem to have been no priests in Crete; no one can believe that priestesses had no political influence. Moreover, excavations in caves bear witness to a feminine world: numerous representations, ex-votos are consecrated to Eileithya, goddess of childbirth, who later became a goddess of the last category in classical Greece. To help women go through their pregnancy, to assist them in childbirth, can hardly be regarded as an exercise in masculine creativity, especially in a matrilineal system. Men seem not to have entered some of the goddess's sacred caves. Centuries later, Pausanias (II, 35, 3sq) spoke of a cult, in Argolid, consecrated to a very ancient Demeter Chthonia, to whom only women made sacrifices, and to Eileithya whose statue men were not allowed to see.

Bearing in mind the fierceness with which men keep religious objects to themselves in African tribes, and the energy with which they barred women from performing sacrifices in classical Greece, we can measure the distance travelled from this feminine religious authority and the stakes inherent in the mastery of the divine.

Mycenaean society reveals yet more contradictions: goddesses apparently remained more numerous than gods and held a dominant position. Charles Picard points out the central role played by Hera, surrounded by gods identified as Zeus and Dionysus, who appear as father and son under the goddess's authority. Obviously much was borrowed from Crete: the Demeter cult, identical representations of the *potniai*, and, as we have already pointed out, the importance of priestesses. The reason for the semi-victory of Crete over the Indo-European gods lies in the cultural superiority of Cretans over the Achaean warriors, and ancient man's caution before foreign deities: the gods of the vanquished are not destroyed, they are assimilated or added to one's own gods. Nonetheless, the undeniably patriarchal character of Mycenaean civilization had to be reflected in the realm of the Sacred; phallic symbols, unknown in Crete, appeared along with male gods.

Thereafter, the gap between the female character of the Sacred, which was, however, declining, and the status of women widened. This gap is apparent in relations between women, and in their relations with men. The female sovereign and the priestesses still derived power from the existence of great goddesses; the Queen was endowed with magic powers; priestesses, who became soothsayers, wielded a determining influence over these superstitious warriors, eager to win the favour of the gods. Priests and priestesses served the royal person; temples guaranteed the king that his world would function properly, from the march of the stars to the obedience of warriors and the fertility of herds.

However, the power of priestesses should not be allowed to hide the fact that Mycenae appears to have performed human sacrifice, as is indicated by Homer, and the list of probable sacrificial victims on the tablets shows a higher number of women. These women were evidently slaves; the sacrifice of the princess (Iphigenia) was probably reserved for exceptional circumstances. The reason for the greater number of sacrificial women is the greater number of female goddesses to whom it is more fitting to offer individuals of the same sex.

To sum up, Mycenaean society remained convinced of women's superiority in relation to the Sacred. But the social deterioration of most women made them into mediators of the divine instead of a group able to organize the religious realm in accordance with its own interests.

The development toward ranking the pantheon of gods in conformity with the terrestrial order took place slowly but inexorably. Gods replaced goddesses: Apollo drives Gaea away from Delphi, Zeus does the same with Dodona; on the Acropolis of Athens, the old statues of goddesses are relegated to the rank of minor deities. The outcome of this process is that religious practices broke up along class or sex lines. This is probably more pronounced in Archaic and especially classical Greece than in Crete, or even in Mycenae, where the official pantheon was ruled over by Zeus, sovereign, celestial and political god *par excellence*. The other great deities were male (Poseidon, Hades, Apollo), were masculinized goddesses (Artemis, Athena) or were demoted: Hera whom Zeus hanged by the feet; Aphrodite whom a mere mortal could wound with impunity; Demeter, a Cretan heritage, whose name means Mother-Goddess, restricted to the domain of agrarian fertility; Hestia made to embody the permanence of the household. Thus, goddesses were no longer 'deities of the entire society', but incarnations of functions and values that had devolved to women. Even Athena was woman in that she was the craftswoman of weaving. It was during this period that there clearly emerged what have been described as the archetypes of femininity. The identification of women and the earth, because both are possessed and dominated by man, was indeed commonplace: 'I give you this girl in the hope of a plowing which will produce legitimate children', a father would say at wedding agreements. But this identification was the opposite of a valuation of femininity and took place at a time when, as we have pointed out, women were most removed from work and the ownership of land. Femininity, even in the divine order, was henceforth restricted to the area of reproduction of men and nature; Hera sponsored legitimate marriage, Demeter wheat growing.

Concerned to break away from the persistent ambiguities of mythical thought, some went further. From the second half of the sixth century onwards, philosophers condemned mythology and endeavoured to build a rational system of thought based on the opposition of contraries. Dualist classifications, inevitably symbolized by male and female, gradually gained the upper hand. Woman became, in essence, all that is most alien to man. The elements of the cosmos were themselves organized in hierarchical order. For the pre-Socratics, the earth and water were the lowest on the value scale; and they were precisely elements with feminine connotations; on the other hand air and fire were endowed with a superior value and were 'masculine'. Plato believed that the body, the prison of the spirit, was earthly. Aristotle perfected a construction (which had a most brilliant future) opposing Femininity/Matter to Virility/Spirit, Passivity to Activity, Water to Fire.

This dualist thought did not, as is generally assumed, come in the wake of great myths; it was by no means inherent in the human spirit. For a Cretan, the goddess was *also* the Earth, but at the *same time* the heavens; she was the active principle *par excellence*, and not passive Matter.

However, alongside official religions and the philosophical interpretations, there existed a 'third religion', which Hellenists designate by the expression 'native cults', 'local deities', 'popular rituals': a religion that was a great deal more archaic and in which some remnants of the ancient *potniai* survived. Rituals had sometimes become incomprehensible to followers; the gods themselves were 'odd'; for example, one Zeus Stratios in Mylassa in Caria, dressed as a woman (hairstyle and necklace), endowed with false breasts — we do not know whether he was a former goddess masculinized, or whether he represented a desire to appropriate the powers of femininity.

Women, Greek authors tell us, are closer to ancient deities and they will become closer to new ones, like Dionysis. Throughout the Greek and Roman world, women found in non-official religious sects a possibility of refuge and an opportunity for protest.

At the end of this inevitably schematic study, several facts should be underlined:

1) The concept of a natural division of labour is contradicted by reality. Women do everything that men do, at different periods. The division of labour therefore appears as eminently historical.

2) The nature of the labour performed by each of the sexes is of far less importance than the social relations within which it is carried out. Whether women are more or less 'productive', more or less responsible for activities essential to the community, is a minor factor. Their status is above all determined by their overall situation in the community.

3) In the slave societies we have studied, women's subordination works as a model for other forms of domination; this reinforces the idea that dominance over women preceded the formation of classes.

4) The equation 'slave mode of production/State/patriarchal and patrilineal system' was preceded by long periods during which a class society coexisted with various modes of subordination of women. In such cases, there is no mechanical connection between a social formation and the status of women; economically and politically related societies may be more or less oppressive. The relation is dialectical and tendential, although the evolution always went the same way.

5) The interpretation of Greek myths does not imply, as Bachofen and Engels believed, the existence of primaeval matriarchy. On the other hand, it is as much an over-simplification to

read in them the universality and atemporality of male dominance. The major and indisputable element that emerges is that historically women's status deteriorates, in relation to social and political changes, even if this deterioration occurs after a time lag.

6) There is convincing evidence for sexual conflict; its acuteness, even when women had lost out, seems in our view to rule out a peaceful subordination of women.

7) The way women are distributed in classes requires an analysis specific to each social formation. Thus, the Mycenaean Queens or priestesses are undeniably part of the ruling class. On the other hand, the wife of an Athenian aristocrat, denied any economic control and political role, confined in a *gynaeceum*, cannot be classified as a member of the ruling class. Nor does she live the lot of a slave. A specific concept is needed to define her status, particularly given the fact that it could apply to other modes of production. This problem lies outside the scope of this article but could be the object of subsequent research.

Bibliography

Adams, Robert McC. *The Evolution of Urban Society* (Chicago: Aldine, 1966).

Ardrey, Robert *African Genesis* (New York: Atheneum Press, 1961).

Ardrey, Robert *The Territorial Imperative* (New York: Atheneum Press, 1966).

Bachofen, Johann Jacob *Myth, Religion, and Mother-Right: Selected Writings of J. J. Bachofen* (Princeton: Princeton University Press, 1967).

Barash, David *Sociobiology and Behaviour* (New York: Elsevier, 1982).

Bleir, Ruth 'Myths of the Biological Inferiority of Women' in *University of Michigan Papers* in *Women's Studies* 2 (1976).

Blumberg, Rae Lesser *Stratification: Socioeconomic and Sexual Inequality*, (Dubuque, Iowa: William C. Brown Company, 1978).

Boserup, Ester *The Conditions of Agricultural Growth* (Chicago: Aldine, 1965).

Boserup, Ester *Woman's Role in Economic Development* (New York: St. Martin's, 1970).

Briffault, Robert *The Mothers* (London: George Allen and Unwin, 1952).

Brown, Judith 'Iroquois Women: An Ethnohistoric Note' in Reiter, pp. 235–51 (1975).

Campbell, Joseph *The Masks of God: Oriental Mythology* (New York: Viking Press, 1962).

Campbell, Joseph *The Masks of God: Occidental Mythology* (New York: Viking Press, 1964).

Caulfield, Mima 'Universal Sex Oppression? A Critique from Marxist Anthropology' in *Catalyst* 10–11, pp. 60–77 (1977).

Chagnon, Napoleon 'Yanomamo: The True People' in *National Geographic* 150, pp. 211–23 (1976).

Childe, Gordon C. *What Happened in History* (Hammondsworth, England: Penguin, 1942).

Childe, V. Gordon *Social Evolution* (London: Watts, 1951).

Chodorow, Nancy 'Family Structure and Feminine Personality' in Rosaldo and Lamphere, pp. 43–66 (1974).

Chodorow, Nancy *The Reproduction of Mothering: Psychoanalysis and the Sociology of Gender* (Berkeley: University of California Press, 1978).

Cohen, Ronald and Middleton, John (eds.) 'Comparative Political Systems' in *Natural History*, (New York: Garden City, 1967).

Coontz, Stephanie 'Insult and Injury: Growing Old in America' in Coontz and Frank (eds.) *Life in Capitalist America*, (New York: Pathfinder, 1975).

Coontz, Stephanie 'Fallacies of Matriarchal Theories', unpublished paper, (The Evergreen State College, 1979).

Coontz, Stephanie and Reed, Evelyn 'Two Views of Women's Evolution' in *International Socialist Review* (February 1978).

Dahlberg, Francis *Woman the Gatherer* (New Haven: Yale University Press, 1981).

D'Andrade, Roy G. 'Sex Differences and Cultural Institutions' in Maccoby, Eleanor D. (ed.) *The Development of Sex Differences*, pp. 174—204 (Stanford: Stanford University Press, 1966).

Davis, Elizabeth *The First Sex* (Baltimore: Penguin Books, 1971).

Dawkins, Richard *The Selfish Gene* (New York: Oxford University Press, 1976).

Davis, Shelton and Mathews, Robert *The Geological Imperative* (Cambridge: Anthropology Resource Centre, 1976).

Deavey, C. A., Katz, P. A., and Zalk, S. R. 'Baby X: The Effects of Gender Labels on Adult Response to Infants' in *Sex Roles* 2, pp. 103–11 (1975).

The Dialectics of Biology Group, Steven Rose, (ed.) *Against Biological Determinism* (New York: Allison and Busby, 1982).

The Dialectics of Biology Group, Steven Rose (ed.) *Towards a Liberatory Biology* (New York: Allison and Busby, 1982).

Diner, Helen *Mothers and Amazons* (New York: Julian Press, 1965).

Divale, William and Harris, Marvin 'Population, Warfare and the Male Supremacist Complex' in *American Anthropologist* 78, pp. 521–38 (1976).

Douglas, Mary *Purity and Danger* (London: Routledge and Kegan Paul, 1966).

Ember, Carol 'The Relative Decline in Women's Contribution to Agriculture with Intensification' in *American Anthropologist* 85, pp. 285–304 (1983).

Engels, Frederick *The Origins of the Family, Private Property, and the State* (New York: International, 1972).

Faithorn, Elizabeth 'The Concept of Pollution Among the Kafe of the Papua New Guinea Highlands' in Reiter, pp. 127–40 (1975).

Fjellman, Stephen 'Hey, You Can't Do That: A Response to Divale and Harris "Population, Warfare and the Male Supremacist Complex" ', paper delivered at the meetings of the Society for Cross-Cultural Research, East Lansing, Michigan (1977).

Fluehr-Lobban, C. 'A Marxist Reappraisal of the Matriarchate' in *Current Anthropology* 20, pp. 341–48 (1979).

Frieze, Irene; Parsons, Jacqueline; Johnson, Paula; Ruble, Diana and Zelman, Gail *Women and Sex Roles: A Social Psychological Perspective*, (New York: Norton, 1978).

Godelier, Maurice 'Modes of Production, Kinship, and Demographic Structures' in Bloch, Maurice, *Marxist Analysis and Social Anthropology*, pp. 3—28 (New York: John Wiley and Sons, 1975).

Goldman, Irving 'Status Rivalry and Cultural Evolution in Polynesia' in Cohen and Middleton (1967).

Gough, Kathleen 'The Modern Disintegration of Matrilineal Descent Groups' in Schneider, David M. and Gough, Kathleen (eds.), pp. 631–54 (1961).

Gould, Stephen Jay *Ever Since Darwin*, (New York: W.W. Norton, 1977).

Gould, Stephen Jay 'Biological Potential vs. Biological Determinism' in *Natural History Magazine* (May 1976).

Gould, Stephen Jay *The Mismeasurement of Man*, (New York: W. W. Norton, 1981).

Gould, Stephen Jay 'Genes on the Brain: Review of Charles J. Lumsden and Edward O. Wilson, "Promethean Fire: Reflections on the Origins of the Mind" ' in *New York Review of Books* (June 1983).

Hahn, Emily *On the Side of the Apes*, (New York: Crowell, 1971).

Hampshire, Stuart 'The Illusion of Sociobiology: Review of E. O. Wilson, "On Human Nature" ' in *New York Review of Books*, (October 1978).

Harper, Edward 'Fear and the Status of Women' in *Southwestern Journal of Anthropology* 25, pp. 81–95 (1959).

Hays, H. R. *The Dangerous Sex: The Myth of Feminine Evil*, (New York: Simon and Schuster, 1964).

Hirschfeld, Lawrence; Howe, James and Levin, Bruce 'Warfare, Infanticide, and Statistical Inference: A Comment on Divale and Harris' in *American Anthropologist* 80, pp. 110–5.

Hubbard, Ruth and Lowe, Marian *Genes and Gender Two*, (New York: Gordian Press, 1979).

Lancaster, C.S. 'Women, Horticulture and Society in Sub-Saharan Africa' in *American Anthropologist* 78, pp. 539—64 (1976).

Lancaster, Chet and Lancaster, Jane B. 'On the Male Supremacist Complex: A Reply to Divale and Harris' in *American Anthropologist* 80, pp. 115–7 (1978).

Lancaster, Jane *Primate Behaviour and the Emergence of Human Culture*, (New York: Holt, Rinehart & Winston, 1975).

Lancaster, Jane 'Carrying and Sharing in Human Evolution' in *Human Nature*, pp. 82–9 (1978).

Leacock, Eleanor 'Myths of Male Dominance' in *Monthly Review*, (New York, 1981).

Leacock, Eleanor (forthcoming) 'Women, Power, and Authority' in Dube, Leela, Leacock, Eleanor, and Ardener, Shirley (eds.) *Visability and Power: Essays on*

210

Women in Society and Development, (Delhi: Oxford University Press).

Leacock, Eleanor, and Nash 'Ideologies of Sex: Archetypes and Stereotypes' in *Annals of the New York Academy of Sciences* 285, pp. 618–45 (1977).

Lederer, Wolfgang *The Fear of Women*, (New York: Grune and Stratton, 1968).

Lee, Dorothy *Freedom and Culture* (New Jersey: Prentice-Hall, 1959).

Lee, R. B. and De Vone, Irven (eds.) *Man the Hunter,* (Chicago: Aldine).

Leibowitz, Lila 'Perspectives on the Evolution of Sex Differences' in Reiter, pp. 20–35 (1975).

Leibowitz, Lila *Females, Males, Families: A Biosocial Approach*, (Massachusetts: Duxbury Press, 1978).

Lewontin, Richard 'Sociobiology — A Caricature of Darwinism' in Asquith, P. and Suppe, F. (eds.) *PSA*, v. 2, pp. 22–31 (1977).

Lewontin, Richard 'The Corpse in the Elevator: Review of Books on Biological Determinism' in *New York Review of Books,* (January 1983).

Lowie, Robert 'Political Organization Among the American Aborigines' in Cohen and Middleton (1967).

Lumsden, Charles J. and Wilson, Edward O. *Genes, Mind and Culture: The Evolutionary Process*, (Cambridge: Harvard University Press, 1981).

Lumsden, Charles and Wilson, Edward *Promethean Fire: Reflections on the Origins of Mind*, (Cambridge: Harvard University Press).

Maccoby, Eleanor and Jacklin, Carol *The Psychology of Sex Differences*, (Stanford: Stanford University Press, 1974).

MacCormack, Carol 'Proto-Social to Adult: A Sherbro Transformation' in Mac-Cormack and Strathern, pp. 95–118 (1980).

MacCormack, Carol and Strathern, Marilyn *Nature, Culture and Gender*, (Cambridge: Cambridge University Press, 1980).

Martin, M. Kay and Voorhie, Barbara *Female of the Species*, (New York: Columbia University Press, 1975).

Martin, Kay 'South American Foragers: A Case Study in Devolution' in *American Anthropologist* 71 (1969).

McGrew, W. C. 'The Female Chimpanzee as a Human Evolutionary Prototype' in Dahlberg, pp. 35–74 (1981).

McGuigan, Dorothy (ed.) *New Research on Women and Sex Roles,* (Ann Arbor: University of Michigan, 1976).

Mead, Margaret *Sex and Temperament in Three Primitive Societies*, (New York: William Morrow, 1963).

Mellaart, James *Catal Huyuk: A Neolithic Town in Anatolia*, (New York: McGraw Hill, 1967).

Morris, Desmond *The Naked Ape*, (New York: McGraw Hill, 1968).

Morris, Desmond *The Human Zoo*, (New York: McGraw Hill, 1969).

Murdock, George P. 'Comparative Data on the Division of Labour by Sex' in *Social Forces* (1937).

Murdock, George P. and Provost, Caterina 'Factors in the Division of Labour by Sex: A Cross-Cultural Analysis' in *Ethnology* 12 (1973).

Nance, John *The Gentle Tasaday*, (New York: Harcourt, Brace, Jovanovich, 1975).

Nash, Jill 'A Note on Groomprice' in *American Anthropologist* 80 (1978).

Oakley, Ann *Sex, Gender, and Society*, (New York: Harper and Row, 1972).

Ortner, Sherry 'Is Female to Male as Nature is to Culture?' in Rosaldo and Lamphere, pp. 67–88 (1974).

Ortner, Sherry and Whitehead, Harriet (eds.) *Sexual Meanings: The Cultural Construction of Gender and Sexuality*, (Cambridge: University of Cambridge Press, 1981).

Parkes, Seymour and Parker, Hilda 'The Myth of Male Superiority: Rise and Demise' in *American Anthropologist* 81, pp. 289–309 (1979).

Paulme, Denise *Women of Tropical Africa*, (Berkeley: University of California Press, 1960).

Pilbeam, David 'An Idea We Could Live Without: The Naked Ape', in Montagu, Ashley (ed.), *Man and Aggression*, pp. 110–21 (New York: Oxford University Press, 1973).

Poewe, Karla *Matrilineal Ideology* (1981).

Pogrebin, Letty *Growing up Free*, (New York: McGraw Hill, 1980).

Pomeroy, Sarah *Goddesses, Whores, Wives and Slaves: Women in Classical Antiquity*, (New York: Schocken, 1975).

'The Predatory Baboons of Kekopey, Harden, and Strum' in *Natural History* (March 1976).

Quain, B. H. 'The Iroquois' in Mead, Margaret (ed.), *Co-operation and Competition Among Primitive Peoples*, (Boston: Beacon, 1961).

Quinn, Naomi 'Anthropological Studies on Women's Status' in *Annual Review in Anthropology* 6, pp. 181–225 (1977).

Reed, Evelyn *Women's Evolution: From Matriarchal Clan to Patriarchal Family*, (New York: Pathfinder, 1975).

Reiter, Rayna (ed.) 'Toward an Anthropology of Women' in *Monthly Review*, (New York, 1975).

Reiter, Rayna Rapp 'The Search for Origins: Unraveling the Threads of Gender Hierarchy' in *Critique of Anthropology* 3, pp. 5–24 (1977).

Richmond-Abbott, Marie 'Early Socialization of the American Female' in Abbott, Richmond (ed.), *The American Woman: Her Past, Her Present, and Her Future*, (New York: Holt, Rinehart and Winston, 1979).

Rohrlich-Leavitt, Ruby 'Peaceable Primates and Gentle People' in Watson, Barbara (ed.), *Women's Studies: The Social Realities*, (New York: Harper and Row, 1976).

Rohrlich-Leavitt, Ruby; Sykes, Barbara and Weatherford, Elizabeth 'Aboriginal Women: Male and Female Anthropological Perspectives' in Reiter, pp. 110–

212

126 (1975).

Rosaldo, Michelle Zimbalist 'Women, Culture and Society: an Overview' in Rosaldo and Lamphere, pp. 17–42 (1974).

Rosaldo, Michelle Zimbalist and Lamphere, Louise (eds.) *Women, Culture, and Society*, (Stanford: Stanford University Press, 1974).

Rose, Robert; Gordon, Thomas, and Bernstein, Irwin 'Plasma Testosterone Levels in the Male Rhesus: Influences of Sexual and Social Stimuli' in *Science* 178, pp. 643–45 (1972).

Rowell, Thelma 'Forest-Living Baboons in Uganda' in *Journal of Zoology* CLXXXII, pp. 790–96 (1966).

Rowell, Thelma E. 'The Concept of Social Dominance' in *Behavioural Biology* II, pp. 131–54 (1974).

Sacks, Karen 'State Bias and Women's Status' in *American Anthropologist* 78, pp. 131–54 (1976).

Sacks, Karen *Sisters and Wives: the Past and Future of Sexual Equality*, (Westport: Greenwood Press, 1979).

Sahlins, Marshall *Stone Age Economics*, (Chicago: Aldine, 1972).

Sahlins, Marshall D. *The Use and Abuse of Biology*, (Michigan: University of Michigan Press, 1976).

Sanday, Peggy *Female Power and Male Dominance*, (Cambridge: Cambridge University Press, 1981).

Schacter, Stanley and Singer, Jerome 'Cognitive, Social, and Physiological Determinants of Emotional State' in *Psychological Review* 69, pp. 379–99 (1962).

Schneider, David M. and Gough, Kathleen (eds.) *Matrilineal Kinship*, (Berkeley: University of California Press).

Science for the People: Sociobiology Study Group 'Sociobiology – Another Biological Determinism' in *BioScience* 26, 3, pp. 182–90 (1976).

Simmons, Leo *The Position of the Aged in Primitive Society*, (New Haven: Yale University Press, 1946).

Slocum, Sally 'Woman the Gatherer: Male Bias in Anthropology' in Reiter, pp. 36–50 (1975).

Steward, Julian *The Theory of Culture Change*, (Urbana: University of Illinois Press, 1955).

Strathern, Marilyn 'No Nature, No Culture: The Hagan Case' in MacCormack and Strathern, pp. 174–222 (1980).

Suderkasa, Nicera 'Female Employment and Family Organization in West Africa' in McGuigan, pp. 48–63 (1976).

Tanner, Nancy *On Becoming Human*, (Cambridge: Cambridge University Press, 1981).

Tanner, Nancy and Zehlman, Adrienne 'Women in Evolution, part I' in *Signs* I (1976).

Tavris, Carol and Otis, Carole *The Longest War: Sex Differences in Perspective*,

(New York: Harcourt, Brace, Jovanovich, 1977).

Thomas, Elizabeth Marshall *The Harmless People*, (New York: Vintage, 1959).

Thompson, George *Studies in Ancient Greek Society: The Prehistoric Aegean*, (New York: Citadel, 1965).

Tiger, Lionel *Men in Groups*, (New York: Random House, 1969).

Turnbull, Colin *The Forest People*, (New York: Clarion, 1962).

Turnbull, Colin 'Mbuti Womanhood' in Dahlberg, pp. 205–19 (1981).

Van Allen, Judith ' "Sitting on a Man": Colonialism and the Lost Political Institutions of Igbo Women' in *Canadian Journal of African Studies* 6, pp. 165–81 (1972).

Washburn, Sherwood and Devore 'Baboon Social Organization' film, Educational Materials Corporation (distributor) (1963).

Washburn, Sherwood, and Lancaster 'The Evolution of Hunting' in Lee and Devore (eds.) (1968).

Webster, Paula 'Matriarchy: A Vision of Power' in Reiter, pp. 141–56 (1975).

Weiner, Annette B. *Women of Value, Men of Renown: New Perspectives on Trobriand Exchange*, (Austin: University of Texas Press, 1976).

Whyte, Martin King *The Status of Women in Pre-industrial Societies*, (Princeton: Princeton University Press, 1978).

Williams, B. J. 'Have We a Darwin of Biocultural Evolution?' in *American Anthropologist* 84, pp. 848–52 (1982).

Wilson, E. O. *Sociobiology: The New Synthesis*, (Cambridge: Belknapp Press of Harvard University Press, 1975).

Wilson, E. O. 'Human Decency is Animal' in *New York Times Magazine*, (12 October, 1975).

Wilson, Edward O. *On Human Nature*, (Cambridge: Harvard University Press, 1978).

Zelman, Elizabeth 'Pollution and Power' in McGuigan, pp. 183–93 (1976).

Zihlman, Adrienne L. 'Women in Evolution, Part II: Subsistence and Social Organization Among Early Hominids' in *Signs* 4, 1, pp. 4–20 (1978).

General Index

Aegean, 149,173,180,182,190,194
age-class, age-group, 98
aggression, 2,3, 9–11, 28, 113
agriculture, female role in (see also horticulture), 5, 37, 77–80, 84, 87, 88, 174–6, 178,179, 183–5
agriculture, male role in, 5, 78, 79, 115, 179
Akan, 95
alienation, relation of, 84–6, 89, 92–4, 96, 99, 107, 166
ancestor worship, 127
Anglo-Saxon society, 150
Arapesh, 10
aristocracy (see also ruling class), 42, 143, 144, 147–50, 152, 154, 186, 189, 195
arms, taboo on women bearing, 91, 92, 181
Ashanti, 23, 95
Athenian democracy, 183, 192, 194, 196
Athenian tragedy, 39, 150, 190, 181, 194–9
Athens, 22, 149, 157, 164, 176, 193, 194
Australian aborigines, 15, 116
avunculocality see residence rules
Aztec society, 142, 145

Babylonia, 147, 154

Bakongo, 98
balanced reciprocity see reciprocity
Bambara, 104
Bamilke (Cameroon), 147, 160
Bandia, 159
Baoulé, 95
Bari, 195
Baruga, 90, 91, 103
Bellacoola see Native American societies
Bedik, 91, 104
Béti, 83
'big man', 33, 130
bigamy, 186
bilineality, 94, 95, 100
biodeterminism, biological determinism, 6,. 10, 49, 50, 60, 86
brideprice, bridewealth, 83–5, 122, 127–8, 137–9, 140, 149, 163, 167, 184
Bushmen (San), 19, 21, 24, 116

Canadian Indians see Native American societies
captives, 157–8, 160–2
– 'captifs de core', 161
Carolingian Europe, 151, 154
Catal Huyuk, 19, 134, 138
Chad, 89
chiefs, chiefdom, 124–5, 144, 148, 156
China, 164

children
 – legitimacy of, 167, 188
 – of rulers, 165–6
 – of slaves, 157–61
 – status of, 158, 166–7
clan, 32, 76–7, 94, 99, 143, 151, 176–7,
  181, 189, 195–6
class society
 – its impact on women, 109–12,
  142–3, 145, 153, 170
 – rise of, 33, 37, 41–2, 77, 107, 110,
  112, 129, 142, 144, 155, 168, 205
classical drama *see* Athenian tragedy
client, clientage, 143–4, 149, 160
Code of Hammurabi, 153
Code of Gortyn, 177–9, 182
colonization, colonialism, 18–9, 25,
  121, 125
concubines, 165, 178, 190
Congo, 78
conical clan, 128, 134
creation myths, creation symbols, 104
Crete, 22, 108, 142, 146–7, 173–4,
  177–80, 182–3, 185, 190, 200–4

Dahomey, 92, 114, 146
descent, rules of, *see* bilineality;
  matrilineality; patrilineality;
  unilineality
dimorphism, sexual, 2, 9, 20, 44–6, 51–
  7, 59, 63, 67, 69, 71–2, 74
division of labour
 – biological, 5
 – by age, 57, 59, 65, 116
 – 'natural', 55, 88–9, 205
 – by sex, 5, 7, 20–2, 32, 34–5, 37–9,
  43–9, 51–2, 55, 57, 59, 62, 64–9, 71–
  4, 77–9, 86–9, 92, 100, 105, 110, 112,
  114–6, 119, 125–6, 129, 139, 182,
  184, 205
divorce, 82, 84, 93, 164, 177, 192
dowry, 83, 160, 163, 167, 176–7, 184,
  192
dual sex systems, 120

egalitarian society (*see also* communal

society), 33, 35, 37, 40, 76–7, 108–
  10, 121, 126–8, 133, 140, 143
Egyptians, 14
endogamy, 145, 178–9, 181, 186, 188
Eskimo, 30, 114
exchange (*including* exchange of
  women), 38, 43–4, 47–50, 60, 62–4,
  67–8, 71–4, 83, 92–4, 96–7, 99, 115,
  121–4, 128, 131, 159–60, 167, 170,
  181
exogamy, 68, 73, 81, 83, 92, 96, 98, 167,
  188, 192

Fang, 83
fertility, 17, 56–9, 63, 66, 115, 121, 175,
  200
feudal society, 174
fishing, 30, 79–80, 87, 101, 115
food, female production of (*see also*
  agriculture, female role in), 77–8,
  80, 134
food, male production of, 67
food taboos, 85
foraging societies, 9, 13, 32, 35, 45, 49,
  50, 55–7, 59, 60, 62–3, 65–6, 69, 71,
  73, 108, 111, 113, 118
functionalist theory, 18

Gabon, 78
gathering, 19, 21, 27, 47, 50, 87, 101,
  113–4
goddesses, 102–4, 152, 169, 183, 199–
  205
Greece, 150–2, 154, 164, 169–205
 – ancient or Archaic, 169, 173–5, 177,
  189, 191, 201, 203
 – classical, 174–6, 184, 186, 196, 199,
  201–3
 – Homeric, 142, 146, 173
 – primitive, 169, 173, 189
groomprice, 122, 140
groomservice, 122
gynecostatism, gynecostatic societies,
  93, 99

Hadza, 50, 116

Hagan, 15–6, 141
Hausa, 163–4
heirs *see* inheritance
Hellenic civilization *see* Greece
Hittites, 88
home base, 63, 113
hominids, 42, 47, 51, 55, 59, 69, 70
Hopi *see* Native American societies
hormones, 10–12
horticulture, 19, 21, 35, 78–80, 108, 115–6
hunting, 5, 19, 27–8, 30, 38, 47, 49, 50, 59, 64–8, 70–3, 79, 80, 87–8, 101, 112–5, 122, 132, 134

Iatmul, 91, 103
ideology
 – matrilineal, 41, 133, 134
 – in primitive societies, 17, 20, 65, 104, 127, 133–4, 151–2
 – patriarchal, 104
Inca society, 142, 145–6
incest, incest taboo, 43–4, 48, 68–9, 73–4, 167, 170
Indo-Europeans, 173, 180–2, 199, 202
infanticide, 17–8, 20
inheritance, 33, 82–3, 95, 151, 177, 184, 190
initiation
 – male, 89, 90, 103, 107, 186
 – female, 89
Iroquois *see* Native American societies
Ivory Coast, 95–7

Jivaro, 80, 83–4

Kavirondo, 92
kin corporate societies, kin corporations (*see also* lineage societies; mode of production), 36, 40–2, 110–12, 116–26, 129, 130–2, 135–6, 139, 141–4, 146, 150
kingdom, 92, 108, 112, 142, 147–8, 156, 158–60, 162, 165, 178
kinship (*see also* lineage societies; matrilineality; patrilineality), 60–1,
74–6, 94, 100–1, 112, 116, 127, 129–30, 133, 142, 150, 154, 159, 167, 171, 195
Kotoko, 161–2, 165
Kung, 113, 116

labour, labour-power, 38–9, 41, 85, 102, 107, 128,, 132, 137, 139, 145, 147
labour-service, 85
labour-value, 85
law
 – of adultery, 15, 153
 – African customary law, 81–2, 166
 – Islamic law, 166
 – Roman law, 166
legal incapacity of women, 82, 166
levirate, 83
lineage societies (*including* lineage organization, lineage relations of production) (*see also* kin corporate societies), 36, 40, 76–9, 81, 83–5, 87–9, 91–2, 94, 96, 100, 105–6, 119, 126–8, 131, 133–4, 136–9, 141, 143–4, 156–62, 167–8
Lovedu, 122

Mandan, 14
marriage
 – marriage and exchange, 68, 73, 121, 137, 139
 – marriage rules, 76, 81, 97, 98, 111, 121–2
 – cousin marriage, 163, 167
matriarchy, 26, 106, 169–71, 177–8, 186, 205
matricide, 193
matrilineality, 26, 36, 39, 40–1, 81, 94–102, 105–6, 108, 119, 130, 133, 138, 140, 144, 169, 170, 178, 180–2, 185–7, 190
matrilocality *see* residence rules
Mauritania, 157
Mbuti, 25
Mediterranean, 26, 102, 161–2, 173, 183, 198

Melanesia, 24
Mesopotamia, 148, 150–1, 154
migration, 30
Minoan civilization *see* Crete
mobility, 21, 87, 101
mode of production, 39, 40, 86, 112,
    118, 180
    – kin corporate mode of p., 39, 118,
    122, 143, 148
    – lineage mode of p., 85–6, 99
    – slave mode of p., 205
Montagnais Naskapi *see* Native
    American societies
Mossi (Yatenga), 160
Moslems (*see also* law, Islamic), 159
motherhood, 50, 57, 66–7, 87, 114
Mundugamor, 10
Mycenean civilization, 173–4, 179,
    182–3, 185, 191, 202–3
myth, mythology, 26, 29, 39, 102–5,
    140, 169, 171–2, 176–9, 185, 187–9,
    191, 193, 196, 199, 201, 204–5

Native American societies, 7, 102
    – Bellacoola, 30–1
    – Cheyenne, 30
    – Hopi, 93–4, 120, 123
    – Iroquois, 9, 14, 22, 30, 120–1, 132
    – Montagnais Naskapi, 32
    – Northwest Coast Indians, 118
    – Plains Indians, 135
Nazis, 165
Neolithic revolution, 17
neolocality *see* residence rules
New Guinea, 13, 90–1, 103, 123, 142
Northwest Coast Indians *see* Native
    American societies
nuclear family, 154
Nuer, 78, 93, 123
Nupe (Nigeria), 161

paternity (legal), 167
patriarchy, 16, 22, 32, 105, 107, 154–5,
    169, 170, 178–80, 182–3, 192, 201,
    205
patrilineality, 17–8, 26, 32, 36, 81, 94–8,

101, 119, 122, 133–6, 140, 144, 146,
    148, 152, 182, 192, 201, 205
patrilocality *see* residence rules
Plains Indians *see* Native American
    societies
political leadership
    – of females, 125, 131
    – of males, 15–16, 125–6, 131
pollution beliefs, 12–13, 142
polyandry, 136
polygamy, 17, 183
polygyny, 130, 134–7, 139
Polynesia, 94
population, 17, 25, 43, 63, 66, 70–1,
    105, 120
priestesses, 178, 182–3, 196, 201–3, 206
primates
    – dominance among, 2, 3, 11
    – learning capacity of, 4, 57
    – mating behaviour of, 2, 52, 54
    – sex-roles among, 2, 52–3
private sphere, 14, 153
production (*see also* mode of p.), 33, 35,
    37, 42–5, 47–51, 59–62, 70–1, 73, 79,
    80, 105, 125, 141, 154–5
projectile weapons, projectile
    hunting, 37–8, 45, 64, 66, 71–3, 112
property
    – kin corporate *see* kin c. mode of
    production
    – collective, 105
    – private, 109–11, 149, 184
psychoanalytical theory, 13, 171, 173,
    202
puberty, 54, 57–8, 71
public sphere, 14, 152–3

queens, 23, 96, 177, 190–2, 196, 203,
    206

rank, ranking, 33–4, 96, 110, 119, 126–
    7, 129, 139, 141
reciprocity, 30, 61, 93, 127–9
    – balanced r., 89, 93, 118, 124
    – reciprocal exchange, 48, 124
    – generalised r., 48, 57, 60–1, 85, 124

redistribution, 33, 115, 121, 124–5, 130–4, 139, 141
religion (*see also* goddesses; priestesses), 82, 134, 151, 170, 180–1, 195, 199–201, 205
reproduction (*see also* fertility), 12–13, 35, 44, 63, 72–4, 120, 126, 135, 141–2, 155
residence rules, 36, 39, 81, 111, 122, 129
 – and avunculocality, 76, 138, 140
 – and matrilocality (uxorilocality), 39–41, 93–4, 96, 99, 100, 102, 105–6, 111, 122–4, 126–7, 129–33, 136–40, 170, 178, 180–2, 188
 – and neolocality, 138
 – and patrilocality (virilocality), 17, 36, 39–41, 81, 92–4, 96–100, 106–7, 111, 122–3, 126–7, 129–42, 170, 182
Rome, Roman Empire, 146, 154, 157, 164, 166
ruling-class men, 42, 107, 142
ruling-class women, 42, 107, 145–8, 152–4, 163, 206

San *see* Bushmen
Sara (Chad), 89, 90
Saudi Arabia, 164
segmentation, 85, 96, 127
seniority, 119, 127, 133
sexual dimorphism *see* dimorphism, sexual
sexual segregation, 13, 28
sharing, 3, 7, 31, 49–51, 70, 88, 118
Sherbro, 15
slaves, slavery (*including* system of slavery, slave formation), 22, 31, 33–5, 42, 76, 85–6, 95, 144–5, 147, 149, 154, 156–68, 170, 178, 180, 185, 199, 205–6
 – slaves, female, 144–5, 162, 166, 168, 174–6, 178, 181, 191, 203
 – wage-slavery, 76, 86
sociobiology, 4–8, 61
South America (*including* Latin America), 24, 79, 81, 91
Sparta, 192–3
state societies
 – impact on women of, 32, 34, 40, 109–11, 151–5
 – rise of, 37, 148–50, 155
stratification (*see also* ranking), 42, 105, 109, 111, 129, 138–9, 143–4, 155
structuralist theory, 74–5, 170–1
succession, 76, 95–6
Sumer, Sumerians, 14, 108, 142, 146, 149, 151
surplus, 139

taboo against women bearing arms, 91–2, 181
Tasaday, 25, 46
Tchambali, 10
technology, 30, 37–8, 43–4, 65–6, 135, 181, 200
Tiwi, 50
Trobriand islanders, 7, 103
Truk, 133
Tuareg, 95
Tupi-Guarani, 79

unilineality, 110, 119, 133
Upper Volta, 82
uxorilocality *see* residence rules (and matrilocality)

virginity, 145, 201
virilocality *see* residence rules (and patrilocality)

Waalo, 162, 164
war, warfare, 17, 19, 25, 30, 33, 79, 80, 100, 110, 114–5, 119, 121–2, 132, 143, 152, 176

Yanomano, 18
Yao, 132
Yoruba, 24

Index of Authors

Adams, R., 150
Aeschylus, 150, 193, 196, 198
Anaxagoras, 193
Aristotle, 177, 193, 195
Awori, Thema, 77–8

Bachofen, Jacob J., 169, 170, 193, 205
Balandier, Georges, 77, 98
Briggs, J., 114
Brown, J., 113

Chagnon, Napoleon, 18
Childe, Gordon, V., 27, 115
Chodorow, Nancy, 13–4
Clastres, Pierre, 79, 81

Dah, Michael Monuel, 82
de Beauvoir, Simone, 172
Delcourt, Marie, 186–7
Diamond, Stanley, 150
Divale, William, 17–20
Draper, P., 113
Durkheim, Emile, 62

Engels F., 26, 32–3, 108, 117, 170, 193, 205
Euripides, 190–2, 197
Evans-Pritchard, E. E., 78

Faure, Paul, 200–1

Finley, M., 180
Fluehr-Lobban, C., 27
Freud, S., 171
Fried, Morton, 33, 124
Friedman, J., 126–8
Frisch, Rose E., 57–9, 63

Gernet, Louis, 181, 186
Gessain, Monique, 98
Godelier, Maurice, 90–1, 103

Harris, Marvin, 17–20
Haupt, Lehman, 88
Heath, D. B., 114
Hendrix, 131
Herodotus, 177–8 187, 189, 198
Hesiod, 174–5, 180, 184, 193, 195, 198
Homer, 174, 177, 183–4, 187, 192, 203

Jaulin, Robert, 85, 89, 90
Jewsiewicki, D., 133
Johnson, 131
Jung, C. G., 171

Kabore, Brigitte, 82
Kelly, Raymond, 13, 142

Lacan, J., 202
Leacock, Eleanor, 27, 32–4
Leakey, L. S. B., 55

220

Leboeuf, A., 161
Lee, R., 116
Leibowitz, Lila, 9
Lévi-Strauss, C., 74, 100, 170, 172
Lewontin, Richard, 6
Levin, H., 11
Ligon, J. David, 61
Ligon, Sandra H., 61
Loraux, Nicole, 193–4

Maccoby, E. E., 11
Mair, Lucy, 144
Mann, A., 55–7
Martin, K., 135
McKinley, Kelton R., 56–7
Mead, Margaret, 10, 103
Meillassoux, Claude, 102, 118, 122
Morin, Edgar, 88, 102
Moscovici, Serge, 88, 102
Murdock, George P., 111, 114

Nadel, S. F., 161
Nance, John, 25
Nash, Jill, 123

Ortner, Sherry, 14, 153

Parker, Hilda, 20–3, 113
Parker, Seymour, 20–3, 113
Parsons, Talcott, 62
Paulme, Denise, 16, 77, 98
Pausanius, 202
Penn, William, 125
Pericles, 188, 193, 195

Picard, Charles, 200, 202
Plato, 177
Poewe, Karla, 135–7
Pomeroy, Sarah, 26
Provost, C., 114

Quinn, Naomi, 25

Rapp, R., 27
Rosaldo, Michelle Zimbalist, 24
Rowlands, M. J., 126–8

Sacks, K., 118, 122
Sahlins, Marshall D., 124, 129
Sappho, 194
Schlegel, A., 131
Semonides, 198
Singer, A., 123
Smith, Mary, 163
Smith, Pierre, 104
Spears, R. R., 11
Strabo, 177
Suderkasa, N., 24

Tanner, Nancy Makepeace, 57

Vernant, Jean-Pierre, 175, 195, 198
Vidal-Nacquet, Pierre, 185
Voorhies, Barbara, 135

Whitehead, Harriet, 14
Wilson, E. O., 4, 5

Xenophon, 175